Contesting the
Global Order

SUNY series in New Political Science
―――――――
Bradley J. Macdonald, editor

Contesting the Global Order

The Radical Political Economy of Perry Anderson and Immanuel Wallerstein

GREGORY P. WILLIAMS

Published by State University of New York Press, Albany

© 2020 State University of New York

All rights reserved

No part of this book may be used or reproduced in any manner whatsoever without written permission. No part of this book may be stored in a retrieval system or transmitted in any form or by any means including electronic, electrostatic, magnetic tape, mechanical, photocopying, recording, or otherwise without the prior permission in writing of the publisher.

For information, contact State University of New York Press, Albany, NY
www.sunypress.edu

Library of Congress Cataloging-in-Publication Data

Names: Williams, Gregory P., author.
Title: Contesting the global order: the radical political economy of Perry Anderson and Immanuel Wallerstein / Gregory P. Williams, author.
Description: Albany : State University of New York Press, [2020] | Series: SUNY series in New Political Science | Includes bibliographical references and index.
Identifiers: ISBN 9781438479651 (hardcover : alk. paper) | ISBN 9781438479668 (pbk. : alk. paper) | ISBN 9781438479675 (ebook)
Further information is available at the Library of Congress.

Library of Congress Control Number: 2020937137

10 9 8 7 6 5 4 3 2 1

For Colleen

Contents

Acknowledgments	ix
Introduction: Radical Political Economy for an Age of Uncertainty	1
Chapter 1 Cosmopolitan Beginnings	17
Chapter 2 Ideational Lineages	37
Chapter 3 The Year that Changed Everything	55
Chapter 4 Ideas Need Institutions	67
Intermission I: Immanuel Wallerstein's New Pair of Glasses	91
Chapter 5 There Is No Alternative	99
Chapter 6 Shed a Tear for East European Communism?	121
Intermission II: Perry Anderson's Clear-Headed Radicalism	141
Chapter 7 Do Not Believe What Great Powers Say	147
Conclusion: The Point Is to Interpret, and Then Change, the World	165
Notes	179
Bibliography	227
Index	245

Acknowledgments

Writing may be solitary, but books remain collective endeavors. I now have a sense of the impact of others' ideas and support.

It is a pleasure to see this book as part of SUNY Press's series in New Political Science. I thank Michael Rinella at SUNY Press and Bradley J. Macdonald, the series editor, for their support. I also thank Yvonne Deligato at Binghamton University Archives for her help with the Wallerstein Papers collection. The Rare Book and Manuscript Library at Columbia University kindly supplied a digital copy of an important text. Another source supplied documents on the condition of anonymity. In addition to the reviewers, several others read manuscript chapters or entire drafts, including Robert Denemark, Georgi Derluguian, Jane Anna Gordon, Martin Jay, Mladen Medved, and Bryan D. Palmer.

I thank my protagonists, who inspired this study. Perry Anderson, preferring that scholars emphasize textual analysis, declined to be interviewed but wished me well. Immanuel Wallerstein sat for an interview. Sadly, he has since passed. Others will be contemplating his, and Anderson's, ideas for some time.

This book began as a dissertation at the University of Connecticut. I am especially grateful for my advisor, Cyrus Ernesto Zirakzadeh, a kind soul with an original mind. At a time of change in the discipline, Ernie showed that political science research can be both academically and personally meaningful. Other committee members also contributed advice and ideas that helped the work come together. They included Shareen Hertel, David L. Richards, Mark A. Boyer, and Charles R. Venator Santiago. I also learned a great deal from the late J. Garry Clifford, an original member of the committee, whose writings and lectures were captivating.

As this study became a book project, colleagues in my department at the University of Northern Colorado offered wise advice, both intellectual and practical. I am especially indebted to Richard Bownas and Stan Luger.

My family offered words of encouragement. I thank my parents, James and Elizabeth Williams, as well as my brother, Andrew Williams. The loving support of my wife, Colleen O'Connell Williams, made this project enjoyable and worthwhile.

Introduction

Radical Political Economy for an Age of Uncertainty

On September 24, 2008, four months before the end of his presidency, George W. Bush gave his first prime-time televised address on economic affairs. It was a Wednesday. The economy was in crisis. One after another, large financial institutions were collapsing or requesting government assistance. Countrywide fell in January, followed by Bear Stearns in March. That summer, several European banks folded. Governments in North America and Europe coordinated efforts on monetary policy. Then came September. Within weeks, disaster struck Merrill Lynch, Lehman Brothers, A.I.G., and Washington Mutual.

The president announced that he would lead a bipartisan effort to restore stability to the economy and confidence in markets. He promised that the government, during this extraordinary time, would act quickly and without partisanship. President Bush attributed the successive collapses to instability brought on by irresponsible lending and overly optimistic assessments of the housing market. Regulatory agencies, he noted, should have done more to head off this economic emergency, which, even though it had struck suddenly, should not have taken officials by surprise.[1]

Over the coming months, two accounts of the crisis would emerge. For convenience, we can call these the prevailing explanation and the unconventional explanation. Although they were generally quite different, and although individual opinions clashed, these accounts were not mutually exclusive. In fact, they shared an important trait: each represented a genuine merger of economic and political modes of inquiry. They were, in other words, in the tradition of political economy.

The prevailing explanation attributed what came to be known as the "Great Recession" to a confluence of relatively recent factors. It explained that the banks had underestimated financial market risk, households had saved too little, and mortgages were too easily approved. Moreover, according to this account, some bankers were manipulating not only the price of loans between banks but also currency exchange rates. Simultaneously, many big banks were overleveraged, which meant that they had taken on large amounts of debt to buy assets (betting that an asset's value would grow faster than interest would accumulate). In addition, foreign debt, coupled with a decline in U.S. hegemony, weakened the American economy. Then, according to the prevailing narrative, a series of events sent the system into a tailspin: a spike in oil prices, followed by a housing crash, followed by a stock market crash. This narrative was valuable because it accounted for a specific chain of events leading up to catastrophe.[2]

The unconventional account attributed the events of that year to capitalism's propensity for crisis. It highlighted longstanding global economic interconnections and patterns of faster and slower growth. It emphasized materials used for industry and the decline of natural resources in the twentieth and twenty-first centuries. This narrative also thought about the legacy of colonialism and an unfair relationship between laboring classes and those that owned factories, banks, and other businesses. It conceptualized the 2008 crisis from a bird's eye view—at the level of the global capitalist system.[3] It was valuable because it accounted for long-term patterns that gave rise to the crisis.[4]

This work is a journey into the second narrative. It arrives amid growing concern that the international order (economic and political), widely considered stable, has been greatly shaken. This study does not address the 2008 crisis in detail, which is merely a recent example of global capitalist instability. Instead, this book investigates the intellectual tradition that produced the unconventional narrative through an analysis of two of its pioneers, the American sociologist Immanuel Wallerstein and the British historian Perry Anderson. Wallerstein founded the Fernand Braudel Center at Binghamton University, the journal *Review*, and was a main force behind the development of world-systems analysis. Anderson edited the *New Left Review* (NLR) for decades and remains an influential force at the journal and its book publishing house, New Left Books (which publishes as Verso). With careers that stretched beyond six decades, their responses to major political events can provide insights into the study of political economy today. Each left an important mark on our scholarly understanding of political economy. Each struggled to break free from traditional historical and social scientific thinking, and then struggled against misunderstandings and criticism. By virtue of their scholarly efforts and institutional positions, each left a legacy that generations of researchers have followed.

Wallerstein, Anderson, and other scholars of political economy work in a field with a rich and diverse history. It used to be that governance and economics were regarded as a single subject of study. But since the late nineteenth century, specialization has meant that economics and politics were often studied apart from one another. In order to make sense of a complex world, specialization seemed sensible. But disciplinary divisions also made it appear as though issues of trade and currency were distinct from bureaucracy and lawmaking. In Western universities, economists turned their attention to the functions of capitalism, while political scientists focused their efforts on the state and the concept of democracy. Yet for almost as long as politics and economics have been studied in isolation, there have been intellectuals who rejected such specialization. In the twentieth century, many sought to avoid choosing between politics or economics. Political economy came to be an intellectual resistance against increasing specialization. In the study of global politics, this resistance was called international political economy (IPE). It took institutional form in the 1970s, when a group of economists and political scientists sought to formally bridge their fields. They conceived of IPE as broader than any specific discipline because it encompassed all the ways that politics and economics interacted on a world scale.

For Benjamin Cohen, the "Magnificent Seven" of IPE were Robert Cox, Robert Gilpin, Peter Katzenstein, Robert Keohane, Charles Kindleberger, Stephen Krasner, and Susan Strange.[5] These intellectuals created journals such as *International Organization*. And they established institutional homes for IPE in organized sections of the British International Studies Association (BISA) and its American counterpart, the International Studies Association (ISA). Soon, IPE had its own university courses and textbooks.

Some scholars of IPE, including Cox and Strange, were critical of capitalism. But many others saw the anticapitalist writings of social historians to be ideologically biased, and thus flawed. This was especially true for the American tradition of IPE.[6] This group of intellectuals often favored short-term trends derived from observational, empirical data, which, over time, led practitioners to embrace quantitative methods or formal models.

Many American scholars adopted what they believed to be an unbiased, scientific approach to political economy. Its members hoped that their data-driven orientation could lead to the production of covering laws, true for all times and places. Perhaps as a consequence, many adherents to the American tradition assumed a narrow understanding of political economy. According to one study, *International Organization* published fewer and fewer articles dealing with big questions (of interdependence or regimes) relevant for international development; by the 1990s, articles on the applications of game theory on liberal democracies were much more common.[7] After the 2008 crisis, generally, though not without exception, adherents to the American tradition espoused the prevailing explanation.

The British tradition was very different. It avoided scientism and what it considered the American fetishization of evidence testing. But mostly, the British tradition was different because it tended to ask different questions about hegemony and systemic transformation—what Cohen has called the Really Big Questions of political economy.[8] British IPE favored description and often normatively positioned itself against U.S. hegemony and capitalism. In response to 2008, therefore, adherents to the British tradition were more likely to espouse the unconventional explanation.

Emerging simultaneously to the British and American versions of IPE was a tradition of radical political economy (RPE).[9] Its members, almost without exception, espoused the unconventional explanation of the 2008 crisis. But it was nonetheless a lively intellectual assemblage. Among the writers who pioneered this tradition were British Marxists such as Anderson, along with Robert Brenner, Eric Hobsbawm, Tom Nairn, and E. P. Thompson. Others were world-systems scholars like Wallerstein, along with Samir Amin, Giovanni Arrighi, and Andre Gunder Frank. RPE is sometimes referred to as the "Left Out" tradition because, in addition to its ideological orientation, many radicals were omitted from Cohen's intellectual history of IPE.[10] RPE is not, however, a discreet category: some scholars may prefer the label Critical IPE, since radicalism is also an "emancipatory" project, broadly defined;[11] and others could be labeled part of the British tradition.[12]

However classified, radicals have always thought about systemic transformation, hegemony, and the growing interconnectedness of nation-states. Radical writings were different, however, in three respects. One, they descended from an older lineage of social history that was concerned with class struggle, social injustice, and the material foundations of power relationships (among social groups and among nations). Marx was, of course, an influence, but many radical writers avoided self-identifying as "Marxist" precisely because they had moved so far away from Marx's own views. Marxism is commonly associated with a preference for economic forces (such as wages or trade) over political institutions (such as the state). Social historians had a richer view of this relationship, one that conceived of the interplay between political and economic forces. Furthermore, British Marxism and world-systems analysis were each influenced by social history that came after Marx. Some scholars self-identified as Marxists, and some did not. But all thought about justice in society, and often took up issues of class disparities, labor rights, and other populist concerns. These authors included Hungarian thinkers such as Karl Polanyi and Georg Lukács, French writers such as Fernand Braudel and Jean-Paul Sartre, and Italians such as Antonio Gramsci. The American C. Wright Mills and other Columbia Essayists influenced the development of world-systems.

As social historians, radical writers often avoided disciplinary labels and sought to influence the wider public. Many thought of themselves as public intellectuals, which Stanley Aronowitz defined as a persistence at espousing "unauthorized ideas."[13] Radical writers alternated between writing for an academic audience and a general readership. Some shunned the academic world altogether (although the truly independent intellectual has become rare).[14]

Two, radical political economy was also different in that its practitioners were activist intellectuals, concerned with the emancipation of peoples. As part of the New Left that emerged in the 1950s and 1960s, radicals wished for a more egalitarian, noncapitalist future. They wrote in support of subordinate groups in society, and they were skeptical of governments, large businesses, and other actors wielding power. They were outraged at how narratives of equality and democracy veiled realities of global injustice and the suppression of the lower strata. In their opinion, most social scientific tools of investigation in the 1960s simply did not account for the gap. They distrusted the pro-capitalist West and were disappointed by the social democracies and socialist parties of Western Europe, yet they were also angered by the brutality and absurdity of Stalinism. Inspired by the global protests of 1968, many came to believe capitalism was unstable. As scholar-activists, many thought they could transform the system from within (or at least fashion a replacement as it disintegrated).

The political activist stance of radical political economy in some ways made them more like philosopher-historians from earlier generations. They shared with thinkers Friedrich Nietzsche, E. H. Carr, and

John Garraty the view that self-proclaimed neutrality was elusive and potentially dangerous.[15] The economist Gunnar Myrdal made this point when he wrote: "Useful economics can never be free of ideology and value judgements. The problem is to keep them in harness."[16] Radicals took this notion a step farther by contending that scholars could not be separated from their findings. Radicals worried about histories that had no meaning other than the delivery of facts.[17] They thought that the solution to the problems of history could only be solved with more history. Many embraced Nietzsche's category of critical history:[18] by interrogating the origins of our present circumstances, radicals thought that the condition of humanity could be improved.[19] In fact, radicals believed that their political commitments enhanced the objectivity of their studies. Like James Rosenau, they acknowledged a simple truth: even though science teaches that research should be value free, it is the observer who gives meaning to facts.[20]

Alongside their sense of justice, a third distinguishing characteristic of radicals was their embrace of totalities, which they interpreted to mean a commitment to the social whole. By social whole, radicals meant the collective impact of all of the various parts of society. They conceived of institutions, social norms, trade relations, diplomacy, or even war as interconnected, and, likewise, avoided studying any one factor individually.

In writing about totalities, radicals thought a great deal about long-term historical processes, considering political phenomena over decades, centuries, and even millennia. If most scholars can accept the notion of short-term trends, they thought, then why should long-term trends be any different? Radical political economy also tended to favor large-scale spatial analysis: political, economic, and cultural changes did not occur at the level of the nation-state, but at the regional or world scale. Therefore, although they thought the notion of stages in political and economic development was critically important, they conceived of that development in terms of stages of entire social systems.

These intellectuals were positivists in the sense that they believed the past and present could be objectively understood. They debated, however, about their ability to know the future, not because they doubted their understanding but because many considered the future to be inherently uncertain. Still, their objective standing did not mean a nomothetic orientation; they did not think social laws, applicable in all places at all times, were possible. Yet neither was radical political economy idiographic in orientation; its adherents did not think that findings from one place and time were inapplicable to other places and times. Thus, radical political economy generally held the view that social regularities could be found with geographical and temporal boundaries. The character of feudalism in Asia, for example, was different than that of Western Europe.

Prior to 2008, a symbol of capitalist instability, it may have seemed as though the radical tradition was obsolete. In the 1960s, many of its proponents believed that capitalism was on the verge of collapse and that socialism would take its place. Yet in the eyes of many commentators, in Western governments as well as in academia, history has moved in precisely the opposite direction. East European communist party states, exposed for their cruelty, fell apart in democratic revolutions. Simultaneously, advanced capitalist nations saw a decline in socialist parties, a rollback of the welfare state, and an increase in the popularity of free market capitalism. These developments, according to supporters of the capitalist West, would not only reduce the likelihood of interstate war but create opportunities for peaceful cooperation. Furthermore, proponents said, economic advancement would improve living conditions everywhere. This narrative became so prevalent that even its opponents had to admit its widespread appeal. By Anderson's own admission, the 1990s was a "grand slam" for capitalist advancement.[21] At the end of the twentieth century, many believed that there were no rivals to capitalism.[22]

Yet the crisis of 2008 demonstrated the continued relevance of the radical tradition, as crises tend to do. When times are prosperous, or at least arguably prosperous, the radical critique of capitalism may be less convincing. During times of difficulty, radicalism becomes more appealing. Events of the twenty-first century have called into question the principles of free market capitalism. Far from symbolizing an age of sustained peace and cooperation under a unifying market, recent years have been turbulent. Many postcolonial nations remain politically and economically troubled, and face crises of governance, clean water, and rising seas. Wealthy regions have seen growing wealth and wage inequality as well as aggressive austerity programs. The Occupy Movement and the Arab Spring, as well as electoral expressions of dissatisfaction with ruling parties, are indicative of restless citizenry. Far Left and Far Right parties and candidates have gained a level of prominence that, not too long ago, would have been unthinkable. For some, commonly associated with the "Left," populism has manifested in demands for wages, welfare, or rights. For others, considered part of the "Right," populism has come in the form of demands for immigration restrictions, often in xenophobic terms. These movements, though with different impulses, reflect the sentiment that, perhaps, the post–Cold War world did not match up with the rhetoric used by European and American policymakers and intellectuals. Suddenly, the international economic and political order appeared not to contain crises but to itself be in crisis.

Some may find it tempting to claim, or accuse radicals of claiming, that earlier predictions of socialism had been vindicated. In 2012, one journalist for BBC's *Newsnight* suspected as much in an interview with Eric Hobsbawm. He thought that the historian, in light of the economic crisis, was clutching at straws, looking everywhere for the death of capitalism and the birth of socialism. Yet nothing could be farther from the truth. Hobsbawm replied: "I'm not clutching any straws because I'm pessimistic. . . . I suspect that we are looking forward to a rather stormy period in the next twenty or thirty years."[23] This in fact was a common conclusion for radicals. Such a view may seem self-defeating, but, as clear-headed intellectuals, radicals preferred accuracy (even depressing accuracy) over fantasy (however good it may feel).

Although previously known for their seemingly constant predictions of the arrival of global socialism, many in the late twentieth and twenty-first centuries spoke somberly about future prospects for socialism. Instead of encouraging potential revolutionaries to take action, some have suggested that now is the time for contemplating alternative futures.[24] Socialists, in other words, should more thoroughly develop their plans for postcapitalist governance.

This work takes the position that political failure, and the subsequent dearth of optimism, was an opportunity for intellectual growth. This book argues that although the course of history in the twentieth century did not move in the direction they predicted or wished, Wallerstein's and Anderson's sensitivity to current events made their works relevant for the study of international political economy as well as for those populations who did not have vocal or powerful advocates. Reflecting on the present, in other words, can lead to creative interpretations of the world. Political failure can become a kind of laboratory for revision.

In the 1960s, both Wallerstein and Anderson were hopeful about the progress of labor movements at home and nationalist movements abroad. Protests of 1968 led them to believe that socialism could soon become a reality. Yet the resurgence of free-market capitalist ideology in the 1980s demonstrated that their predictions were not about to come true. Wallerstein responded by rejecting optimism and pessimism altogether. He also stopped making predictions about a socialist future. A postcapitalist system, he thought, might indeed be less exploitative; but the odds were just as good that it would be more exploitative. Anderson's response was quite different. He was greatly disappointed by the ever-increasing dominance of capitalist ideology in the twentieth century. The best the Left could do, he thought, was to weather the storm and wait for an organized socialist movement or for capitalism to somehow fall apart on its own accord.

Though not optimistic, Wallerstein and Anderson did not give up. They neither clung to old beliefs in imminent socialism, nor acquiesced to capitalism's seeming dominance. They continued to write about international transformations, from the ancient world, to feudalism, to the modern capitalist interstate system, and to some kind of postcapitalist system. They took to explaining current events and cultural attitudes, and to exposing the ideology of powerful governments. Political events forced Wallerstein and Anderson to confront the reality of capitalism's continuation despite its predicted demise.

Such a study is valuable because Wallerstein and Anderson stayed focused on those Really Big Questions of IPE. Scholars of political economy and international relations have long pondered the issue of order in the international system and how it changes over time. The economic crisis of 2008 renewed the pertinence of such questions. Are we witnessing a crisis *within* capitalism? Or, are we witnessing a crisis *of* capitalism? Symbolically, 2008 represents doubt in the stability of capitalism as well as the nation-state system. An investigation into two thinkers devoted to the transition to and away from capitalism can offer some practical advice for the present.

Specifically, this work deals with three topics relevant for the study of international transformation. These are: totalities as an object of study; the origins and operations of capitalism; and the role of agency in determining behavior. On the first, this work reviews options for the study of totalities. As I shall point out, Wallerstein saw totalities as *closed*, which meant that he conceived of totalities as defined by historical and geographical boundaries. Another name for Wallerstein's totalities was world-systems. Anderson pursued totalities in an *open*-ended process he called totalization; he saw current events as the culmination of centuries or millennia of historical forces. Both visions can be of value to scholars of political economy, many of whom question the utility of the nation-state for the study of transnational activism, trade, and environmental regimes.

Second, Wallerstein belonged to that relatively small group of scholars who defined capitalism functionally and as requiring the endless accumulation of capital (or, stored value). He saw capitalism's origin as a historical accident which could just as easily have not happened. Anderson did not explicitly and systematically define capitalism, but he typically (though not always) used the term to refer to the private provision of goods and services produced by wage labor. Capitalism, for him, was the inevitable outcome of the West European dialectic between slavery in the ancient world and feudalism in the Middle Ages. Consequently, Wallerstein and Anderson viewed late capitalism differently, and also had opposite reactions to the fall of East European communism. Like the study of totalities, this back-and-forth between Wallerstein and Anderson offers lessons to scholars on the consequences of alternative ways of conceptualizing capitalist processes.

Third, Anderson and Wallerstein developed complex accounts of the relative ability of individuals to affect the world around them. Wallerstein believed that individuals could not overthrow a system when it was healthy, and argued that human agency increased during times of systemic crisis.[25] Anderson, even though he stressed the causal power of structures in history, believed that human agency had increased over time. In his opinion, if Left groups could develop strong organizations they could potentially overthrow the capitalist system. Wallerstein and Anderson thus shared somewhat similar views on the power of individuals. With a convergence of their (historically contingent) interpretations of human agency, there may be reason to think, in the twenty-first century, that we can choose our economic system.

This work also reflects on the unification of theory and practice in the social sciences. In recent years, scholars of international political economy have pursued unification.[26] Many have drawn inspiration from Alexander George's *Bridging the Gap*, and, more recently, the writings of Joseph Nye and Robert Jervis,[27] both of whom have expressed concern over a breach between scholarship and policymaking. One scholar has criticized the "cult of irrelevance" in academia, and has gone so far as to recommend that the policy usefulness of one's research be a criterion in tenure decisions.[28] But for whom should scholarship be relevant? Should scholars, for example, direct their research to the needs of non-policymakers? To subordinate groups around the world? To the wealthy?

The works of Wallerstein and Anderson point to an alternative way to unify theory and practice in the social sciences. They represent a type of intellectual who believes that scholarly endeavors should aid groups excluded from the political process. They sought to bridge theory and practice, but not on behalf of governments.

An examination of Wallerstein and Anderson can uncover visions of capitalism, totalities, and agency, and can provide models for writers of twenty-first century IPE who are concerned with the concept and practice of transformation. This study seeks to learn from its protagonists and apply those lessons to the twenty-first century.[29] It looks at how political circumstance informed and shaped their thinking. It does not inspect the effect of popular culture on Anderson or Wallerstein, nor does it investigate their private lives. It instead describes the political events of their day, the political projects they participated in and led, and the problems that they as radicals faced in the academy.[30]

This investigation of ideas employs an interpretivist approach, in which the goal is not to isolate variables or develop causal hypotheses but to clarify actors' understandings. It assumes that intellectuals do not employ ideas with prepackaged meanings, but wrestle with old ideas and create new ones to make sense of the puzzling experiences that they confront. What were the content and character of the political imaginations of Wallerstein and Anderson? How did they articulate these views? Although interpretation can come in many forms, this interpretivist analysis rests on two pillars: meaning making and contextualization.[31]

Interpretive research assumes that humans are meaning-making actors, which is to say that the issues and ideas that Wallerstein and Anderson wrote about do not have fixed connotations. Instead, Wallerstein and Anderson gave meaning to concepts. It is up to the researcher to grasp how people understood a concept at a particular time and a particular place. Often, Wallerstein's and Anderson's ideas were expressed in the public sphere. They sought to shape scholarly and public conversations by influencing how people thought about the Cold War, capitalism, and socialism. Both intellectuals thus engaged in social narratives—that is, the stories of society—and how these stories affect the present.[32] They found the dominant Western Cold War narratives about development and capitalism not only unconvincing but harmful for society. They thought society needed more accurate explanations of the past, even the distant past, to better grasp the present.

Likewise, context is important for interpretive research. In this study, context refers to the political events and intellectual environments that surrounded Wallerstein and Anderson. It assumes that scholars do not write from some abstract space removed from the everyday world. They react to and are shaped by the political and scholarly scene in which they live. Yet scholars are not mere reflections of their context. They also shape their milieu.[33] (This style of research closely follows Anderson's and Wallerstein's own methods: they, too, looked to context for clues into what writers or statesmen may have been thinking at a given time.) One must think about how humans envisioned the world around them, and how certain actions were possible or impossible.[34]

Biographers also interact with their subject matter. In personality, in writing style and location, in presuming to include some facts while leaving out others, researchers make an imprint on their material. Today, social scientists often use the term *reflexivity* to refer to biographer-subject awareness.[35] Carr perhaps anticipated this idea when he wrote, straightforwardly if imprecisely: "[The] work of the historian mirrors the society in which he works. It is not merely the events that are in flux. The historian himself is in flux."[36] This portrayal of Wallerstein and Anderson is written with the present in mind. The major themes of this study—on totalities, capitalism, and agency—are addressed intermittently, appearing and reappearing at points when Wallerstein and Anderson refined their scholarly views.[37]

Through developing a history of radical lives, this study may help others chart a course forward. The assumption is not, absurdly, that any single book could transform international politics. The assumption is merely that all people, regardless of class or education, rely on ideas about how the world works and how it ought to work. As the columnist George Monbiot put it: "Ideas, not armies or even banks, run the world. Ideas determine whether human creativity works for society or against it."[38] From where do we get ideas for the twenty-first century? This work originates with the view that we should step back and reconsider twentieth-century radicals. Wallerstein and Anderson were among those who sought to create a more peaceful and egalitarian society and a vibrant, critical intellectual culture. By appraising their life trajectories, we subsequent thinkers can understand why they believed what they believed about scholarship and politics. And by building on their research, it may be possible to shape the world and how we study it.

Two books have been written in English about Anderson; a third is a history of the *New Left Review*.[39] All of them discuss his contributions to Marxism and his impact on Marxist historians. This work emphasizes other aspects of Anderson, especially his methods and their relevance for political economy. No comprehensive inquiry of Wallerstein exists in English, although many articles take stock of his influence on social science.[40] Scholars of international relations are often familiar with a subset of Wallerstein's writings, but very few may know how his world-systemic orientation grew out of his earlier personal and professional experiences, or how he elaborated on world-systems late in life. In fact, the intellectual trajectories of Anderson and Wallerstein were more complex and nuanced than has been generally acknowledged.

Chapter 1 describes the ideological battles of the interwar and postwar periods, which were the historical backdrop to Wallerstein's and Anderson's formative years. For Wallerstein, the place was New York, which became home to the United Nations when he was a teenager. New York felt like the "capital" of the world-economy: although he traveled, Wallerstein believed he experienced other cultures and perspectives largely because of the city. By contrast, Anderson achieved his cosmopolitanism through constant travels: China, America, Ireland, and Britain. Both paths enabled these curious minds to think about the world's poor and politically deprived. And in their early writings, Wallerstein and Anderson used their global orientations to criticize policies at home and to contemplate the decolonizing world. They wrote soberly about the tough road ahead for socialists. But as young intellectuals, they remained optimistic about the prospects for progressive forces around the world.

Next, this work explores those radicals with a major influence on Wallerstein and Anderson. Both read Karl Marx. Both regarded more recent Marxists as more significant for their development. For Wallerstein, it was Frantz Fanon, Fernand Braudel, and Karl Polanyi who, collectively, taught that conclusions reached in the European context were a poor fit for the decolonizing world. They prompted a reconsideration of how social science conceived of history and geography. For Anderson, it was Edward Gibbon, Jean-Paul Sartre, Georg Lukács, and Lucio Colletti, whose work enabled thoughtful deliberation about humanism and structuralism. It was through notable minds that Wallerstein and Anderson came to develop their own understandings of the world.

The third chapter discusses 1968 as a major turning point for Wallerstein and Anderson. Each had grown frustrated at the lack of progress of Left parties at home and shortfalls in newly independent states abroad. Yet the revolutions of 1968 altered their thinking. Socialism now seemed possible. Anderson's enthusiasm, however, exceeded Wallerstein's. As editor of the *New Left Review*, Anderson was surrounded by like-minded comrades, and believed his journal could be part of the vanguard for revolution. Wallerstein, who served as a negotiator between student protesters and Columbia University's administration, considered 1968 as that time when the Left temporarily stopped the Right from advancing (in universities, and in society). Both intellectuals welcomed global protest as an expression of dissatisfaction on the part of everyday citizens. Symbolically, 1968 represents the peak of Wallerstein's and Anderson's optimism.

Chapter 4 is devoted to their reinterpretations of modern capitalism. The protests of 1968 led Wallerstein and Anderson to believe socialism was a real possibility. In response to that year, Wallerstein wanted to ensure that universities remained places from which the Left could encourage third world nationalist movements. Anderson wanted to aid socialist strategy. For each, the path to success was the same. They were convinced that the crucial problem was a lack of knowledge about how humanity came to its modern circumstances, characterized by global capitalism and national states. Thus, through scholarly writings and institutional activities, they reinterpreted modern European history. In 1974, they separately published what are called "totalizing" histories of modern capitalism. And as of 1976, the year Wallerstein became the inaugural director of Binghamton University's Fernand Braudel Center, they each led cultural institutions too. Paradoxically, as they sought to initiate change, their respective research programs and institutions were imbued with a worldview that greatly minimized human agency.

Twice, this manuscript takes a break from its larger narrative to delve into related issues. In the first intermission, Wallerstein's evolution from state-based to world-systemic analysis is portrayed in three snapshots, from 1967 to 1973. Here, readers see the issues with which he wrestled to make sense of the surrounding world.

Chapter 5 discusses how Wallerstein and Anderson responded to the decline of the excitement of 1968 and to the emergence of neoliberalism in the 1980s. Each came to new realizations about the relative power of humans within an overarching capitalist structure. Wallerstein's and Anderson's nuanced visions of human agency grew more complex in the 1980s. Neoliberalism caught each by surprise, but their reactions to Thatcher and Reagan could not have been more different. Each came to new realizations about the relative power of humans within an overarching capitalist structure. Wallerstein saw the very concepts of optimism and pessimism—and subsequently, the actions of activists—as irrelevant to the longevity of the system. For him, nothing could stop the system from undoing itself. Anderson, by contrast, thought that capitalism's demise would come at the hands of committed revolutionaries. Internal journal documents reveal that he was greatly disappointed by the lack of socialist advancement and doubted his ability to lead the *New Left Review* as a vanguard organization. Thus, as Wallerstein grew more committed to the study of the operations of capitalism, Anderson saw the dream of socialism slipping away.

Chapter 6 compares their different responses to the end of East European communism. Wallerstein remained certain that capitalism was endangered, but Anderson was shaken by the apparent lack of cohesiveness of the Left and the great organization of the Right. Despite their opposing viewpoints, Wallerstein and Anderson returned to their intellectual projects of the 1970s. The end of one-party communism in Eastern Europe deepened the divide between Wallerstein and Anderson. In fact, they had opposite responses to the movements of 1989. Wallerstein was sure that 1989 revealed the weaknesses of liberalism, and he became more convinced that capitalism would collapse. For his part, Anderson's pessimism increased. Though not supportive of communist parties, he was nonetheless shocked by the speed at which free-market thinking spread through the former Warsaw zone. But he was perhaps more disappointed at fellow leftists who seemed to have given up their resistance to capitalism. Ironically, this was also a criticism directed at Anderson. The comparison demonstrates how intellectuals who imagine capitalist processes in similar ways can have such divergent interpretations on its future.

The second intermission shows Anderson's pessimism, labeled as a clear-headed radicalism, through his understanding of hegemony. A recurring theme, though never in the foreground, Anderson drew an intellectual sketch of hegemony across time, raising eyebrows that he had given up on the possibility of world-historical change. Little evidence suggested capitulation. A more surprising outcome was his implication that powerful political leaders can choose hegemony, albeit partially dependent on structural economic conditions.

Chapter 7 uncovers some surprising similarities in their reasoning and conclusions. At the turn of the twenty-first century, Wallerstein's and Anderson's research converged once again. They returned to their macro-historical projects of the 1970s, writing histories of the modern world. And, improbably, they began expressing similar views of human agency.

Wallerstein, who considered capitalism to be in its final stage, argued that humans had the ability to create a postcapitalist world-system. And Anderson, who thought capitalism was as strong as ever, nonetheless maintained that human agency had increased in the modern world. Strangely enough, if the twentieth century can be characterized by Wallerstein's and Anderson's differences, the early twenty-first can be characterized by their similarities.

This study closes by taking stock of Wallerstein's and Anderson's relevance for the twenty-first century, and points to radical political economy's continued relevance for social science today. Although this story strives to remain optimistic, it is ultimately about political hardship. It describes Wallerstein's and Anderson's optimism for a better world, which they believed would be realized by the destruction of capitalism and the implementation of socialism on a world scale. In the 1970s, they saw their writings on the history of capitalism as a commentary on Cold War politics. In particular, they thought that a shift away from state-centric perspectives to the study of totalities could produce more accurate portrayals of the present. Their projects and their optimistic attitudes, however, came to a halt in neoliberalism's rise to dominance in the 1980s. Each thinker was forced to confront a political reality far from what he expected. Yet political disappointment is fertile terrain for observers today, who can learn how intellectuals such as Wallerstein and Anderson adjusted to failed expectations. For Anderson, adjustment meant acknowledging capitalism's dominance while maintaining his political determination. For Wallerstein, adjustment meant that he stopped predicting the arrival of future socialism and yet continued to anticipate the end of capitalism. When they returned to their macrohistorical projects begun in the 1970s, they did so with diminished expectations. Still, their new writings had a heightened sense of the ability of humans to change the world. Far from being a product of the past, radical political economy has been continually remade by its innovators in light of contemporary problems.

Chapter 1

Cosmopolitan Beginnings

In geography and lineage, the life stories of Immanuel Wallerstein and Perry Anderson were rather different. Wallerstein, a self-described "complete New Yorker,"[1] found the city to be his entry to the world. New York was full of diverse peoples and languages, and became the home of the United Nations in Wallerstein's teenage years. Anderson, by contrast, achieved his cosmopolitanism through constant travels: China, America, Ireland, and England. Both paths, however, enabled these curious minds to think about the world's poor and politically subordinate. From their earliest writings, Wallerstein and Anderson used their global orientation to criticize policies at home and contemplate the future of the decolonizing world. Wallerstein wrote about the American backlash against national self-determination and assessed various independence movements in Africa. Anderson examined the historical roots of domination in the world and within Britain. Whereas the former considered future prospects for postindependence stability, the latter was predominantly concerned with how social hierarchies were established.

The Capital of the World-Economy

The 1930s was a time of great political change. A global economic depression undermined public confidence in the stability of capitalism, and, in the West, the Soviet experiment divided Left public intellectuals. Fissures between pro-Stalinists and anti-Stalinists deepened throughout the thirties as disenchantment with Stalin grew. After Hitler and Stalin signed a nonaggression pact in 1939, many pro-Stalinists dropped their support. In U.S. public debate, America's participation in World War II, allied with the Soviet Union, temporarily reversed this trend, although further disappointment, and eventually shock, over Stalin would become the prevailing view of the Left.

Oscillation between pro-Stalinism and anti-Stalinism was due partly to a lack of information about Stalin's leadership, coupled with the hope that communism could be realized in the Soviet Union. Much of the American Left was preoccupied with antifascism rather than championing communism. Stalin, moreover, very ably garnered widespread support in the United States by positioning the Soviet Union as the only truly antifascist government. In fact, the peak of Stalin's popularity in the West corresponded with his Revolution from Above, which ranks among the most brutally repressive domestic programs in history.[2] Stalin's crimes were not widely understood in the United States, where intellectuals debated whether reports of repression were exaggerated for political purposes. There was also a reluctance to think that the Soviet Union, which had been a beacon of hope for workers and those advocating for equality, had turned on its own people. This was not mere denial: the most critical of reports failed to capture the scale of Stalin's crimes.[3]

This debate raged fiercely among leftists in New York City, where Immanuel Maurice Wallerstein was born on September 28, 1930. He described New York, with its diverse culture, as being "absolutely essential" for his intellectual development.[4] His parents were Lazar and Sara (Günsberg) Wallerstein. From separate places in the Austro-Hungarian Empire, they met in Berlin, and had a child, Robert. (Though born nine years apart, Robert and Immanuel would become close as adults.) Lazar, a rabbi who became a physician, grew concerned about life in Berlin. The family moved to New York in the early 1920s. As a boy, Immanuel took an early interest in languages. His parents mostly spoke English at home, but they conversed with friends and relatives in German and other dialects from Central Europe. He was exposed to German, Spanish, Portuguese, and French.

For Wallerstein, being Jewish meant that his family was on the Left. In his mind, to be Jewish also meant that one was sensitive to the rights of peoples and to the principles of national self-determination. However, he considered himself unusual in that he never saw a logical distinction between the rationale for an Israeli state and the rationale for a Palestinian or an Algerian one. Later, he reflected: "[O]ne of the reasons why I felt a great empathy for the Palestinian cause from the beginning was because I couldn't see any difference between their arguments and those that the Jews had made."[5]

As a youth, Wallerstein was conflicted in the disputes among interwar leftists. He sympathized with the anti-Stalinism of social democrats, who worried about willingness of Western communists to adopt positions of East European communist parties that betrayed genuine communist principles. He also sympathized with the American communists, who accused social democrats of being unwilling to mount a genuine opposition to capitalism. These arguments, according to Wallerstein, "created dilemmas with which I have had to wrestle ever since."[6]

One such dilemma for Wallerstein was how peoples could be freed from constraints imposed by great powers. He thought the world federalist movement might have ideas for how to provide a more equitable distribution of power. Wallerstein's first article, "Revolution and Order," appeared in *Federalist Opinion*, the publication of world federalists.[7] The piece, which appeared in print the same year he received his BA from Columbia University, displayed an early concern for the interests of subordinate peoples. At the time, global federalists thought mostly in terms of creating peace between the United States and the Soviet Union. Wallerstein believed his fellow federalists should consider world government from a third world perspective. In his opinion, world federalists needed to address the "legacy of hostility, suspicion, fear and wounded dignity" imposed by the West onto the third world. An appeal to order would not be enough, nor, he thought, should it be enough to quell the third world's revolutionary passions. For him, it was up to federalists to truly understand the issues of the dispossessed.[8]

One avenue Wallerstein took to understand the world's poor was through organizations such as the Young Adult Council (YAC) and the World Assembly of Youth (WAY). In 1951, WAY met in the United States. The following year, the meeting was held in Dakar. It became one of many trips he took to the region. Membership in the organization enabled Wallerstein to meet politically active people, many of whom would go on to lead African states after independence.[9] Although he took several trips to Africa in the fifties and sixties, Wallerstein also maintained his contacts by virtue of living in New York. Ghana was admitted to the United Nations in 1957. Guinea joined in 1958, followed by several others in the sixties. Every fall, delegates would come to the General Assembly. Wallerstein was often invited to United Nations receptions, and, as an adult, deepened ties forged in his youth. To him, New York seemed like "the center of Africa."[10]

Wallerstein spent much of this time in New York. He earned his undergraduate degree in 1951. Wallerstein was then unhappily drafted into America's Korean War, and sent to defend the Panama Canal.[11] (He had previously attended meetings of the American Veterans Committee because it was politically active.) Afterward, he returned to New York and Columbia University for graduate school.

The sociology department was a leading institution for a new field of study that came to be known as political sociology. The faculty included Seymour Martin Lipset, Daniel Bell, Paul Lazarfeld, and C. Wright Mills, who became a mentor for Wallerstein. According to Wallerstein, the department "thought of itself, and was thought of, as the center of the sociological world."[12] Yet he differed from many of his colleagues on ideological and methodological grounds. With regard to the latter, he was different in that he neither sought universal laws nor did he advocate case uniqueness in his studies.[13] He would later describe his vision of research as heretical to social science at the time.[14] Still, his position within the institutional framework of Columbia University, as well as its location in New York, provided a stable place from which he could espouse radical ideas.

Though he was encouraged by the strength of postwar independence movements, Wallerstein worried about their prospects for success in light of U.S. hegemony. He expressed these reservations in a 1954 master's thesis on the xenophobia of America's Far Right.[15] With the advent of the Cold War, anti-Stalinism and anticommunism came to prominence in the United States. Wallerstein thus joined the community of New York intellectuals who wrote about extreme anticommunist attitudes espoused by some conservatives.[16]

Wallerstein saw a deep fissure within American conservatism. He saw *sophisticated conservatives* under attack by *practical conservatives*, categories he borrowed from Mills.[17] The tradition of sophisticated conservatism descended from Puritanism, and stressed individual self-reliance and self-worth through work and honest practices. Sophisticated conservatives, according to Wallerstein, were also likely to favor the protection of civil liberties and local governance.[18]

The practical conservative, on the other hand, came from a place apparently beyond rationality. This political style was an appealing rhetorical device because it seemed to make simple and sensible propositions.

For example, the practical conservative would act as if there were no harm in asking citizens to take loyalty oaths, something Wallerstein saw as fundamentally dangerous. The practical conservative, he wrote, "would abolish the Fifth Amendment, because it stands in the way of cleaning out the Reds."[19] The practical conservative was, in other words, fearful, kneejerk, and suspicious.[20] By advocating dramatic change in the name of protecting the homeland, practical conservatives had declared "war" on their sophisticated counterparts.[21]

At the time, Wallerstein thought that Senator Joseph McCarthy most embodied the rhetoric of the practical conservative. McCarthy declared that the United States faced both foreign and domestic threats, but noted that citizens should be especially mindful of the latter. In the age of McCarthy, the chief domestic threat to America was the Left, but all political opponents were potential targets.

Methodologically, Wallerstein studied McCarthyism by analyzing the senator's speeches and polling data. In an attempt to gain access to records of speeches, he sent a letter to the senator. Not without a sense of humor, he posed as a devotee: "I am a veteran just out of service and returned to school. I have been discussing with some of my fellow veterans your fight for Americanism in government. As soon as we tried to find out more information about what has been going on while we were in service, we discovered the papers were not being fair in reporting your great work. We are very anxious to get hold of copies of speeches you have made since 1950 when you first exposed the mess in Washington. We want to study these speeches, reproduce them and circulate them."[22] It is not clear if the senator's office responded, but in the meantime Wallerstein performed content analysis on several speeches. The data came from records held by Daniel Bell.[23]

To explain McCarthyism, Wallerstein emphasized two main factors: status politics and the paradoxical foreign policy of isolationist-interventionism. On the former, Wallerstein directed readers to the people McCarthy routinely attacked: Anglo-Saxon political elites, well educated and in positions of power. On the latter, which Wallerstein referred to as the *anti-military militarist*, we find that the practical conservative was suspicious of the powers of the Army, but also spoke of the "inevitability of the third world war."[24]

The heart of McCarthyism, as Wallerstein told it, was anti-intellectualism. Intellectuals were nice targets because they both occupied decision-making positions in the State Department, and were the ones sympathetic to communism during the 1930s. Practical conservatives portrayed intellectuals as phony elites, with fake British accents and practicing diplomacy while lavishing in their femininity and homosexuality. Practical conservatives questioned the ability of State Department intellectuals to fight communism.[25] According to Wallerstein, intellectuals may have been unusual scapegoats, but they were, in a post-Nazi world, easier scapegoats than Jews. McCarthy, in fact, worked hard to avoid being seen as anti-Semitic and as an offshoot of Nazism.[26]

For Wallerstein, McCarthyism thus sought to start a kind of counterrevolution against the developing postwar scene. He categorized McCarthyism as an antirevolutionary, regressive force, aimed at suppressing nationalist, anticolonial, movements. Wallerstein worried that practical conservatism might displace sophisticated conservatism: "The decision, whichever way it ultimately goes, will have a decisive impact upon the world situation."[27]

Wallerstein believed that the final outcome was important because it could "contribute to the solution of man's problems here and now."[28] Thus, although the thesis was an analysis of the United States, he saw it as connected to the postwar international order.[29]

The most pressing problem in the world, according to Wallerstein, was the transition of the colonized zones to national self-governance. Dominant powers such as the United States had a choice: they could be effective facilitators of such a transition, or, they could slow or damage the process. Spending time in Africa made Wallerstein more aware of the influence of great powers on the rest of the world. Transfixed, he stayed at Columbia, took a doctorate in 1959, and then joined the faculty. During these years, Wallerstein concentrated on African decolonization and independence. "It was Africa," Wallerstein recalled, "that was responsible for challenging the more stultifying parts of my education."[30]

Preparations for a doctoral dissertation, "The Emergence of Two West African Nations: Ghana and the Ivory Coast," shaped Wallerstein's research agenda for more than a decade.[31] Drawing on interviews with some two hundred leaders of voluntary associations in Accra and Abidjan (the capitals of Ghana and Ivory Coast), he examined the role of nationalism in the formation of the two then-newly independent states. At the time, nationalist movements in Africa were about reducing inequality and achieving some measure of political fairness.[32]

Notably, Wallerstein attributed the social structure of Ghana and Ivory Coast to European imperialism. As he saw it, the differences in how Britain and France managed their colonies were minimal in comparison to the difference between European rule and self-rule. At first, colonial administrators kept to their forts. But when European powers carved up Africa in the late nineteenth century and assumed direct control, they profoundly changed the colonized peoples. As he saw it, postcolonial governance was a product of the total and fundamental change imposed by outsiders.[33] In Ghana and Ivory Coast, these changes came in the form of a market economy and urbanization.

Wallerstein's dissertation demonstrated that he conceived of development as *relational*. By relational, one means that a city, a state, or a region does not change mostly on its own but as the result of its relationships to other places. Wallerstein saw tribal elites, nationalist leaders, and even European colonial administrators as operating within a larger, historically contingent, international structure, produced by an interaction between the two worlds. The relationship was not simply one of independent development, or one of pure domination and subordination. Instead, the Westernization of Africa had been complex, and took place within what he called a "changing world context."[34]

Though Wallerstein stressed interconnections, his research relied on the national state. Unlike Anderson, who was drawn to states by the devotion they inspired, Wallerstein found the state to be a useful tool. To him, nation-states simply appeared to be the most consequential actors in the world. He wrote: "[T]he nation is the most significant unit of social structure, the only complete social system existing in the modern world."[35]

Wallerstein recognized the great uncertainty that lay ahead for Ghana and Ivory Coast. One difficulty was that African states had a truncated revolutionary period. Europe had hundreds of years to process its changes, but in Africa, revolutions of politics, society, and technology happened at once. Nonetheless, he remained optimistic about their prospects, which he saw as representative of the prospects for the continent.[36]

Wallerstein's orientation, shown through his writings on McCarthyism as well as African decolonization, was toward the world's political subordinates. Wary of U.S. power, supportive of African nationalism, he never considered social research to be dispassionate or detached from the current events. The years spent living in New York, interacting with other cultures, followed by trips to Africa, shaped Wallerstein's identity. Yet even though Wallerstein's childhood cultivated cosmopolitanism, it was very much a New York cosmopolitanism. Later, Wallerstein concluded that New York was in fact the "capital" of the world-economy.[37]

British Marxism, Not Nationalism

Perry Anderson failed to identify with any particular city or country. Although born in London, Anderson believed he should have been born in China.[38] His father spent the major part of his career working for Chinese Maritime Customs (CMC), and it was only by coincidence that, on September 11, 1938, Francis Rory Peregrine Anderson was born in London.[39] His family called him Rory.[40] Anderson's sentiment of being out of place, even at birth, is illustrative of his vision of world politics. Childhood experiences, he thought, led him to avoid adopting the national allegiances or patriotism that people commonly develop in their youth. To the contrary, he believed that he took on a cosmopolitan identity, removed from any particular national state. Thus, Anderson's cosmopolitanism was the product of experiencing diverse peoples absent a central meeting place, such as New York.

Anderson's Left orientation came in part from an inherited intellectual curiosity and a familial disposition toward the oppressed. The first born was Richard Benedict "Ben" O'Gorman Anderson, then Perry, and the youngest was Melanie Catherine Sainthill Anderson.[41] Perry's mother, Veronica (Bigham) Anderson, descended from a line of English businessmen and civil servants. His father, James Carew O'Gorman "Shaemas" Anderson, came from a mix of Irish and English folk that were more politically engaged. The O'Gormans were Catholic Irish nationalists that, according to Anderson's brother Benedict, made it all but impossible to identify as English.[42] Shaemas Anderson supported Sinn Fein in Ireland, criticized fellow Britons working in Chinese Maritime Customs, and empathized with the suffering of local Chinese. Of the three Anderson children, however, only Benedict later became an Irish citizen, a decision he made more out of love for father than love for country.[43]

In the 1940s, a natural sensitivity for the downtrodden combined with potent life experiences, which would shape Anderson's intellectual views. In 1941, under pressure from Veronica and unhappy with his post in Shanghai, Shaemas Anderson decided to head home. The Andersons traveled by way of San Francisco and spent the rest of the war in California and Colorado. The war in the Atlantic made passage home too dangerous.[44] Moreover, the war in the Pacific and Japan's takeover of Chinese Maritime Customs likely ruled out any consideration of returning to China. While in the United States, Anderson's father worked for the California bureau of Britain's Office of Political Warfare. The family moved to Ireland in 1945. Shaemas Anderson, whose health had been in decline for some time, died the next year.[45]

The Anderson brothers attended Eton. In Benedict's recollection, their mother had a low opinion of the Irish educational system and pushed her sons to attend an English boarding school. She also noted that they would need scholarships now that family income mostly came from their late father's pension.[46] Most works describe Perry and Benedict as coming from means, a conclusion supported by their father's position and their ability to rescue the *New Left Review* (discussed later in this chapter).[47] Benedict's remarks, however, suggest that family resources were not unlimited, especially when it came to paying for a prestigious boarding school. The brothers won spots on the limited roster of scholarship students, and they quickly found that their Eton experiences were rather different than sons of rich Britons and what Benedict called the "brown-skinned 'princes' from the ex-colonies." The rich boys looked down on their lower status peers, and the scholarship boys regarded their rich peers as dumb and lazy. Both groups were "snobbish" in their own way, Benedict noted.[48] Perry recalled how, by this point, his accent had changed several times: in California, he was regarded as English; then in England, he was regarded as American; then in Ireland, he was regarded as English once again; and finally, while at school in England, he was regarded as Irish. Frequently relocations, in addition to teasing from fellow schoolchildren, reinforced his cosmopolitanism.[49] Equally significant was the influence of books (while on breaks, he and Benedict would read sometimes seven to eight hours a day),[50] as well as art (the theatre and radio programs).[51]

In 1956, Perry Anderson began his first year at Oxford. Within weeks, two events happened that changed his life forever. He and other members of the university's student Left would refer to the year as a conjuncture, which, according to one-time comrade Stuart Hall, meant that 1956 was "not just a year."[52] It was a seminal moment, for international Left and for twentieth-century world politics. That year, the Soviets suppressed the Hungarian Revolution, and the British and French occupied Suez. The campus was alive with activity. Divisions and political allegiances were exacerbated within the student population, which was already debating the expansion of European communism, colonialism, Vietnam, and turmoil in the Middle East. Anderson reflected: "It was virtually impossible, I think, for any lively young person not to be very quickly and deeply politicized by that experience."[53]

Although many students supported Britain's war on Egypt, Anderson and the student Left opposed both their own government and the Soviets. Anderson considered himself New Left because he rejected old binaries, social democracy versus one-party communism. He and the other students did not think they could trust Western capitalist governments, which suppressed workers at home and subjugated peoples abroad. They also could not trust Soviet leaders. Stalin had been dead for three years. Yet Moscow had not genuinely reversed course under Khrushchev, and the clampdown in Hungary was antithetical to the principles of socialism. Nor did Anderson and others think they could trust Western socialist governments. France was led by the socialist Guy Mollet, who, they thought, betrayed his international Left supporters by siding with Great Britain in the Suez. Quite simply, they declared the trusted model of the Old Left dead; in their opinion, it needed to be replaced by a more sophisticated understanding of world politics. In short, they thought of themselves as "new" because they did not trust either side of the Cold War Establishment. For Hall, 1956 marked the end of a "political Ice Age."[54]

The student Left was frustrated by what they perceived to be an inattentiveness by the British government. They expressed their views in the journals *New University* and *Universities and Left Review* (ULR). Based at Oxford, ULR was edited by Stuart Hall, along with Gabriel Pearson, Raphael Samuel, and Charles Taylor. They considered their position to be a fresh perspective on the British welfare state, which had proven itself "monstrously irrelevant" to those who came of age in the postwar years.[55] In 1960, *New University* published an essay by Anderson and Robin Blackburn, who would remain a friend and ally of Anderson's for decades. In the same issue, Anderson, who thought English audiences should read continental thinkers, also translated an article by Jean-Paul Sartre.[56]

The Oxford Left arrived at a time of declining public support for the Communist Party of Great Britain (CPGB). Waning interest came after two decades of popular and intellectual enthusiasm for Left ideas and organizations. In the 1930s and 1940s, the number of radical publications in poetry, literary studies, science, economics, and politics multiplied.[57] Groups like the Left Book Club published popular radical texts, while the Communist Party Historians Group provided an institutional home for radical intellectuals.[58] Public opinion in Britain shifted to the Left during the war, an experience duplicated in the United States, with opinions about Stalin and the Soviet Union becoming more favorable. In 1942, the British Communist Party boasted 65,000 members. The party held two seats in Parliament in 1945, and was looked upon favorably by a number of sympathetic Labour members.[59] The Left's mood in the early postwar years was quite optimistic: fascism had discredited the Right, and the wild swings of capitalism had shaken the Center.[60]

The temporary alliance of the West with the Soviet Union was forged by a common commitment against fascism. After the war, with fascism eradicated, relations dramatically shifted once again. Chances for the Left's ideological triumph also declined. In the way that the Right had been harmed by proximity to fascism, the Left was harmed by proximity to Stalinism. In truth, Stalin had upended the values of communism. Beliefs in classlessness and equality suddenly became associated with their opposite: tyranny, cronyism, and a lack of individual freedom. Stalin's success lay in that he praised communist principles while subverting those principles in practice. Thus, a standard narrative played out on both sides of the Atlantic, one that associated Stalin with Marxism. To this day, public discourse (especially in the United States) often identifies one with the other.

Notwithstanding Attlee's Labour government from 1945 to 1951, the Left did not win the day. Over a five-year period, the Communist Party lost half its members, and faced public hostility.[61] Still, the Left's ideas were not eradicated. Despite the Right's resurgence, Marxist intellectualism expanded. Even as the Party lost influence, Left journals continued to open up.

In addition to Oxford's student-inspired journals, new publications such as *Past and Present* and the *New Reasoner* became a home for diverse ideas. The Historians Group created *Past and Present* in 1952, with John Morris as editor and Eric Hobsbawm as assistant editor. The *New Reasoner* (for three issues, named the *Reasoner*) was founded in 1956 by John Saville and Edward (E. P.) and Dorothy Thompson. Unhappy with the Communist Party's supine support of Soviet policies, and unable to publish their criticism in established Party publications, they wanted the journal to be an unfiltered outlet for Party members. The explosion of journals, in other words, was a sign of divisiveness among Leftists. The CPGB could not quell dissent within its ranks, even by threatening expulsion. Several prominent intellectuals resigned, including Saville, Thompson, Christopher Hill, and Rodney Hilton.

Anderson became active as an intellectual at this moment of turmoil. There was friction between the established Left and the student Left. The conflict was more than a clash of personalities: it was a contest over the meaning of the New Left and what its members would do to advance socialism. For some, the difference between the Historians Group and the Oxford Left was not just age, but political context: World War II separated their political generations, and, with the threat of fascism seemingly gone, younger Leftists were less willing to support even the strongest antifascist governments.[62]

By 1959, the declining sales and financial troubles incentivized the merger of *Universities and Left Review* and the *New Reasoner*. The new journal was the *New Left Review*, often called by its initials, NLR, or simply the *Review*. It was a marriage of necessity. As far as the participants were concerned, the publications came from different worlds. Yet despite the two journals being very different, every editorial board member except Ralph Miliband, who strongly protested the merger, voted in favor of combining their resources.[63] Hall became the journal's new editor and worked with an editorial board of twenty-five members.

Despite his inexperience, Anderson ascended quickly within the NLR's organizational structure. With his time at Oxford over, he was perhaps looking for the kind of institutional home that academics such as Wallerstein enjoyed. But unlike Columbia University, the NLR was not a place for associating with ideological opponents.

In 1960, Anderson did not contribute a single piece to the NLR (nor had he published in either of its predecessors). In 1961, he published three articles.[64] Late that year, with declining sales and increasing bills, Hall resigned to write on his own.[65] The *Review* was in serious financial distress, and Anderson, as a figure of relative means, was able to help. Therefore, Perry and Benedict Anderson, along with Ronald Fraser, paid off the NLR's debts in return for some editorial concessions.[66] In 1962, Anderson became principal editor with the right to reduce the *Review*'s large editorial board and appoint new board members.[67] That year, he had published in every issue.[68]

Even with some financial relief,[69] the NLR's editorial transition was not smooth. The new team was inexperienced, and, as editor, Anderson intended to take the journal in a very different direction. Previously, the NLR served as a place for organizing and activism.[70] Hall conceived of the NLR as a social enterprise and as a leader of New Left clubs around Britain. The journal was secondary to the movement. It was not overly centralized and did not wish to be. It purposefully lacked, he reflected, "tight organization structure" and "rules, regulations, party programme or 'line.'"[71] The journal was not simply a forum for interpreting the world. Yet Anderson believed it should concentrate on the ideas that inspired activism. Others could organize protests or recruit activists. What the New Left needed, according to Anderson, was a proper understanding of the present. Political commitments of the present ought to be understood by engaging the past in a structural and all-encompassing way. The present did not appear haphazardly, but through a series of historical events, which if understood properly, can aid those who wish for change. To be a part of the New Left, Anderson later reflected, meant that one should think "through a series of public questions which are also intellectual and theoretical questions about the history of the New Left, but also about empire, the Soviet Empire and the British Empire."[72] In Anderson's worldview, a deep understanding of the past was required in order to shape the present.

In the sixties, the British New Left was no longer unified as it once had been. The moment of 1956 had faded.[73] The Left's dysfunctional state could most prominently be seen, Anderson thought, by the Campaign for Nuclear Disarmament (CND). This was a political program the Left should have won. After witnessing the advent and spread of nuclear weapons (by now, in two types, atomic and hydrogen), many young people felt compelled to protest.[74] CND became very popular for a few years but declined just as quickly. The CND failed, he explained, because it could not provide a general theory of the Cold War. Capitalist states, on the other hand, had a very strong explanation: the Cold War was a battle against communist dictatorship, just as World War II had been against fascist dictatorship. The West's explanation, according to Anderson, was popular for its simplicity: "Communism became synonymous with evil and dangerous."[75]

It would be the job of the NLR, Anderson believed, to help fashion a counternarrative that the Left could use against the capitalist West. The New Left needed to show that the Cold War was not an ideological battle with Marxism. It needed to show that Stalin did not represent genuine Left ideas, and that communism was not really a threat to human freedom.[76]

With this ambition, Anderson and the NLR published in three areas: British society; the third world; and bringing continental Marxism home to Britain. The new editors thought that they could shift what they perceived as the British public's narrow-mindedness and self-satisfaction by importing continental Marxism and by emphasizing political change in the third world. The editors announced this new direction in a note to readers, calling it "irresistibly obvious" that prospects for socialism at home were caught up in the larger global struggles for freedom. They wrote: "Socialism remains the vocation of our time; the dethronement of capital has proved both possible and necessary."[77] The NLR should be international because the major socialist revolutions were outside Europe and the decolonization movement possessed great potential for socialism. Thus, Anderson and the editors saw their international perspective as consistent with classical socialism and as allowing for objective analysis of various countries, including Great Britain.[78]

Yet the NLR's writers considered themselves outsiders, "as if [Britain] were a 'foreign' country."[79] Anderson's childhood moves gave him a certain distance. Without such "romantic attachments" to a place, Anderson's perspective was, in many respects, hardly different from that of a foreign visitor. Great Britain might as well have been China or France. In part, this was a logical extension of an existing practice. Many members of the British Left in the 1950s had spent much of their lives outside Britain. Two notable examples are Hall, who was Jamaican, and Sadiq al-Mahdi, who was Sudanese; others too, had joined the student Left at Oxford, while away from their home countries.

In 1964, the NLR began running a series of articles on Britain by Anderson and Tom Nairn. Though published individually, their writings became known as the Nairn-Anderson theses.[80] The theses were the NLR's first attempt at developing a narrative of England's past to shape its present trajectory.[81] For Nairn and Anderson, developing such a history also meant utilizing thinkers from the continent, and thus, in their view, breathing new life into British intellectualism.

They began with a startling premise: that Western Marxism had not penetrated British intellectual life. It was not that Anderson recognized no existing English Marxism, but that he regarded its formation as a radical liberalism rather than a genuine Marxism. A few thinkers, such as Christopher Hill, Eric Hobsbawm, and Raymond Williams, stood out to Anderson as notable exceptions. But even as he acknowledged a limited role for an indigenous English Marxism, he sought to minimize its significance. For example, one essay from 1968 recognized Hill as genuinely Marxist, but it strangely suggested that only in the sixties did he produce what English socialism thus far had not: "a serious, scientific, intellectual achievement."[82] By the time it was reprinted decades later, in *English Questions*, Anderson had softened his tone, describing all three as significant thinkers whose contributions to English Marxism began before the arrival of the New Left.[83]

Still, there may be some truth to thought that the NLR was importing ideas previously "external" to most of the British Left.[84] Nairn and Anderson wanted to replicate the national-identity projects of Gramsci, Sartre, and Lukács, and bring to Britain what their forebears had brought to Italy, France, and Germany.[85]

Most influential in this period was Antonio Gramsci.[86] From the Italian thinker, Nairn and Anderson learned about hegemonic power, rooted in notions of force and consent (or, fear and love, in Machiavelli's terms). Gramsci deemed the bourgeoisie a hegemonic class, a term Anderson applied to elites (aristocratic and bourgeois) in the British context. As Anderson understood hegemony, political power was closely connected to the realm of culture, the latter being essential to the former. If socialists were to win the state, they would have to win the culture too. Still, Anderson's overall relationship with Grasmci's writings was complicated. He later attributed the "Gramscian direction" of the theses to Nairn, noting that his own use of Gramsci was really infused with "Sartrean and Lukácsian subtones."[87] In the seventies, Anderson wrote an article on the "extreme contradictions" within Gramsci's writings that, apparently, Nairn-Anderson had missed.[88] Even though Anderson was no Gramscian, he would return to discuss Gramsci's writings over subsequent decades, a sign of the importance (and, for Anderson, frequent misuse) of Gramsci's concept of hegemony.[89]

Unlike Wallerstein, who focused on the American Right's rhetorical strategies, Anderson's writings on Britain emphasized the historical forces that gave the Right an advantage. The problem Anderson described in his 1964 essay "Origins of the Present Crisis" had to do with an "increasing entropy" of British society.[90] For him, the decline of empire led to the stagnation of British industry, education, infrastructure, and morale. International economic decline, beginning with the completion of imperial expansion, was the chief factor precipitating the crisis. As entropy increased, so too did nationalist fervor and the celebration of past achievements. In Anderson's opinion, Conservative leadership in the 1950s took on an aristocratic character of "neo-Edwardianism," projecting a diplomatic attitude of supremacy whose only relevance was its historical legacy. By the 1950s, Anderson wrote, the upper class had been reduced to play-acting, wistfully conjuring past global dominance.[91]

In such circumstances, Anderson remarked, one should expect the Left to be more popular. Why did the working class *not* achieve ruling supremacy despite its "great numerical superiority" over other classes?[92] The answers to these questions, he thought, would help the Left assess the strength of capitalism in Britain as well as the ability of hegemonic classes to maintain their hegemony despite the revolts of the working class. He came to think that the relative weakness of the British Left, and, in particular, the Labour Party, had to do with the historical character of the bourgeoisie and proletariat.

According to Anderson, the merchants in Britain only halfheartedly revolted against the nobility in the seventeenth century. The bourgeois revolution was, in reality, a limited uprising that became co-opted by the aristocracy. Instead of overthrowing its master, the bourgeois class was rather easily tempted by the aristocratic lifestyle and limited opportunities for joining its ranks. (It was a bourgeois revolution "only by proxy" among factions of rural landowners who disputed the role of the monarchy.)[93] For Anderson, the revolution succeeded in bringing about the transformation to capitalism, but left "almost the entire social structure intact."[94]

Elites (bourgeois and aristocratic), in Anderson's argument, constituted a *hegemonic class,* capturing a force of power based on cultural norms of identity. Here, he borrowed Gramsci's definition: hegemony was "the dominance of one social bloc over another, not simply by means of force or wealth, but by a wider authority whose ultimate resource is cultural."[95] The hegemonic class was unusual in that it could form its own identity, the identities of lower classes, and the national image as a whole.

Anderson found that a hegemonic class might block ideologies produced by bourgeois and working classes. The ruling class in Britain perpetuated what he likened to a quasi-feudal arrangement of social echelons that were reinforced by cultural cues. Aristocratic styles, attitudes, and behavior provided the standard for upward mobility, which seemed unattainable to most workers yet appeared just within reach for labor leaders. Ideologically, the ruling classes (eventually a fusion between the bourgeoisie and aristocracy) developed a conservatism characterized by a desire for wealth and reverence for institutions.[96] The establishment in Britain, in other words, set priorities for the lower classes to keep them from upending the political order. Simultaneously, elites adopted a cloak of equality in the political realm: domestic leaders, unlike those in the empire, took on an appealing egalitarian character. They were not identified as professional politicians, bureaucrats, or military leaders, an amateurism that worked to their advantage. Social norms, ideology, and leadership made the upper class culturally attractive and, through its appeal, hegemonic.

For Anderson, to the extent that the hegemonic class was strong, the working class was weak. British proletarians never seemed quite capable of revolution. The aristocratic-bourgeois fusion made upward mobility of the proletariat naturally more difficult. Furthermore, Anderson commented, England's workers had the unhappy distinction of being the world's first industrial proletariat. Consequently, it had to devise an organizational structure and plan of action from scratch. He believed this fact made the proletariat not immature, but "premature," with no socialist thinking or strategies at its disposal.[97] Thus, workers in England had no precedent or theory to follow.

Over time, leaders of working-class organizations became, for Anderson, unable to envision a radically different world. Britain's working class was thus a *corporate class*. Unlike the hegemonic class that remade social and political relations in its own image, the corporate class sought to increase its power within conditions it did not create and, most terribly, did not fundamentally question. The proletariat in England achieved consciousness, he admitted, but never an accompanying political will. In fact, Anderson thought the proletariat's lack of self-direction could be summed up by the party tasked with representing its views. Unlike any of the other European working-class parties, Britain's proletarian party was not called Socialist, Communist, or Social Democratic. The Labour Party was a declaration of interests, not an expression of how British society ought to be structured.[98]

The empire, moreover, had since the nineteenth century been an additional barrier to meaningful Left reforms. Though members of the working class did not materially benefit from colonialism, they, like any group, were susceptible to imperial romanticism. According to Anderson, the ruling classes successfully played on nationalist sentiments to quell proletarian restlessness. In the twentieth century, world wars served this same purpose, just not as effectively.[99] After World War II, Anderson explained, Labour's postwar parliamentary majority created institutions such as the National Health Service. Yet this success was short-lived. Paradoxically, Keynesian capitalist programs had wiped out widespread unemployment and buoyed the working class. This undermined the Left's case for socialism: for the previous half-century, he noted, the Left had portrayed capitalism to be incapable of preventing poverty.[100]

Anderson concluded that for Labour to transform Britain in the 1960s it must first become a genuine socialist party.[101] However small, there was an opportunity for the working class to achieve some political standing proportional to its demographic size. An awareness of barriers was a prerequisite to surmounting them. The Left, consequently, would do well to encourage Labour to set its sights higher. The only way to success, Anderson believed, was not for Leftists to hope for incremental improvement. The way forward was to transform the corporate class into a socialist one, which would then go about dismantling the hegemonic class looming above. The future of Leftists, from any class position, was caught up in the future of workers. By pairing the entirety of socialism with Stalinism, Western Cold War rhetoric instilled negative attitudes about socialism at home.[102] The capitalists' narrative was so compelling, in fact, that it threatened the survival of Left organizations and journals. For Anderson, the Left should stand up for its convictions. Its survival depended on it.

Anderson did not discuss the global implications of Conservative electoral success, perhaps because of Britain's decline on the world stage. Nonetheless, he, like Wallerstein, saw a close connection between domestic class struggles and the struggles between the developed and postcolonial worlds. Earlier in the decade, Anderson published a three-part series on the conclusion of Portuguese colonialism.[103] What he found was that, unlike the upper classes in Britain, which placed cultural and political barriers in front of potentially insurgent workers, Portugal's ruling apparatus had not found a way to manage its potentially restless colonies in Africa. Portugal did not sufficiently invest at home or in its colonies in Mozambique and Angola, nor did it have an ideological program in place to pacify the public. There was virtually no co-option, at home or abroad. The state was unprepared for the age of decolonization. As soon as nationalist movements erupted in neighboring areas, anticolonialism broke out in Portugal's territories too.[104]

The contrast between Britain and Portugal, although never directly addressed by Anderson, was clear: narratives could mean the difference between co-option and revolution. Anderson believed that liberation, whether of class or nation, required narratives of liberation. The absence of any defense by Portuguese imperialists ensured that the European power had virtually no African support. But in Britain, the ruling elite's complex program of nationalism and anticommunism, along with a widespread material increase in well-being, ensured that the hegemonic class retained its status. As postcolonial history has demonstrated, a revolutionary mindset is only a starting point for reform. Still, Anderson and the NLR were convinced that if the Left were to have any success it needed a more compelling historical narrative.

Conclusion

With dissimilar childhoods, Wallerstein and Anderson adopted similar extranational political stances. Furthermore, they used their cosmopolitan orientations to criticize conservative domestic politics and write about opportunities (and difficulties) for the postcolonial world. They wrote soberly about the tough road ahead for socialists. Yet, as young intellectuals, they were hopeful about the future. It seemed possible for the Left to advance in the West and for colonial retreat to give way to vibrant, independent, nations. Wallerstein and Anderson took note of obstacles, but, after witnessing the great political and ideological changes from the 1930s to the early 1960s, they had reason to believe that better days lay ahead.

Chapter 2

Ideational Lineages

Born into families on the Left, Immanuel Wallerstein and Perry Anderson became teenagers at a time of hopeful anticipation for the working class at home and for colonized peoples abroad. Political events encouraged optimism, albeit a cautious optimism. As they contemplated current events, their thinking was also informed by notable American and European leftists whose writings encouraged complex views of the past and present.

Wallerstein and Anderson have at various points identified major sources of inspiration, many of whom they also got to know personally. Yet it was a thinker long past, Edward Gibbon, who had a profound impact on a teenaged Perry Anderson. Gibbon proved to be a captivating writer across six volumes of *Decline and Fall of the Roman Empire*. It is noteworthy that neither Wallerstein nor Anderson looked primarily to Karl Marx, though Anderson conceived of his writings as updating Marx's theories for the twentieth century. Although both young radicals would later be identified as Marxists (in words of praise and accusation), Wallerstein never found the label appealing; instead, he took a page from Frantz Fanon in adopting and discarding Marxist terminology as he wished.

Neither modeled his scholarship mainly on twentieth-century English intellectual circles. The geographical center of influence was farther east, in Paris and Budapest: Wallerstein derived his concept of the totality from Fernand Braudel and Karl Polanyi; for Anderson, it was Jean-Paul Sartre and Georg Lukács, especially the former's term *totalization*. The four thinkers, who conceived of totalities in divergent ways, believed that true understanding of our collective past and present came through holism, through seeing the world as complex, made up of interrelated economic, political, social, and cultural parts. A proper discussion of the totality, and how Wallerstein and Anderson gave meaning to this term, is saved for chapter 4. Here, we see how France, Hungary, and the decolonizing world, among other places, contributed to radical thought in divergent ways. We also see how influential writers neither replicate the ideas of their forbears nor invent the world anew. In applying the ideas of others, Wallerstein and Anderson needed to invent new ways of thinking, adjusting to the present. This chapter is about old ideas. Subsequent chapters are about modifying those ideas and inventing new ones.

A Reading List for the World (-System)

Several intellectuals inspired Wallerstein to think in unconventional terms. He was drawn to leftists, especially those who resisted disciplinary categorization. The most significant in Wallerstein's twenties and thirties were (in birth order): Karl Polanyi, Fernand Braudel, and Frantz Fanon.[1] Wallerstein knew each of them personally. The Noble Prize–winning chemist Ilya Prigogine was perhaps more influential, although his effect would happen later, since he and Wallerstein did not meet until 1980. Wallerstein also learned much from his colleagues and collaborators. But many of those, at Columbia University and elsewhere, were intellectual partnerships that did not shape his thinking in the same way as a mentor or classic text.[2]

Wallerstein was ambivalent about Marx. He did not write much about the early Marxists, and when he did, he often pointed out flaws or contradictions.[3] He thought Marx was too much in the tradition of classical economics, too deterministic in his expectations. Wallerstein regarded both Marxism and liberalism as children of the Enlightenment in their shared trust in human progress, which enthusiasts perceived as desirable, evolutionary, and inevitable.[4] Of course, Wallerstein and Marx were aligned in their desire to see capitalism end, though here, too, the former parted company: whereas Marx saw revolutionaries as necessary for capitalism to end, Wallerstein would eventually come to see systems as concluding on their own accord (due to internal contradictions). Later in life, when he was asked if he preferred to be labeled a Marxist or a radical, Wallerstein had a standard joke: "I'm perfectly happy with being called a radical, and being called a Marxist depends on what you mean by 'Marxist.' And I usually say there are four views of me as a Marxist:

there are those who say I'm a Marxist and that's a good thing; there are those who say I'm a Marxist and that's a bad thing; and there are those who say I'm not a Marxist and that's a good thing; and there are those who say that I'm not a Marxist and that's a bad thing. I can identify with people who have argued all of these things, and I don't worry about that."[5]

Wallerstein was ambivalent because he thought the world had changed since 1883, the year of Marx's passing. He believed human beings, conditioned by their times, were far less capable of reaching universal conclusions (for all people at all times) than was commonly assumed. And, just as Marx's knowledge was limited to the nineteenth century, Wallerstein considered himself bound to the twentieth.[6] Human understanding, in his view, was mostly confined to the historical epoch in which one lived.

Wallerstein's feelings about Marx mirror those of another mentor, Frantz Fanon, who also resisted such a classification. Frequently identified with Marx or Freud, Fanon, in Wallerstein's telling, always demurred: "[I]f someone accused Fanon of being a Marxist, he would respond by saying that he was a Freudian. But if someone accused him of being too Freudian, he would respond by saying that he really was a Marxist. Fanon didn't care too much of this question of labels, and I think that he was as much of a Marxist as I am and, at the same time, as little of a Marxist as I am."[7]

Wallerstein met Fanon in Accra, when the latter served Algeria's provisional government as ambassador to Ghana. It was 1960, the Year of Africa. Seventeen colonial territories would achieve independence on the continent. Wallerstein thought Fanon was "full of life and passion."[8] He, like Wallerstein, wrestled with Marx's legacy, particularly regarding lessons about class terminology. Fanon's sense of classes was greatly influential to Wallerstein, who nonetheless acknowledged that the former never directly outlined a perspective on class struggle. "And yet," Wallerstein contended, class struggle was "central to [Fanon's] world-view and to his analyses."[9]

In the 1950s, European communist parties mostly spoke about urban classes in conflict, the industrial bourgeoisie and industrial proletariat. But in Africa and much of the rest of the world, these categories hardly seemed relevant.[10] When Fanon applied Marxist terms to the colonial world, he redefined them, diverging from the European context. Wallerstein found that Fanon and his critics spoke past one another on the meaning and effects of bourgeoisie, proletariat, peasantry, and lumpenproletariat. (In one case, he determined that Fanon's use of "peasant" was roughly the equivalent of "proletarians" in the writings of two critics.)[11] Throughout his career, Wallerstein's insistence on defining and debating the meaning of terms paradoxically had the same effect: the occasional dispute that somehow never moved beyond the terms of debate. It was not that Wallerstein wished to get caught up in "the fetish of terminology,"[12] as he called it, but that he believed terms were attached to assumptions about historical processes.

About class, Wallerstein concluded that not only were European concepts a poor fit for the postcolonial world, meanings changed over the centuries. To be bourgeois in the twentieth century meant something different than in the nineteenth or the sixteenth centuries, or in its twelfth-century origins, defined as one who lived in urban areas, free from peasant or noble obligations.[13] In postwar America, the agent of the "new middle class" was the salaried professional, neither the early modern merchant, nor the industrial owner-producer. At the same time, the civil servants running postcolonial African governments comprised an "administrative bourgeoisie," or, alternatively, the "dictatorship of the bourgeoisie," as Fanon liked to call one-party states. The meaning of proletariat was similarly varied. Classes, Wallerstein wrote, regularly changed from their initial formation, being broken apart or combined with others over time.[14]

In addition to *class*, Wallerstein also took to the term *strata*, which he saw as a combination of class and status. Among the many variations of strata included: *upper, middle, lower, working, capitalist, educated, dominant,* and *privileged*.[15] The point, it seemed, was to portray differences in well-being, as well as interests, without getting stuck debating the meaning of class terms. The lower strata, after all, often did not worry so much about the juridical or social positions of their oppressors. Take the case of French peasants at the time of the revolution. According to Wallerstein, "[B]oth the better-off peasants and the rural poor often made less distinction between the 'aristocracy' and the 'bourgeoisie' than either the latter themselves or subsequent scholars have been wont to do. To rural workers, both aristocrats and bourgeois were part of the 'privileged classes.'"[16]

Nevertheless, he believed class concepts were reflective of enduring interests. Exploitative processes of capitalism corresponded to three tiers: the top was an exploiter of others; the middle was both subject to and creator of exploitation; and, the bottom was exploited. Those at the top wished to retain three tiers (as well as ensure that the middle had an interest in maintaining the status quo), while those at the bottom wished to shift to a two-tiered situation (to most effectively endanger the privilege of those at the top). Later, Wallerstein came to identify these three tiers in a variety of contexts: the globe, in terms of core, semiperipheral, and peripheral areas; the national state, in terms of what is sometimes called socioeconomic status; and in the production of goods.[17]

In 1961, Wallerstein again met with Fanon. It was fall in Washington, D.C. Fanon, dying of leukemia, was "still full of life and passion."[18] Fanon was interested in the United States, its hegemonic power abroad and the civil rights movement at home. Sick and irritated, he remarked: "You Americans do not engage in dialogue; you still speak monologues."[19] Wallerstein frequently thought about this scolding, even though he realized that "it was not directed at me personally."[20] He took the lesson to heart, however, and would make similar comments about America's foreign policies in the decades to come. Furthermore, Wallerstein adopted Fanon's attitude about European ideas, which we may call *particularistic*, originating from a specific locale, and the sentiment that those ideas have *universal* applicability. According to Wallerstein, Fanon chose to "be particular and be universal."[21] In doing so, he chose not to jettison all European ideas, such as those about class, but rather to reform and rethink them in the colonial and Algerian contexts. Algerians, in his view, preferred to be "liberated" (e.g., to remove the veil, or to embrace modern medicine) by fellow Algerians, even if presented with the same arguments and ideas from Europeans.[22]

Throughout the decade, Wallerstein concentrated on decolonization and the experiences of the emerging nation-states in Africa. He was interested in the challenges facing "new" nations and wanted to draw on the experiences of Europe's "old" nations, learning about their "young" sixteenth-century histories. His plan assumed that all nation-states more or less followed the same trajectory, that is, that they "modernized" in the same way.[23] Wallerstein would come to reject his assumption (shared by many other social scientists) that postcolonial nations could follow the same paths as European states centuries earlier. According to Wallerstein, it was Fernand Braudel who was responsible for cultivating an interest in early modern Europe, and for demonstrating the irresolvable flaws of modernization theory. It was Braudel, he noted, who "pointed" him in the direction of world-systems analysis.[24]

Braudel's impact on Wallerstein could perhaps not be overstated,[25] though the two thinkers did not use concepts such as "society" in identical ways or have the same sense of historical change. Nonetheless, Braudel's works convinced Wallerstein that social scientific findings about society, the economy, or politics were confined by history and geography.[26] There could be no standard model of "development" because apparent rules governing social and political activity were impermanent. Braudel shared this opinion with others in the *Annales* tradition, a French historiographical perspective represented by the journal *Annales ESC*.[27] Marc Bloch and Lucien Febvre, who became Braudel's mentor,[28] founded the journal in 1929. For them, *Annales* was an act of resistance against most French historiography, which they judged as devoid of substance, of synthesis, the mere chronological recapitulation of events.[29] To borrow Peter Burke's description, Febvre was particularly opposed to "any history that was less than total."[30] Yet *Annales* also rejected the notion of general covering laws, applicable for all places and times. Its adherents examined long-term structural patterns (even if some disliked the term *structure*). Many, also, did not self-identify as Marxists.[31] Like Fanon, Braudel and many in the *Annales* tradition were inspired by Marx's ideas yet also innovated upon them.

One way that Braudel struck out on his own was through utilizing long-term historical analysis in addition to shorter time scales. He believed that there were multiple, coexisting, ways that humans perceived the passage of time. The concept of historical "layers" or what some have called the "plurality of social time" was meant to show the variety of ways that history affects human life in the present.[32] In his most famous article, "History and the Social Sciences" (1958), Braudel divided notions of time into three categories—short, medium, and long—that must be combined to properly understand the past.[33] "For me," he wrote, "history is the sum of all possible histories"; one should not study one type of history "to the exclusion of others."[34]

By short term, Braudel meant the timespan around an event (something that was event-*ish*, in Wallerstein's description).[35] Though certainly an important timeframe, the short term may also be the most deceptive. Braudel warned: "Do not think only in the short term. Do not believe that only those actors who make noise are the most authentic."[36] The medium term referred to cyclical phenomena such as periods of faster or slower economic growth.[37] But how long? Questions of translation have led to divergent interpretations. For some, it has meant "conjuncture," a popular concept among the English-speaking Marxists that marks a critical turning point in history, often symbolized by a single year. Wallerstein conceived of it differently. He thought a *conjoncture*, "a cyclical phase," meant a somewhat longer timeframe, a series of events over a period, up to a few decades.[38]

The long term or *longue durée* became Braudel's most well-known timespan. He credited Marx for being the first scholar to utilize long term analysis in social modeling. Yet Braudel also believed that many of his contemporaries applied Marx's models too rigidly, as if they were laws.[39] On this point, Braudel closely resembled Wallerstein's own description of Marxism, as well as Anderson's. Braudel saw the *longue durée* as a rebuke to much of the standard practice of social science, which he viewed as unwilling to consider the impact of long-term forces on the present. For support, Braudel noted that despite political changes, European societies from the fourteenth to the eighteenth centuries retained consistent economic attributes, including: the significance of the merchant class, which used precious metals; repeated agricultural crises; and a reliance on external trade (such as through empire building).[40]

Braudel also commented on the possibility of a fourth timespan, the "very long term." He did not mean "very," however, as an extension of the *longue durée*, but rather as a timespan that was (virtually) immoveable. In one interpretation, the very long term existed to show that the *longue durée* was not permanent, not ahistorical, but merely lengthy.[41] In this sense, the two timespans were significantly different: one permanent (or almost permanent), the other historical.[42]

Still, Braudel's general ideas about methods could be interpreted in a variety of ways, especially about how his sense of time corresponded with an understanding of space.[43] "History and the Social Sciences" did not discuss (at least in detail) how geography aligned with his idea a plurality of social times.[44] Students had to read a bit more closely for such lessons about space. One instructive source, however, was Braudel's two-volume work on *The Mediterranean and the Mediterranean World in the Age of Philip II* (1949), which combined layered times with a concept he called a world-economy, identified as a "self-contained universe." He later elaborated in the 1970s, explaining in depth the relationship between geography and time, though after Wallerstein had drawn his own conclusions.[45]

Whereas Braudel taught expansive ideas about the plurality of social times and how, esoterically, time was associated with space, Karl Polanyi taught specific ideas about how economies functioned. Of importance was Polanyi's distinctions among "modes of economic behavior," as Wallerstein called them, especially the difference between modern capitalism and precapitalist economies.[46]

For Polanyi, the modern *market economy* contrasted sharply from premodern societies. Espoused by thinkers such as Adam Smith, Ludwig von Mises, and Friedrich von Hayek, the notion of a market economy, in Polanyi's description, "implies a self-regulating system of markets; . . . it is an economy directed by market prices and nothing but market prices."[47]

Such a mode of economic organization was neither natural nor the inevitable product of social evolution. To the contrary, premodern economies functioned according to other logics, and, he contended, the modern market economy was fashioned by states.

Prior to the age of Smith (or least the age he symbolizes), economic aspects of life were part of and constrained by other aspects of life, such as familial, political, and religious structures. The assumption that all societies were predicated on individual acquisition (an idea born in the nineteenth century) was what Polanyi called the "economistic fallacy."[48] Of course, Polanyi did not mean that premodern societies had no markets, but merely that the rest of the economy and society was not built upon the market. The notion of a market had existed for millennia, but, he clarified, before the modern age "its role was no more than incidental to economic life."[49] Instead, the realm of economics was controlled by logics of *reciprocity* or *redistribution*. The former was usually small in scale, with crops and other foods traded in person: the head of household, frequently male, knew that his civic reputation depended on quality and honest dealings with his extended family; his family would be paid back, so to speak, with other services. Such a system was not, however, merely altruistic. Survival depended on reputation. Redistributive economies were somewhat larger, with trade moving through at least one intermediary. Prominent members of the group (whether tribal leaders, aristocrats, or heads of bureaucracies) would use their positions to acquire political power. Polanyi pointed to feudal systems as examples of redistribution and the interconnectedness of economics and social relationships.[50] Polanyi's categories greatly influenced Wallerstein. In the seventies, in fact, he would base his perspective of world politics off Polanyi's typology, with adaptations.[51]

Was the market economy the inevitable outcome of the decline of feudalism? Was it bound to happen?[52] To the contrary, Polanyi considered the modern state necessary to the modern market economy and commodification. States cleared away restrictions on open markets. State policies instilled the commodification of land, of money, and of labor.[53] Wallerstein later expanded upon this concept, claiming that capitalism involved the "commodification of everything."[54] Far from seeing political and economic variables in competition, Polanyi shared with Wallerstein a vision of unity between state development and capitalist development. For both scholars, modern political and economic sectors developed in a mutually reinforcing dynamic.

Polanyi's holism also influenced Wallerstein. Like Braudel, Polanyi conceived of the interrelationships among variables to comprise social organizations. He admitted that reciprocity and redistribution were not conventional economic principles,[55] but, as Block and Somers note, the Hungarian was also pushing back against social science specialization. Instead of emphasizing narrow market principles, Polanyi thought that scholars ought to be using the notion of holism, by which he meant thinking about ways in which economics, politics, and society were interconnected.[56] And, much like fellow leftists from Hungary and France—Lukács, Braudel, and Sartre—Polanyi framed his orientation in the vocabulary of totalities. According to Block and Somers, Polanyi saw himself following in the footsteps of Aristotle, relating "all questions of institutional origins and function to the totality of society."[57]

Stylistically, Wallerstein's prose was reminiscent of Polanyi, Braudel, and Fanon. Though Braudel's works were often extensively documented (a trait Wallerstein also acquired), Braudel, like the others, retained the style of an extended essay. Their writings varied between dense historical analysis and public expositions of ideas, with prose accessible to readers without disciplinary expertise. In this respect, the European and African thinkers Wallerstein admired shared with the New York intellectuals a commitment to writing for general audiences. Following C. Wright Mills and Richard Hofstadter, both at Columbia, Wallerstein wrote social history that, he hoped, would be meaningful for everyday people living in the present.[58]

A Reading List for Olympian History

Like Wallerstein, Perry Anderson wanted to affect the lives of people in his own time. And much like Wallerstein and others who published at a young age, Anderson's perspective on the world came from life experiences and from works he read, in some cases, in his early teens. In the years prior to assuming editorship of the *New Left Review*, Anderson had developed a sense of cosmopolitanism reinforced by frequent relocations and an Eton education. At Oxford, political turbulence and especially the events of 1956 taught Anderson an enduring lesson: to answer practical questions about the present, one must engage in historical and philosophical investigation. Activism, therefore, was considered inseparable from academic intellectual enterprises. With the correct explanation, the correct narrative, of history, the Left could compete against the false narratives of the capitalists. As shown in the last chapter, some of Anderson's peers did not share his view, but he remained confident (at least reasonably confident) in his plan for the NLR. Like any independent mind, Anderson had found sustenance in several authors, including Edward Gibbon and twentieth-century Marxists such as Georg Lukács, Louis Althusser, and Jean-Paul Sartre.[59]

Anderson has said that of all authors, Gibbon had the greatest impact during his formative years. One can see why. Like Gibbon, Anderson developed a preference for viewing history in terms of grand trends, had a breadth of reading interests, and a penchant for combining philosophical and historical questions.[60] Anderson's writings moved from political history to philosophical commentary. In one work, he digressed into a six-page commentary on the political thought of Machiavelli, using the thinker to flesh out a discussion of Italian Absolutism.[61] Gibbon, too, was comfortable with, in the words of one account, "penetrating the mentality of every nation and people."[62] He wrote with rich descriptions and images, conveying a sense of familiarity on a multitude of subjects, a characteristic reminiscent of the so-called *Olympian universalism* for which Anderson became known.[63] Serenity seemed to be an act of emotional control.[64] Like Gibbon, Anderson's persuasiveness was derived in part from convincing his readers that there was little he had not read on the topic at hand. It was not uncommon for readers to find him referencing disciplinary debates in the fields of history, economics, political science, or political theory, with summary and criticism. And he displayed his erudition with confidence.[65]

Anderson's macrohistory of Europe, a demonstration of the ancient world's effect on modernity, was conceived as a continuation of *Decline and Fall of the Roman Empire*.[66] Anderson relied on Gibbon's account at crucial turning points, such as: the underlying structural problems amid the Golden Age of Antiquity; the Catholic Church's role in the fall of Rome; and, the stagnation of the Byzantine economy.[67] Yet Anderson also found that, occasionally, Gibbon's accuracy may have been sacrificed for a well-turned phrase.[68]

Still, Gibbon's effect was confined to historiography. Anderson was also influenced by European Marxists, mostly continental thinkers, though his debates with English Marxists no doubt also affected his thinking. He never fit neatly into a singular Marxist tradition, shifting his views as editor of the *New Left Review*. Instead of seeing Marxism as dogmatic or even limiting, as Wallerstein did, Anderson saw the project of historical materialism in terms of intellectual liberty. For him, taking "'liberties' with the signature of Marx is in this sense merely to enter into the freedom of Marxism."[69] Such freedom meant borrowing from contrasting traditions and rethinking assumptions, which culminated in an original if paradoxical combination: a Marxism forged from humanistic and structural sources. Yet Anderson was not unique in this regard. His contemporaries at the NLR and elsewhere also borrowed from various corners of the Marxist tradition. Thus, he did not borrow heavily from Marx. In *Considerations on Western Marxism*, Anderson devoted only a few pages to Marx and Engels before moving on to their successors (though he did reference Marx and Engels frequently throughout).[70] He favored Marxists who revised and expanded upon Marx's economic thought on imperialism and political theory.[71] Yet in Anderson's writings was a mostly supportive tone toward Marx, peppered with frequent alternative interpretations or notes on historical accuracy.[72] He considered Engels a superior historian.[73]

The Hungarian Marxist Georg Lukács was a major influence on Anderson's early professional life.[74] The two came to similar conclusions on the importance of ideas and of narratives in the lives of everyday people. Lukács considered the norm of impartiality, when applied to the social world, to function as an "ideological weapon of the bourgeoisie."[75] By this, he meant that class struggle was removed from most of social science; there was only the individual and society. In fact, he regarded emphasis on the individual as the cornerstone of bourgeois thought. The goal of bourgeois thinkers, it seemed to him, was to persuade workers to accept their reduced social position as natural, to conceive of it as the byproduct of their individual achievements and efforts. Such behavioral laws conveyed a sense of permanence on present social conditions and instilled feelings of normalcy (or at least helplessness). He found that the fetishization of objectivity made capitalism appear natural and permanent.[76] For Lukács, Marxists needed to tear away this veil by continually demonstrating that workers were victims of bourgeois ideology. Anderson took this lesson to heart. His sense of the *New Left Review*, after all, was that it should challenge conventional explanations of the world.

Lukács taught that the proletarian movement could not be separated from its self-understanding. The way to freedom, so to speak, was through the totality, which Lukács defined as "the all-pervasive supremacy of the whole over the parts."[77] It was up to the intellectual to grasp both the broad historical trends and the particular details, not merely what happened, but the overall placement of an event in the larger historical totality.[78] In his opinion, aspiring to totalities meant developing expertise in class analysis.[79] On the importance of totalities, Anderson concurred. On the centrality of classes, however, Anderson disagreed. Instead, he considered the mode of production the most important element of any social formation.[80]

Although he was already the editor of a prestigious Left journal, Anderson in the early 1960s remained a young scholar whose views were not fully formed. One could add, however, that the tradition of historical materialism also shifted in this period. Increasingly, extending a trend from the 1930s, leftists no longer felt bound to the European communist parties that took their cues from Moscow. Furthermore, political turmoil afflicted the parties themselves. After Khrushchev's "secret speech" of 1956 that criticized Stalinism and sought to reform the Communist Party of the Soviet Union (CPSU), the parties of Western Europe also began to rethink their positions. In addition to the Communist Party of Great Britain (CPGB), communist parties across Western Europe saw enrollment decline. For Lucio Colletti, who left the Italian Communist Party (PCI) in 1964, the institution had proven itself fundamentally antidemocratic. Colletti recounted his decision a decade later in an interview with Anderson.[81] He considered Khrushchev's speech to have been a major turning point, an attempt to recreate the intellectual and political freedom of Leninism, though one that ultimately failed. Hardliners won the struggle over the CPSU, an outcome that for Colletti affected the parties of Western Europe too. In the case of the PCI, a party that never fully abandoned its Stalinist foundation, genuine debate remained limited within an overall authoritarian framework.[82] This was not the experience of the CPGB, however, which fell into disarray, its leaders no longer able to enforce their will onto members. As Eric Hobsbawm recalled: "It was a good deal easier to be Marxist without constantly feeling that you had to toe the line because, by this stage, it wasn't clear what the line was."[83] Nevertheless, the decline in West European communist parties meant, for members and nonmembers alike, the ability to forge a Marxism of one's own.

Communist parties had long been criticized for their mechanistic, ahistorical, Marxism: the mere application of economic and technological theory onto particular class positions. In their accounts of the past, there seemed to be very little room for contingent, historically derived forces, especially those originating from the political superstructure.[84] Humanists such as E. P. Thompson maintained this criticism against structuralism generally. Louis Althusser and others associated with structuralism emphasized the mode of production and its economic, political, and ideological dimensions over an analysis of domestic class conflict.[85] But in the view of Thompson, Raymond Williams, and Stuart Hall, the thoughts and behavior of everyday people mattered more than dispassionate forces like legal codes and economic trends; indeed, humans created those forces which can appear to exist at a distance. As Hall put it: "Can one claim that 'the law' is in the courts and in the law books but not in the contractual bargaining in the marketplace? The law is everywhere."[86] The point was that social formations could not be created apart from the humans who took part in them, in a conscious and complex process intimately linked to human mythmaking about a collective past.[87] The social whole was in essence a "totality of practices," in Hall's description, comprised of "human energy, human practice, the material activity of human beings."[88]

Still, Hall was quick to point out similarities with structuralists, an indication that the gulf between humanists and structuralists in the 1960s was not as wide as one might assume. Hall considered Williams, for example, to be "a genetic structuralist" who perceived an underlying structure that informed cultural practices.[89] Hall also credited Althusser with understanding that social formations were complex entities, comprised of multiple levels: economic, political, and ideological.[90]

For his part, Anderson agreed with humanism's attention to detail, of building theories from historical accounts. Like the humanists, he noted regional variations and the differences among social formations. But he parted company from them on the question of causation. According to Anderson, humanists such as Thompson allowed assertion to suffice for explanation. In place of a causal linkage between human activity and world-historical change, Anderson wrote, Thompson turned instead to discussions of human experience.[91] In Anderson's opinion, the historian ought to have done more.

On the questions of causation and social formations, Anderson jettisoned the notion of a totality of human practices. Rather, he preferred Althusser's structuralist approach as well as the term *complex totality,* which denoted a multiplicity of components within an overarching framework. Juliet Mitchell, who was married to Anderson for a time, wrote that one should think of complex totalities in terms of a multiple sectors: "As each sector can move at a different pace, the synthesis of the different timescales in the total structure means that sometimes contradictions cancel each other out and sometimes they reinforce one another."[92]

Mitchell's summary revealed nuances within Althusserian structuralism. Far from some distant force imposed without regard to historical circumstance, the complex totality was an intricate series of moving parts. Anderson defended Althusser and structuralism against its critics. In *Arguments Within English Marxism* (1980), Anderson took on those who associated structuralism with Stalinism and sought to correct the record, concluding: "[I]n the history of philosophy there is no intrinsic relation between a causal determinism and a callous amoralism."[93] It was in this context that he endorsed Althusser's structuralism, pointing out its utility within Marxism.[94]

Anderson's critique of humanism, if obscured by his ongoing debate with Thompson, was reinforced by an engagement with the ideas of Jean-Paul Sartre. Anderson admired Sartre and French intellectual life of the 1960s;[95] he even modeled his tenure as editor of the *New Left Review* after Sartre's *Les Temps Modernes*.[96] Sartre's ideas both informed and challenged the younger intellectual. In fact, Sartre's preferred term, *totalization*, appeared more frequently than *complex totality* in Anderson's writings.

These facts nevertheless conceal meaningful differences between Sartre and Anderson, particularly on the issue of structures and human agency. The two agreed that human choice, indeed, human freedom, was defined by larger constraints. In an interview conducted by Anderson, Ronald Fraser, and Quintin Hoare, Sartre explained his views by discussing torture, which he called a situation whereby one "either speaks or refuses to speak."[97] How long can the prisoner hold out? Outside forces may have brought torturers and the captured together, but endurance determines whether the captured will give up information. In other words, behavior is not always predetermined, and individual choice plays a role. Sartre clarified: "I believe that a man can always make something out of what is made of him. This is the limit I would today accord to freedom: the small movement which makes of a totally conditioned social being someone who does not render back completely what his conditioning has given him."[98]

But Sartre also conceived of structures as built and maintained by human activity.[99] In any given social formation, in his view, human-made oppositional forces (such as classes) were most responsible for overarching structures. Furthermore, decisions made at the summit of society were recreated by others at lower levels. In the same interview, he gave a few examples. One was that of two armies at war that, through their antagonisms, created an intelligible structure. Another example was that of class cohesiveness, made up of self-interested individuals who together forged a coherent structure. And a third was the Soviet Union under Stalin. The

Boss's policies were reinforced by lower levels of Soviet society, the combined force of which created their relationship to Stalin.[100] For Sartre, each case showed existing structures replicated imperfectly by human actions, which in turn led to the creation of new structures.[101]

Unconvinced, Anderson contended that without an objective force, namely, the mode of production, no totalization could be specified. Take the example of the Soviet Union. Sartre's own account, according to Anderson, rested on the singular force of Stalin, not a web of institutions and personalities. Anderson's interpretation was closer to that of Althusser than Sartre: "It is, and must be, the dominant *mode of production* that confers a fundamental unity on a social formation, allocating their objective positions to the classes within it, and distributing the agents within each class."[102] When it came to causation, Anderson sided with the structuralists.

Still, structuralism did not mean economism. For Anderson, one should look to the economic base as well as the political superstructure.[103] Furthermore, like Wallerstein, Anderson considered empirical investigation to be inseparable from theory building. He thus looked to those Marxists who made bounded generalizations through historical comparison, located in the developmental trajectories of geographic regions. He sought to avoid what was sometimes called "Hegelian Marxism," which for critics meant a difficulty recognizing historical nuance, and thus a tendency to overgeneralize—becoming lost, so to speak, in ideas removed from processes.[104]

In the late 1960s, Anderson came to think highly of Trotsky, thanks to an unlikely friendship with Ernest Mandel. According to his biographer, Mandel was an independent mind, critical of structuralists, but who also took on humanists and Hegelians.[105] Like Thompson, he considered Althusserianism to be the application of grand ahistorical rules onto the past.[106] Nonetheless, Mandel and Anderson had a high regard for one another,[107] an admiration that began when the former published a defense of Trotsky in the *New Left Review*.[108] Anderson and several other (but not all) NLR editors found it to be compelling.

Over time, Anderson accepted that Western Marxists, including Lukács and Althusser, should have done more than merely disagree with Stalin. Western Marxism, according to Anderson, "never completely accepted Stalinism; yet it never actively combated it either."[109] The trouble was that many leftists still had not fully broken with the CPSU: they could simultaneously criticize Stalin's terror and consider his party a symbol of proletarian rule.[110] Anderson concluded that the Left should instead look to Trotsky, who, as a historical materialist that took revolutionary action, exemplified the unification of theory and practice. Trotsky and his heirs (Anderson considered Isaac Deutscher, Roman Rosdolsky, and Mandel among the most notable) maintained their relevance for the working classes.[111] They did so, in Anderson's opinion, by several actions: by focusing on politics and economics rather than philosophy; by staying internationalist, addressing regional and global concerns; by writing in an accessible style; and by avoiding retreat into university life. In a sign of their subversive ideas, their politics often resulted in exile.[112]

Though he endorsed revolutionary practice, Anderson did not model his writings on Trotsky. Instead, Anderson's Marxism remained a mix of Luckács, Althusser, and Sartre. In the 1970s, it should be added, Anderson was also drawn for a time to the ideas of Lucio Colletti. As Paul Blackledge tells it, Colletti's writings were influential in two respects: one, for embodying the revolutionary mindset of Trotsky; and, two, for interpreting historical processes as complex and interrelated, that is, the building of theories from historical description.[113] Like Colletti, Anderson did not find a one-way connection between economics and politics. They instead preferred exploring the multiplicity of ways that economic and political forces could comprise a totality, what Colletti called a "determinate totality."[114] In fact, Anderson's writings have become well known for demonstrating nuances and exceptions while also pursuing a general argument. Yet in avoiding overly abstract narratives, Blackledge explains, Colletti and Anderson often veered into overly descriptive narratives.[115]

Anderson's preference for complexity was coupled with a desire for understanding the long-term. He cultivated a Marxism that favored structures over human practice, and historical over dialectical materialism. Yet in producing a synthesis of many ideas, it was strange that Anderson mostly chose to avoid the writings of the British Marxists who came before him (other than his lengthy rebukes of E. P. Thompson). After all, figures such as Maurice Dobb and Eric Hobsbawm, who were read by the continental theorists Anderson admired, hardly register in the first three decades of his publications.[116] More puzzling was the fact the likes of Dobb and others were dealing with similar issues of transition that Anderson would address in his major works.[117] But Anderson always thought of his task as a writer and editor was to chart new routes. The way to socialism, he thought, depended on ideas. And in his view the most robust Marxism had taken up residence across the Channel.

Conclusion

Though they were already established radical scholars, Wallerstein's and Anderson's intellectual positions remained in formation throughout the 1960s. They were confronted by, or rather allowed themselves to be confronted by, unconventional ideas about power, classes, and the concept of totalities. Wallerstein contemplated time and space, and how social scientists imagined the world. He questioned whether it was really national societies that could move through stages of development, and if they went through similar experiences. Anderson refined his own vision of Marxism, drawing on competing visions of structures and human experience. Their scholarly views, however, emerged against the backdrop of great power rivalry and decolonization. Though neither could have realized it, a major world-historical event was about to shape their positions and opinions for decades. It was a moment of systemic revolt, of feelings of possibility, even the anticipation of triumph. Wallerstein would call it the most important moment of the century.[118] The year was 1968.

Chapter 3

The Year that Changed Everything

At the halfway mark between the end of World War II and the end of the Soviet Union, protests broke out in New York, Berkeley, Paris, London, Bangkok, Cairo, and many other places. The movements were distinct, but many participants felt a common sense of purpose in opposition to the effects of capitalism and the aggression of great powers.[1] For some, the year represented a collective moment of resistance against the global order. In the United States, university protests, riots at the Democratic convention in Chicago, and the Tet Offensive demonstrated the need to reevaluate Cold War policy. The Tet Offensive, in particular, showed that the world's greatest power could not achieve victory over a far weaker nation.

In the early 1960s, Immanuel Wallerstein and Perry Anderson were optimistic about the prospects for radical forces around the world. European powers were forced to relinquish formal control of their colonies, and Labour's win in Britain led many to think that an expansion of social welfare was imminent. Yet as the decade wore on, the pace of social change slowed, and Wallerstein and Anderson, along with many other social historians, grew impatient. The events of 1968, however, reversed their pessimistic attitudes.

The Year in New York

In the sixties Wallerstein was a professor at Columbia University. He married Beatrice Friedman in 1964. Politically, he championed decolonization and took frequent trips to Africa. In the early part of the decade, he was optimistic about African nationalism (and pan-Africanism), and defended postcolonial nations from critics who, he thought, had set expectations too high.[2] In his opinion, de-linking from colonial rule would be a long and slow process. Vibrant party systems, strong institutions, and the rule of law needed time to develop. Thus, he thought, observers should for a time tolerate the presence of one-party states and limited political freedoms. The new states had lively political debates and no terrorizing secret police. Postcolonial Africa was more nascent-democratic than anti-democratic. Furthermore, he considered one-party states to be far better at allowing popular participation than if nations had returned to a localized patronage system. After all, Western parliamentary democracies did not emerge overnight.[3]

Yet, over time he became increasingly distressed about the entrenchment of nondemocratic leadership across the continent.[4] Several events were disconcerting: the assassination of Togo's president, Sylvanus Olympio, in 1963; the establishment of white ruling classes in South Africa and Rhodesia; Mobuto's military dictatorship in the Congo; and, the ousting of Ghana's president Kwame Nkrumah, a leader of the movement for African unity. By 1966, there was much to be disappointed about.

Part of the problem, as Wallerstein saw it, was premature integration into the global economy. European states developed in competition only with one another. In the twentieth century, new states did not have the opportunity to grow their industrial or technological bases by themselves. Wallerstein shared the frustration of African leaders, who saw Western economic meddling as an extension of colonial rule. Tanzania's president Julius Nyerere called such meddling the *second scramble* for Africa.[5]

Wallerstein was therefore dismayed by how Western scholars often described the process of economic and political development in the postcolonial world. Their explanation, known as *modernization*, was troubling because it conceived of development at the national level. Although diverse in the details of their arguments, modernization theorists attributed economic stagnation to internal problems of governance and infrastructure, which, the argument went, could be corrected by increasing national linkages with the outside world. Wallerstein thought the opposite: many internal problems, it seemed to him, were the product of extranational forces. He believed that traditions such as modernization could only originate from the developed world. Furthermore, many studies in American social science were amenable to the United States because they did not blame the great powers for lethargic economic and political development in the postcolonial world.

Wallerstein was ready for something different. Dissatisfied with the prevailing tools of analysis, he wanted a social science that kept the interests of governments at a distance. In 1968, events at Columbia provided some clarity to his thinking.

The big change came with protests that began on April 23, a Tuesday that students called their Bastille Day. Students barricaded themselves inside several campus buildings.[6] Wallerstein was among those who wanted to see the university address student concerns and for the conflict to be resolved peacefully.

Students had a long list of grievances about the university's treatment of minorities and workers as well as its increasingly cozy relationship with the federal government. For a while, some students had been troubled by the university's support for U.S. foreign policy through the Institute for Defense Analysis (IDA), the implementation of ROTC, and on-campus CIA recruitment. But the tipping point was the construction of a new gym in Morningside Park, a public strip of land separating Columbia from Harlem. Under a new proposal, the black community's access would be limited, and citizens would have to enter the gym through the back of the building. Some occupying students, already facing prosecution for earlier break-ins, thought that the Bastille Day takeover could be a negotiation tactic for dropped charges. For other students, however, protests were merely the beginning of more widespread collective action. According to Mark Rudd, the chairman of the Students for a Democratic Society, the students were neither disorderly nor nihilistic. In his letter to Columbia's president, Grayson Kirk, Rudd wrote: "You call for order and respect for authority; we call for justice, freedom, and socialism. There is only one thing left to say. It may sound nihilistic to you, since it is the opening shot in a war of liberation. I'll use the words of LeRoi Jones, whom I'm sure you don't like a whole lot: 'Up against the wall, motherfucker, this is a stick-up.' "[7]

As a member of the university's Ad Hoc Faculty Group (AHFG), Wallerstein was chosen to be a negotiator. He was an Africanist, had previously chaired the Faculty Civil Rights Group and, according to the student account of the protests, was considered a trusted figure by the black student community.[8]

The opening negotiating session took place in Hamilton Hall, which was the first building to be occupied. Wallerstein and Samuel Cohen (from the philosophy department) climbed over barricades to meet with student leaders. Wallerstein admired their discipline, but also found it to be an obstacle in the negotiations. "They would only discuss certain things, such as demands," Wallerstein said, "which made it very difficult to have a conversation about anything. The point of the tactic was, I think, that wrapped in mystery, they felt they could get more concessions."[9]

Aside from the issues of class domination and racial discrimination, there were practical issues to address. For the students, these included academic suspension and criminal prosecution; for the administration, these included the soon-to-retire President Kirk, who was worried about his legacy, and Vice-President David Truman, who aspired to replace him. Despite the AHFG's persistence, the dispute was intractable.[10]

Five days into the crisis, with mounting city pressure for police intervention, the AHFG developed a final proposal for a peaceful resolution, described as a "bitter pill" for both parties. Working through Saturday night, the proposal was drafted almost entirely by Wallerstein. One committee member warmly titled him the AHFG's "evil genius."[11] His "bitter pill" proposal involved two main recommendations:

1. That disciplinary measures be conducted by a tripartite commission of students, faculty, and administration, and that all occupying students face the same penalties.

2. That New York's mayor convene a panel, made up of trustees, community members (chosen by the mayor), and faculty members (chosen by the faculty), to develop a new plan for the gym under construction.

In addition, the AHFG wrote that both sides would have to accept these terms without modification: once the president accepted the plan, the students should leave the occupied buildings. If one side agreed, but the other did not, the AHFG pledged to throw its support behind the agreeing party. If neither accepted the plan, the AHFG would stop negotiating altogether.

The AHFG's chairman, Alan Westin, described the following day as "the day of decision for Columbia."[12] After reading the responses, Wallerstein determined that both the protestors and the administration rejected the proposal. Wallerstein, who by this point was seen as "on the verge of complete exhaustion," announced to the committee that the bitter pill solution had failed.[13] And despite their promise to quit, members of the AHFG debated a few last-minute plans to avoid police action. But by midnight the police had readied a sizeable force just outside the university. Shortly after 2:00 a.m. Tuesday, April 30, police officers forcibly cleared the campus, arresting more than seven hundred and injuring almost 150.

More protests and arrests ensued that summer. The administration pended criminal charges against students and dismissed some supportive faculty. President Kirk retired in August. In September, Wallerstein participated in the Radical Faculty Group's "Public Affirmation" that condemned the administration's behavior.[14] According to the group, the administration was duplicitous in their conciliatory rhetoric amidst a heavy-handed response. The group demanded that criminal charges be removed and dismissed faculty be reappointed, and they noted that the students had legitimate reasons to protest.[15] In the eyes of the Radical Faculty Group, interim president Andrew Cordier and the administration, despite withdrawing many of the penalties imposed that summer, were only halfheartedly committed to true reform. Ultimately, Columbia's relationship with the IDA ended, the ROTC stopped recruiting on campus, and, perhaps symbolically most important, the gym was built in another location.

For Wallerstein, the "strain" of 1968 took a toll. The protests divided the sociology department as well as faculty across campus. He said he "reached a point where it was difficult to be there."[16] In 1971, he accepted a post at McGill University and moved to Quebec.

Still, Wallerstein's overall reaction to 1968 was positive. He saw it as a sign of restored hope for the Left. Most encouraging, in his view, was that American society had developed its own, *indigenous*, socialist tradition. The same year he left for McGill, Wallerstein penned an essay, "Radical Intellectuals in a Liberal Society," where he advised fellow radicals to recognize their crucial role for the decolonized world, and also to have patience.[17] He believed that for socialism to become reality, intellectuals in the developed world needed to play a prominent (though subordinate) role vis-à-vis the movements of the underdeveloped world. This role included operating as activists yet evaluating that activism at the same time. But most importantly, radicals needed to acknowledge that change would not come quickly. They needed what Wallerstein called the "passionate calm of one for whom the revolution is not a battle of a day, a year, or a decade, but one of centuries."[18] Though outside observers may not have thought about African development and student protests as connected, in Wallerstein's experience the two were knotted together.

Though encouraged by 1968, Wallerstein's optimism was mitigated by the gravity of the task ahead. The first step was for radical intellectuals to transform the university. In his opinion, scholars at Western universities had become too closely associated with the Western foreign policy interests and, therefore, could not conceive of world politics from a critical standpoint. It was up to the radical intellectual to make the university a place of conflict.[19]

Universities, he wrote, needed to become coliseums for "intellectual combat." Tranquility and peace at a university were dangerous signs that the institution had relinquished its role in society. And in the postwar years, the apparent tranquility was really cheerleading for U.S. foreign policy. In Wallerstein's interpretation, from 1945 to 1965, American universities had moved closer to Washington: they allowed ROTC on campus; supplied class rankings to government Selective Service administrations; and performed national defense research.

In the late 1960s, many universities reduced their close ties to government, albeit temporarily. For Wallerstein, this change was also an inherently political act. Thus, he suggested that universities stop pretending to be apolitical because, no matter how they behaved, they were behaving politically.[20] Yet he also thought that the inescapability of politics should not be feared. Instead, he believed this conclusion was an invitation for universities to become more socially engaged and to take positions on important questions. The very purpose of a university, in fact, was to question established truths. He likened such questioning to acting as a kind of watchdog for society.[21] Without a critical stance, the university abdicated its time-honored role. By failing to question the government, the university lent it legitimacy.[22] In turn, Wallerstein recommended that social scientists also detach themselves from governments. The purpose of research was not to aid U.S. foreign policy, but to work toward a better world through accurate assessments of social phenomena. Such an open pronouncement of intellectual activism was likely jarring to his fellow social scientists. But Wallerstein concluded that the most dangerous position was a proclamation of neutrality.[23] One's public social science research and one's private political beliefs, he thought, were inseparable. Furthermore, Wallerstein did not believe that it was contradictory to be both scholarly and politically engaged: "I am politically committed and active, and regard open polemics as a necessary part of my *scholarly* activity."[24] For him, polemical writing was not a choice between being value-free and value-driven: it was an acknowledgment of the inherently normative act of performing social research.[25] Just as the neutral university was an impossible feat, so too was the neutral intellectual. In other words, value-free scholarship was for Wallerstein merely concealed subjectivity.

The Year in London

Like Wallerstein, Perry Anderson in the early 1960s was heartened by signs of social progress. And, like Wallerstein, Anderson's hopes had started to wane a few years later. Whereas Wallerstein drew sustenance from decolonization abroad, Anderson was encouraged by the promise of an expanded social welfare state at home.

Still, Anderson in the early 1960s was more of a cautious optimist. When Labour swept to victory in October 1964, Harold Wilson became prime minister. Wilson won support from working-class voters, who appreciated his plainspoken attacks on the upper class (despite sending his children to a private boarding school). Anderson and the *New Left Review* endorsed Wilson and hoped that he would realize their dreams of socialism in Britain. But a few weeks before the election, Anderson warned of the limitations of Wilsonism.[26] Labour had promised to transform Britain's tax structure, increase public ownership, expand welfare and pensions, invest in education at all levels (including the abolition of university fees), and increase loans for the underdeveloped world. But Anderson was suspicious about the absence of promises on other issues related to foreign affairs and domestic welfare subsidies. In terms of socialist strategy, Wilson's language on capitalism, although refreshingly critical, stopped short.[27] He generally attacked enterprises and behavior that either predated capitalism, such as nepotism, or were ancillary to the functions of capitalism, such as the parasitic practices of landlords and stockbrokers. Anderson worried that promises of future socialism served to lower near-term expectations and provided cover from taking incremental steps.[28] Anderson's overall mood, however, was hopeful: "The chances for the Left are now tangible. It will take the utmost courage and imagination to seize them."[29]

Months later, Anderson and the editorial board reversed their opinion. Partisan endorsement turned into open disgust. Tom Nairn penned NLR's formal denunciation of the Wilson government. His memorable opening line reflected the editorial board's new attitude: "Unique among governments of the Left, the Labour Government has done more than fail its friends: it has even disappointed its enemies."[30] Nairn argued that the government, despite vocalizing socialist principles, had pathetically embraced economic policies similar to those of its Conservative predecessors. It embraced international loans and currency deflation without meaningful steps to invest in promised areas. Labour speeches became an apology for a lack of change.[31]

By 1968, however, Anderson had new reason to believe Britain was back on the path to socialism.[32] He was particularly amazed by the uprising in France, which was impressive because of its sheer scale. The revolt exceeded previous movements in Britain and Belgium and even, Anderson thought, the 1905 Russian uprising. In one piece, the NLR observed that the movement seemed to be everywhere at once: "More than ten millions stopped work: not only students and industrial workers, but peasants, intellectuals, school children, shop assistants, even TV news-readers, astronomers at the Meudon Observatory and strip-tease girls at the Folies Bergères."[33]

The revolt shook the French government. Preparing for his ouster from office, Charles de Gaulle gathered his papers and briefly left the country. He promised to step down, but then decided to hold onto power if he could. In June his party survived parliamentary elections, although the victory was a short one. The following spring, de Gaulle's proposed reforms were defeated, and he resigned.

The French state, however, was not defeated. An NLR editorial even commented that the state as an institution may have been strengthened. But this fact mattered little.[34] Anderson saw 1968 as a sign of social change on a larger scale. Specifically, he considered the protests a sign of the importation of anti-imperialist sentiment. Previously contained to the third world, the struggle had reached the developed West. In other words, France was psychological emancipation for Anderson and the NLR. Many years later, American social science would coin the term *cognitive liberation*, a phenomenon whereby movement participants think beyond their present condition to imagine alternatives in their movement and in their organization, seeing real chances for success.[35] Anderson and his colleagues had such an epiphany. Although they were well aware of capitalism's power, the opportunity for socialism now seemed real. It also seemed that they could make a meaningful difference. French intellectuals, according to NLR's editors, had created a vibrant Marxism that affected all French students.[36] France, in other words, confirmed that revolutionary culture could be instilled in an advanced capitalist society.

Thus, Anderson did not interpret 1968 as merely a year of symbolic importance. For him, it meant socialism was truly possible, at home and in the world. Wallerstein was content with the cultivation of a socialist tradition in the United States. Anderson's new optimism went farther.

Still, he did not write much directly about 1968. Whereas Wallerstein frequently, even obsessively, returned to the year as the critical turning point of the century, Anderson did not devote much space to the conjuncture. Instead, 1968 became a theme in his writings. His 2009 book on European integration, for example, contained at least seven interspersed references to the year, notable for the strength of his declarations.[37] Anderson called the French revolt "still the largest and most impressive demonstration of collective agency in post-war European history."[38] Elsewhere, he wrote, simply: "1968 . . . The date, and all it implies, says enough."[39]

In one article from 1968, however, Anderson reflected on the mood of the year. "Components of the National Culture" was meant to be an intellectual companion to the student movement in Britain.[40] Like Wallerstein, Anderson thought that universities should be independent of governments. Yet he went farther by asserting that universities should be sites of resistance to reactionary forces. In Anderson's opinion, British universities had previously functioned as agents of controlling classes, steering students away from questions about the nature of political authority.

Anderson wanted to aid the student movement by providing a historical background from which it could criticize higher education.[41] It was necessary to win over students, he thought, for three reasons: one, students were too young to be from the traditional heritage of communism; two, they had skills to process and develop theories; and three, students were a large population, much bigger than any group of intellectuals. Thus, despite its constantly changing nature, the university was an important group for moving toward socialism.

Socialists nonetheless had their work cut out for them. British universities, he remarked in "Components," developed in such a way that students did not question the lifestyle gap between the upper and lower classes. Anderson attributed this development to disciplinary specialization. What he meant was that specialization, at least this form of specialization, tended to ask small, technocratic, questions about the nuances of language, ideas, or swings in the economy. He believed that what the university system really needed were fields of study capable of synthesizing events spread out across time and geography. In his view, asking big questions about the history of economic development would eventually call into question the morality of Britain's class structure. It seemed to him that only the field of literary criticism had proven itself capable of advancing socialist thought.[42] (Anthropology, he commented, employed methods conducive to such a synthesis, but had instead chosen to serve the state.)

Invoking Lenin and Gramsci, Anderson restated his belief that revolutionary culture and revolutionary theory were necessary prerequisites for socialist revolution. Revolutionary culture referred to those practices and beliefs that prime society to overthrow capitalism; in turn, revolutionary theory referred to an understanding of why such an overthrow was necessary. For activists to be successful, Anderson thought they should know the destructive forces of capitalism and be capable of formulating a replacement. In his view, the public needed fields of inquiry that did not serve governments, that were sensitive to long-term historical forces, and that acknowledged the interconnectedness of economic and political developments on a world scale. Not unlike Wallerstein, Anderson believed that intellectuals could provide the tools for cultural awakening. But, in a shift of emphasis, he thought they needed an organizational home for coordinating their efforts. Socialist revolution required a vanguard organization. Addressed only sporadically in public, Anderson's beliefs are support by the NLR's internal documents.

In a document titled "Ten Theses," Anderson elaborated on his socialist strategy. By vanguard, he meant a collective that unified theory and practice in a movement for socialism. The vanguard would speak to diverse groups (such as workers and intellectuals) spread across the world. The vanguard of socialist revolution need not be Western communist parties, which Anderson described as centrist organizations (somehow both anticapitalist and nonrevolutionary, comfortable with a gradual realization of socialism). Instead, he believed that all anticapitalist organizations must also be revolutionary, defined in this context as advocating for the immediate realization of socialism. He faulted the French Communist Party for working against the revolutionary movement in 1968. The Italian Communist Party was split, with some members opposing and some members supporting the protests. And the Cuban Communist Party, which Anderson also described as centrist, sided with the movement of 1968.[43]

The vanguard also need not be a single large party. The size of the 1968 revolutions demonstrated for Anderson that those large-scale organizations of the early twentieth century were no longer necessary. The vanguard, in fact, need not be a single organization. The vanguard may change over time, or, there can be multiple vanguard organizations operating in separate geographic zones at the same time.[44]

With a common commitment to the demise of the state (whose institutions support and perpetuate capitalism), revolutionaries working with Western social democratic institutions could make true socialism a reality.[45] One day, Anderson predicted, the notion of the market could be a historical artifact, much like the notion of the manor. And as capitalism falls, so too will imperialism and the exploitation of peoples.[46]

In response to 1968, the NLR launched a few new projects (in social activism, journalism, and publishing) that overextended its editorial board and led to a period of disarray.[47] Following the May uprising, the NLR collective contributed to the Revolutionary Socialist Students' Federation's (RSSF) first and second conferences. Simultaneously, the decision was made to found New Left Books (NLB) as a complement to the journal, as well as join up with a new monthly publication, *Black Dwarf*.[48]

Anderson thought that the NLR, by interpreting current events in the proper way, could be one of those vanguard organizations. It would help to unify theory and practice by providing large-scale analyses that had been missing from Britain's university system (but also missing from most Western universities). By the 1970s, the NLR committed itself to understanding a neglected area of research: relations between advanced economies and the third world.[49] These struggles were an extension of 1968 in the sense that they questioned the imperialist adventures of the advanced capitalist world. In this way, Anderson as an editor became very much concerned with the legacy of 1968.

Conclusion

The protests of 1968 raised Anderson's and Wallerstein's spirits. Socialism now seemed possible. Anderson's enthusiasm, however, exceeded Wallerstein's. This was partly due to the fact that socialists were more active and vocal in Britain than in the United States. But it was also due to Anderson's institutional location. Surrounded by ideologically supportive comrades, Anderson may have played up signs pointing to socialism and played down signs confirming continued liberal capitalism. It is also possible that Wallerstein's private views were closer to Anderson's than they appeared. Wallerstein's public commentaries usually focused on abstract issues of development or ideology. He, after all, also wrote about the social role of universities, and recommended that they become places for radical intellectuals to express their views (and battle conservative opponents). Yet there was still a clear difference: Wallerstein wanted the Left, through universities, to stop the Right from advancing. Anderson wanted the Left, through universities, to claim victory.

For both intellectuals, 1968 was a tipping point of global social protest. Previously, it seemed as though the West (Western Europe and North America) was resistant to the social upheavals of the third world. Anderson and Wallerstein welcomed the protests as an expression of dissatisfaction on the part of everyday citizens. For Wallerstein, the New York protests taught that many Americans (particularly students) were unwilling to support American Cold War policy, especially toward the developing world. It also called into question state-centric social science. Collectively, the protests showed Wallerstein that the world's peoples were having a common experience, albeit from different perspectives. He suspected the linkage was economic, although he did not yet fully understand how those economic processes worked.

Anderson, conversely, saw 1968 in strategic terms. The protests demonstrated that the West could be transformed from within. It was now up to the Left (and specifically the NLR) to provide direction for this diverse movement. He, therefore, shared with Wallerstein the belief that Western intellectual support was necessary for overturning capitalism.

Although Wallerstein's and Anderson's initial reactions to 1968 show a profound change in their thinking, the full effect of the year would not be seen for another decade. In the intervening years, they would craft the books for which they are most known today.

Chapter 4

Ideas Need Institutions

The protests of 1968 led Wallerstein and Anderson to believe socialism was a real possibility. In response to that year, Wallerstein wanted to ensure that universities remained places from which the Left could encourage third world nationalist movements. Anderson, by contrast, wanted to aid socialist strategy. What remained unclear was how they would pursue their goals. By what means can social scientists detach from governments and aid third world movements? How can the *New Left Review* be a vanguard organization for socialist revolutionaries?

For each, the answer was the same. They were convinced that the crucial problem was a lack of public and scholarly understanding of the historical processes that gave rise to the current international order. Through scholarly writings and institutions, they reinterpreted modern European history. In 1974, they published histories of modern capitalism. And as of 1976, when Wallerstein became the inaugural director of Binghamton University's Fernand Braudel Center, they each led cultural institutions too.

For Wallerstein as well as Anderson, a particular historiography provided the route to achieving their goals. In Wallerstein's case, what was wrong with social science was its methods. In Anderson's case, what was wrong with socialist strategy was its historical understanding. Unifying Wallerstein's and Anderson's efforts was, to borrow an expression from Lukács, an *aspiration to totalities*.[1] A reading of history that adhered to the study of totalities was central to realizing their visions for a better world. Thus, even though their immediate goals and methods were different, Wallerstein and Anderson engaged in remarkably similar courses of action.

The Study of Everything at Once

By expressing their research in terms of totalities, Wallerstein and Anderson shared a fondness for the research tradition of their mentors; not widespread in the twentieth century, such a tradition was frequently employed in prior centuries. According to Martin Jay, totalities were once the most prevalent mode of research.[2] As intermittently discussed in chapter 2, to totalize was possess a sense of holism. For some writers, this meant thinking of society in terms of metaphors, say, of the human soul or the body. For others, holism meant that one conceived of the whole (whether it was the mind, a social class, society, or the world) as an ecosystem comprised of various parts; to study any one part in isolation was to fail to understand the whole. Anderson's definition was perhaps the most succinct: "[A] totality is an entity whose structures are bound together in such a way that any one of them considered separately is an abstraction."[3] It was up to the scholar, however, to identify what parts best signified the social whole.

Despite, or perhaps because of, its historical popularity, ideas of a totality or of totalization have become remarkably difficult to pin down.[4] The distinction between parts and wholes was after all a convenience to make sense of a complex world. Several different usages have already appeared in this work. According to Hall, the totality was one of human behavior and practices.[5] Polanyi sought to connect our understanding of the economy to other aspects of human life, drawing temporal and spatial boundaries around the social whole.[6] In Lukács's interpretation, the totality was expressed through class struggle.[7] Braudel inspired Wallerstein to apply totalities in terms of a summation of times (short, medium, and long) over a given space. Anderson took Sartre's term, totalization, but without much direct attention on Sartre's preferred object, human consciousness; in its place, Anderson described sociopolitical complexes. Yet the applications and definitions are limitless. As Fredric Jameson has noted, discussions of totality have stretched to include the study of political parties, aesthetic commentary, Hegelian ideas, and ethics.[8] Some writers have even disagreed with the notion of contradiction in totalities, central to many of the views expressed above. For Roberto Mangabeira Unger, the totality was harmonious unity, a "view of the world as a whole completely mirrored in each of its parts."[9] Nonetheless, opponents of totalities (and perhaps some supporters) have tended to lump various forms together, even including the phonetically similar "totalitarianism," which Jameson denounced as "the silliest of all puns."[10] The totality as a style of thought has been applied to diverse subjects, ranging from the human mind to the proletariat to global systems.

Though foreign to many in this century, the totality was the dominant mode of thinking in previous eras. Born in ancient philosophy, surviving through the medieval world in the writings of theologians, the totality has taken on many forms in its path to modernity. A few brief examples from the term's historical lineage demonstrates a crucial distinction between Wallerstein and Anderson: that of the *descriptive totality* and the *normative totality*.

According to Jay, a totality in the normative sense may embody the hope one had for a better future—a longing for the displacement of social discord (say, according to class or gender) by a new social harmony, whether realistic or utopian. In the descriptive sense, the totality was a tool for understanding social phenomena. Descriptive totalities came in two types. Closed, or latitudinal, totalities have identifiable temporal and spatial boundaries. The regularities of one totality do not apply to others. Open, or longitudinal, totalities have no specified beginning or end, and are often referred to as totalization.[11]

For Plato and Aristotle, the totality was a frame of reference for comparing the ideal government with reality, expressed as both an aspiration (however impossible) and a description. The drama of the *Republic*, for example, lies in Socrates's ability to convince young Glaucon to aspire to the Good, not to tyranny. Socrates does so by contrasting the metaphorical (or ideal) city of speech with the real city of deeds, a process that makes Glaucon realize the importance of justice. Thus, Plato makes his point in part through a comparison of two totalities.[12]

Medieval theologians went a step farther, relying on normative and descriptive totalities with a logic of historical progression. For instance, the writings of St. Augustine explained the decline of Rome, a city of man, in terms of the corresponding rise of the ideal city of God. For Augustine, man's real nature existed before the Fall; afterward, what survived was an imperfect form that could be perfected through piety and the Church.[13] Later, in the twelfth century, John of Salisbury developed an *organological* perspective, whereby he adopted the metaphor of the body to explain society and political authority.[14] For John, the soul of the body politic was the clergy, the prince was the head, the senate was the heart, soldiers were the hands, and judges and local leaders were the eyes, ears, and tongue. Farmers, close to the soil, represented the feet. And treasurers and record keepers comprised the stomach and intestines that, if corrupted, could make the whole body sick.[15] John believed that society, like the body, could only be understood through the whole. With this metaphor, John noted the importance of farmers and other laborers, concluding that their numerical size and importance for the survival of the society necessitated attention and stewardship by the prince.[16]

Totalities fell out of fashion in the modern world. In their place came Enlightenment reasoning that prioritized individual relationships and inductive reasoning.[17] The tradition of totalities continued in diminished form—to such an extent that by the twentieth century, Marxists could lay claim to the totality as their own. For Lukács, it was the totality that distinguished Marxists from other kinds of thinkers (especially "bourgeois" thinkers).[18] But, as we have seen, the totality as a concept has no inherent ideological leaning. Totalities can be used to justify conserving the rate of social change as readily as they can be used to promote social liberation.[19]

Even among radicals, there was no consensus on totalities. Anderson's preference for open totalities aligned with his perception of social formations as containing overlapping and contradictory impulses. Although history for Anderson was open-ended, he nonetheless placed temporal limits on analysis, albeit some two millennia or so (i.e., the modern capitalist state as the synthesis of ancient and feudal modes of production). The range of Anderson's totalization was so grand that commentators (some supportive, some critical) have called his studies an exercise in "Olympian universalism," that is, the seeming ability to write about world history from "800 BC to last week."[20]

In Anderson's totalization, the unit of analysis was unspecified. Yet throughout his career, Anderson always appeared to treat domestic and international issues from a spatial perspective larger than the national state. He, like Wallerstein, did not assume that states were insignificant actors, but merely that the behavior of states was bound up in other economic and political processes. After the revolution of 1968, Anderson referred to global politics of the twentieth century as a *complex totality* of interconnected sectors.[21] Though not directly addressed by Anderson, context suggests his understanding of "exogenous" and "endogenous" was different than many historians and social scientists who used the terms in reference to the nation-state. Exogenous, for Anderson, meant *outside* of the totality; endogenous meant *inside* the totality.

Anderson and Wallerstein sometimes referred to totalities as *modes of production*.[22] Yet, as shown in chapter 2, they were different from those Marxists who found causation only in the economic base and not the political superstructure. Anderson and Wallerstein considered many factors germane to their historical narratives, including: trade, war, and class conflict, as well as demographic, epidemiological, and ecological change. They did not think much of scholarly works that reduced all causation to one category of variables. But they nonetheless shared with Lukács the idea that totalities were not "neutral" tools, but part of the solution to the problems of capitalism. Wallerstein in particular devoted considerable effort to persuading his fellow social scientists of the virtues of totalities. He hoped, with enough convincing, for his methods to "end up conquering the intellectual world."[23]

Unlike Anderson, Wallerstein in his writings frequently addressed the unit of analysis. He had long questioned social science's reliance on the national state, and, after experiencing Columbia University in 1968 firsthand, developed a new conceptualization of the relationship between national and global processes. He ultimately concluded that state and interstate phenomena were intimately interrelated, part of the same global system. By 1973, Wallerstein's new vision of the world as a descriptive totality was fully formed.[24]

As mentioned above, Wallerstein preferred the study of something called *closed totalities*, which is to say that he thought of totalities as having geographical and temporal boundaries. In other words, he believed there were distinct places and times where the totality existed, and places and times where it did not. The study of modern Europe, for example, meant the study of a particular place at a particular time, however defined; thus, it became important to know where Europe was and when it became modern. And, logically, to talk about boundaries meant that one must also talk about lifespans, for if there were places and times to demarcate the existence of a totality, then there were places and times to demarcate its inexistence. Totalities, for Wallerstein, had a time of formation, a time of stability, and a time of falling apart.

Wallerstein called totalities *world-systems*. On this association, he was unambiguous: "[T]he only totalities that exist or have historically existed are mini-systems and world-systems."[25] He hyphenated the term to indicate that social systems were actually self-contained worlds: some might be geographically very small, say, tribes or kin-based social groupings, while others might encompass whole continents or the planet. The concepts of exogenous and endogenous were important for Wallerstein, and not used in reference to the national state; rather, he used them in reference to world-systems.

In practice, Anderson's open totalities and Wallerstein's closed totalities diverged greatly. Anderson did not worry about bounding his totalities as Wallerstein did. In fact, Wallerstein developed a typology of world-systems, with four basic types: reciprocal mini-systems, redistributive world-empires, the capitalist world-economy, and a socialist world-government.[26] (In an "intermission" following this chapter, we see how he arrived at this perspective.)

Wallerstein thought that for each type, scholars should expect different kinds of behavior (by humans and institutions). The first, reciprocal mini-systems, he admitted was an awkward replacement for what used to be called primitive societies. He understood mini-systems to be small-scale hunter-gatherer or agrarian social groupings, which the world had not seen in some time.[27] And the last type, a socialist world-government, had never existed. But it seemed to him as though the world was moving toward global socialism.

World-empires have historically been more common. These systems, according to Wallerstein, had a single governing organization that extended over the entire economy. He considered ancient Rome and Han China to be noteworthy examples. They contained multiple cultures and a widely varying quality of life among various parts of the system. Conventionally, European colonies of the late 1800s are often called empires; but in Wallerstein's terminology, a nation-state's control of external territories was not indicative of a world-empire. Modern European imperialism took place within the context of the larger capitalist world-system.

Like a world-empire, a world-economy, as Wallerstein understood it, was a system that contained multiple cultures and might have great regional variation in labor and quality of life. But unlike a world-empire, a world-economy had no single governing organization. In other words, economic factors such as currency exchange, trade of goods, and food getting extended beyond any one governing organization. Today, the various political centers are the nation-states.[28] In the past, world-economies had short life spans, and tended to transform into world-empires.[29] Thus, the success of the current world-system, the capitalist world-economy, was unique by historical standards. The modern world-system, according to Wallerstein, formed in Europe and the Americas over the "long" sixteenth century (c. 1450–c. 1640) and since then expanded to cover the entire Earth.[30]

Totalities at the Braudel Center

In his 1973 presidential address to the Africa Studies Association, Wallerstein announced his new methodological perspective. The speech was important because he called upon fellow Africanists and social scientists to think about the postcolonial world in a historically comprehensive way.

Adopting such a methodology, however, would be no easy task.[31] The *American Journal of Sociology* turned down Wallerstein's introductory article on world-systems. According to the editor's rejection letter, the "paper has too many flaws for us to consider further."[32] One reviewer wrote: "It barely misses . . . being a diatribe."[33] The piece, "The Rise and Future Demise of the World Capitalist System," appeared in *Comparative Studies in Society and History*, and is today considered Wallerstein's most famous article.[34] His accompanying book manuscript also took a rocky road to publication. In Wallerstein's description, it was Academic Press and Charles Tilly who took a "chance" on his book.[35] This text was the first volume of his magnum opus on *The Modern World-System*.[36]

To Wallerstein's surprise, his article and book were well received.[37] In 1975, he received many offers to join other universities. Wallerstein considered three schools seriously: Northwestern, UCLA, and SUNY Binghamton.[38] Binghamton was the most attractive because it came with the opportunity to lead a research institute. Unlike Anderson, Wallerstein was not yet part of a collective institutional project. Terence K. Hopkins, a friend and comrade who also left Columbia in 1971, was already established at Binghamton. According to Walter Goldfrank, faculty openings, funding opportunities, and "Hopkins's institutional maneuvers" made the school the most attractive option. In 1976, Wallerstein became a distinguished professor, chair of the sociology department, director of the new research center, and editor of a new journal.[39]

The institute became the Fernand Braudel Center for the Study of Economics, Historical Systems, and Civilizations. The journal, *Review*, published its first issue in 1977. Both the Braudel Center and *Review* were committed to understanding social change over the long term. The institution made two assumptions: one, that any series of events was contained within an overarching structure; and two, that all structures were historical.[40] Although Wallerstein was a professor of sociology, the Braudel Center avoided categorizing itself within a single discipline.

Wallerstein tried to extend the influence of the Braudel Center by inviting prominent scholars to teach part-time or submit articles. Among the visiting scholars was Perry Anderson. And, in its first few years, *Review* published essays by luminaries such as Charles Tilly, Eric Hobsbawm, and Rodney Hilton, as well as translations of Braudel, Polanyi, and the Russian economist Nikolai Kondratieff.[41] It also featured regular pieces by scholars of world-systems, including Wallerstein, Hopkins, Samir Amin, Giovanni Arrighi, and Andre Gunder Frank. The journal became a home for debate on historical systems. Submissions could be of any length, in any language, and concern any time period. Although *Review* was intentionally a space for debate, the editors would not accept articles from authors who presumed their findings applied universally (that is, to all places and at all times).[42]

In the late 1970s, Wallerstein pursued several avenues of research at once. The world-systems approach, which he had struggled to inaugurate only a few years earlier, suddenly became an academic industry. After receiving some recognition and intellectual support, Wallerstein tried to influence public debate on postcolonial issues and the third world. He wrote letters to fellow intellectuals and public figures, as well as the editors of *The New York Times*.

Wallerstein also published prolifically. He produced articles and books at a frantic pace, writing about almost every aspect of world-systems. In the span of a few years, he embarked on a wide-ranging research program that he would pursue in some form for the next four decades. He wrote about contemporary struggles in the third world, but also on the transition away from feudalism, and economic trends of the global economy.[43] In addition, Wallerstein published a series of articles on race and class,[44] as well as on the idea of knowledge accumulation in the social sciences.[45] Then in 1980, he released the second volume of his history of capitalism.[46] Having started a fire, he wanted to make sure it would not go out.

The important thing, for Wallerstein, was that social scientists think and talk in a world-systemic vocabulary. A change in terminology, he thought, could have an impact on the well-being of people in the world. The issue of development remained at the heart of his research. For Wallerstein, to talk about "development" meant the development of the world-system, not of the nation. Likewise, to talk about "stages" (which Wallerstein thought was crucial to the modernization tradition) meant stages of a world-system. (He thought these concepts could be improved by talking about "core," "periphery," and "semiperiphery," which will be discussed later in this chapter.)

Wallerstein believed that world-systemic thinking relieved many of the problems that had plagued his research in the sixties. The struggles of newly independent African states, for example, could be contextualized within their colonial past and the present demands for world trade. He was hardly the first person to suggest that colonialism impeded postindependence political stability.[47] But Wallerstein did want to develop an account of how long-term processes led to the current state of international politics. That is, Wallerstein wanted to explain how Europe's colonization, and subsequent *underdevelopment,* of Africa, was one part of a changing world-system.

Unlike Anderson, Wallerstein considered capitalism to be a historical accident. In his view, there was nothing about premodern Europe that meant capitalism *had* to come about. Although the modern world-system was born out of the demise of feudalism, it could have just as easily not been born. To the contrary, he contended, capitalism formed due to "a fortuitous simultaneity of events."[48]

By fortuitous, Wallerstein meant that it was not capitalism that dethroned feudalism in Europe. In his view, feudalism collapsed, and capitalism was born only later. Yet his account of the transition never fully explored the concept of feudalism.[49] In one place, Wallerstein described European feudal relations in the fourteenth and fifteenth centuries as a collection of mostly self-sufficient politico-economic zones such as a town or manor.[50] Elsewhere, Wallerstein identified feudal Europe as a "civilization" (in quotes), and he later called it a Christian civilization.[51] Yet here, too, he avoided an exact definition. He mused that it might make sense to call feudalism a civilization because it was a group of smaller systems held together to a degree by religion and the Latin language. Civilization therefore implied the presence of a common religion and, to some degree, a common language.[52] (In one essay, he described a civilization as comprised of lightly connected world-empires.[53] In another, he noted that a civilization was something in flux, an evolving umbrella identity that encompassed various ever-changing constituent identities, including culture and language.)[54] The crucial point was that Wallerstein deliberately wanted to avoid labeling late feudal Europe as a single world-system. Instead, there were multiple world-empires in operation simultaneously. The vagueness of the description reflects the complex nature of feudalism: multiple civil political centers, with multiple economies (albeit connected by trade), all contained within the ecclesiastical authority of the Catholic Church.

According to Wallerstein, there were two main European world-economies when the crisis of feudalism hit: one in northern Italy and another spread across Flanders and northern Germany. He noted that, between 1150 and 1300, Europe's feudal system expanded geographically, commercially, and demographically. Then, between 1300 and 1450, it contracted in all three respects.[55] This contraction, part of normal systemic fluctuations, happened while feudalism was reaching its productive and technological limit. Subsequent peasant revolts and wars were indicative of a system that had reached a point of diminishing returns.

The final blow to feudalism, in Wallerstein's narrative, came from an environmental crisis, involving changes in climate, patterns of disease, and soil. Before industrialization, material well-being depended on favorable climatic conditions. Oscillation between cold and mild winter seasons contributed to economic recession and expansion.[56] Europe experienced a series of difficult winters in the fourteenth and fifteenth centuries, which led to a decline in population. Meanwhile, lasting effects of the Black Plague, continued on by hot summers and increased rat populations, took a toll on the population.[57] In addition to climate change and the plague, Europe's soil was reaching its productive limit due to overuse and overconsumption by the nobility.[58]

From these conditions, something different arose. This system was not founded on tribute or feudal-style rents. It was, he wrote, a system based on agricultural or industrial surplus to serve a market geographically larger than any one state could control.[59] This something different was capitalism. As mentioned in this book's introduction, Wallerstein defined capitalism as a system based on the requirement for *ceaseless* or *endless* accumulation of capital.[60] By capital, Wallerstein meant *stored value*, which he thought could take many forms, including currency, goods, or even property.[61] There was certainly capital before the sixteenth century, but there was not the need to ceaselessly accumulate capital. For example, landlords in the middle ages controlled agricultural spaces, from which they could extract a productive surplus with peasant labor. Landlords thus had an incentive to control property. But the meaning of land under feudalism was different than that of land under capitalism. In order to survive, or exercise power, or fulfill other goals, landlords did not have to use the area they controlled (at the will of the prince) to endlessly accumulate capital.

The requirement of ceaseless accumulation incentivized conquest. Emerging European states needed to consume more resources, including foods (sugar, fish, and meat), wood, textiles, and bullion.[62] (The latter remained necessary, despite the predominance of symbolic currency, as a hedge against devaluation or collapse.) Starting with Portugal, European states took to the seas, exploring and conquering news lands. Driven by the functional need for endless accumulation, imperial conquest became the driving mechanism behind geographical expansion of the world-economy. Wallerstein referred to the powerful imperial states as the *core* zone of the world-system, and the colonized areas as the *periphery*. Life varied considerably between core and periphery. The core was a small, well-off collection of nation-states. The periphery, by contrast, contained numerous colonies and nation-states, whose structural existence was to fund the advancement of the core. Though geographically distributed, core/periphery distinctions are determined by function, not merely geographic location. Thus, the political instability of new African nation-states in the twentieth century was not due to some failure of leadership in the 1960s but to several centuries of world-system development.

Wallerstein also devised a new category, the *semiperiphery*, which he saw as positioned between the core and periphery.[63] This was an in-between zone, where life was neither privileged nor disadvantaged. Yet it served as a guarantor of the system, functioning as a conveyor belt of economic exchange between core and periphery. It also served an ideological purpose: on one side, as proof of the possibilities of advancement; on the other, as a warning of potential decline. Since its introduction, the semiperiphery has been used by scholars in diverse ways.[64] In the twentieth century, the semiperiphery was characterized by heavy manufacturing, including steel production, chemicals, and consumer home and office supplies.[65] Wallerstein, perhaps because of the shifting nature of production over the centuries, chose not to identify the semiperiphery with specific products.[66] Instead, he emphasized the political and ideological significance of such states.

The modern world-system, Wallerstein noticed, was prone both to cyclical behavior (ups and downs) as well as enduring phenomena called secular trends (which have increased over the life of the system). The former caused the latter, he reasoned, because cycles within capitalism could never quite return to their starting points. Though scholars have identified numerous cycles,[67] some were more prominent than others. Two notable cycles included economic "long waves" and the rise and fall of hegemonic powers (discussed in chapters 5 and 6, respectively). Among the major secular trends were the geographic expansion of the world-system, the trend toward a proletarianized labor force, and political revolts.[68] Ecological exhaustion and laborer demands incentivized expansion to new zones, outside of the world-economy (almost always, new incorporated lands joined the periphery). Then, for a time, the system went through growing pains as it adjusted to its new geography. After a long phase of consolidation, the world-economy would heat up again. Phases were normal, indeed natural, for the system, but also led to long-term consequences such as climate change. The internal processes of world-systems ultimately cause their undoing.[69] Wallerstein would continually return to discussions of cycles and trends in subsequent writings.

From his account of the modern world-system as historical accident, we can identify three counterfactual opinions Wallerstein held about the capitalism. First, capitalism *could* have started outside of Europe. Second, capitalism *could* have fallen apart in its early history and transformed into a world-empire. And third, capitalism *could* have had a different membership in its core, semiperiphery, and periphery. For each of these, we must ask: How was it that history unfolded as it did?

If capitalism could have formed in any region of the world, what explains the absence of its formation elsewhere? Why did it not form in, say, China? For these questions, Wallerstein believed that it was important to note that world-economies were often disorderly. Any system with multiple political centers was prone to conflict and unpredictability. The absence of a centralized political institution in Europe meant greater political instability (in terms of outward danger from other states and inward danger from peasant rebellion). China—even though similar to Europe in population, geography, and technological development—was more politically stable. China, in fact, began its maritime adventures at roughly the same time as Portugal but abandoned the project after three decades. For Wallerstein, China simply did not need to engage in the kind of risky behavior the capitalist system encouraged in Europe. China remained a world-empire, with an effective bureaucracy and the ability to prioritize its system-wide objectives. If Europe had been a *world-empire*, it too may have had greater priorities than territorial expansion.[70]

Second, if capitalism was not the inevitable consequence of the death of feudalism, and, if it was unstable and unpredictable in its early years, why did it survive? In fact, Wallerstein found it rather amazing that the capitalist world-economy lasted beyond infancy. Historically, world-economies often transformed into world-empires because powerful political leaders preferred controlling an entire economic system than one small piece. Wallerstein interpreted Spain under Charles V and his decades-long struggle against France as such an attempt. But instead of creating a Spanish world-empire, Charles V failed. In 1557, Spain (and France) went bankrupt. The world-economy, though young, had proved to be stronger than any particular state organization.[71]

And, third, why did the core emerge in one place and the periphery in another? Wallerstein described the early core as Western Europe (including the English, northern French, and Dutch zones), and the early periphery as Eastern Europe and eventually Hispanic America. Why was the core not located in Eastern Europe? For Wallerstein, it could have been. An Eastern core would have worked for the modern world-system just as well as a Western core. Wallerstein saw the early difference between core and periphery as only marginal, writing: "Either eastern Europe would become the 'breadbasket' of western Europe or vice versa. Either solution would have served the 'needs of the situation' in the conjuncture."[72] Western Europe had more developed towns and more intensive (and therefore more productive) land cultivation. Eastern Europe, by contrast, had less developed towns and less productive lands. Eastern Europe also faced the almost constant threat of external invasion by the Mongol-Tatars. The sizeable twenty-first-century core-periphery gap took centuries to form. Wallerstein explained: "[T]he *slight* edge of the fifteenth century became the great disparity of the seventeenth and the monumental difference of the nineteenth."[73]

One should bear in mind, however, that Wallerstein was writing about core and peripheral zones of a single world-system. It was not just by circumstance that the West became powerful and rich. Rather, its membership, and indeed the core's very existence, was the outcome of relations with the periphery (and vice versa). As he wrote about the early core and periphery, twentieth-century notions of development must have been on Wallerstein's mind. For he believed that if social scientists and policymakers conceived of development at the level of the world-system (and over its entire lifespan), they could better grasp why leaders of newly independent states so mistrusted leaders in the core. Furthermore, he thought a world-systems perspective would aid leaders in the West to better formulate policy responses to challenges in the third world.

Wallerstein's policy objectives were grand indeed. Nothing better demonstrates the scale of Wallerstein's goals than his 1977 appearance before the House International Relations Committee.[74] In his prepared testimony on African development, Wallerstein told House members to keep in mind that the fates of Americans and Africans were interconnected, and that the current economic system would not work to the United States' favor forever.[75]

At one point in his testimony, Wallerstein turned provocative: "I could mumble that 'pride goeth before the fall,' and predict the steady relative decline of the United States within this system over the next hundred years. But Congressmen are and perhaps should be more oriented to the present and nearer future. The case that even the presently privileged would be better off in a more egalitarian world society, in that it would release their human potential as well as those presently oppressed, is one in which I believe. . . . And we have to get our values straight: is development more quantity, or more equality?"[76]

By claiming that the present should remain the top priority of House members, Wallerstein may have meant the opposite. If policymakers neglected the long term, the United States would be worse off. It was a warning of a slow but irreversible decline on the world stage. If policy toward the developing world did not change, and if the hegemonic power did not transform the system, the United States would decline to a suboptimal place. In such a system, U.S. businesses would no longer benefit from uneven trade relations. Therefore, policymakers should be focused on their long-term foreign policy goals.

Wallerstein warned of a long-term economic downturn in the world economy, one that he thought would last until about 1990. Policymakers should expect the quality of life of Americans to decline. Thus, he advised: "The only alternative . . . is a still more fundamental transformation of the world-system."[77] According to him, it would be in the interests of the United States to alter the rules of a game it was on the verge of losing. Therefore, it was both the moral high ground and in the material interests of policymakers to transform the very system they dominated.

Wallerstein must have assumed his plea would be ignored. He recommended, after all, that the United States approach its international development program from the perspective of human development. But his testimony shows that he regarded world-systems analysis as a device for transforming the world, in addition to being a tool of social science.

Totalization at the *New Left Review*

As discussed in chapter 1, Anderson in the sixties did not think the Left was best served by day-to-day activism, but rather that social progress was best achieved through ideas. With frustratingly persuasive Cold War rhetoric emanating from Western governments, radicals needed a more compelling theory.[78] That theory would come from understanding the totality of history, as Anderson had explained in an essay from 1965: "It amounted to nothing less than a 'totalization' of world history in the 20th century. No other movement or doctrine has so far provided this. It remains the insurpassable horizon of all thought and action in our time."[79] In short, the NLR considered itself part of the vanguard precisely because it totalized.

Leading up to 1968, the editors sought out pieces on British society, the third world, and commentaries and translations of continental Marxists for English speakers. After 1968, Anderson and the editors expanded the project. They believed that the dismantling of capitalism would be in the economic, political, and cultural realms. It would be a revolution of production, education, familial relations, artistic expression, and sexuality. Anderson was motivated to articulate a history that explained and contributed to such an interconnected movement. Therefore, by explaining the history and processes of capitalism, he could help create an anticapitalist revolutionary bloc of activists led by the working class.[80]

In some ways, the story Anderson and the NLR sought to tell was not too different from the one crafted by Wallerstein and the Braudel Center. Anderson began with the premise that 1968 was a *revolution* and not simultaneous *revolutions*; the year's seemingly separate events could not be considered in isolation. The complex totality of the late twentieth century was comprised of the capitalist West, the Soviet Union, the third world, and China. Protests broke out in all four sectors, and, should therefore be understood in terms of the sectors' interrelations.[81] Specifically, the sectors were interconnected by the effects of capitalism: class divisions and inequality. Capitalism originated in Western Europe. Yet through imperialism, industrial production, and class struggle, capitalism (and its consequences) spread from continent to continent.[82] Like Wallerstein, Anderson believed that understanding the present global condition required a history of the region that conquered the world.

Although the NLR and its book publishing house were quite active, Anderson took it upon himself to write an account of the origins of capitalism. The ultimate goal of socialists, he believed, was a socialist economy and free society, which could be achieved via the seizure of state power. The socialist movement could therefore benefit from a history of the modern state and how it operated within global capitalism. In 1974, he released the first part of his large-scale study. The manuscript was so long that he was convinced to break it into two volumes, *Passages from Antiquity to*

Feudalism and *Lineages of the Absolutist State* (or, *Passages-Lineages*).[83] He had not published since 1967, at least without a pseudonym.[84]

Anderson's totalization produced a history of capitalism like Wallerstein's in its emphasis on stages, which for them was the principle that totalities change over time and take on new attributes. (Of course, both thinkers remained opposed to stages for national states, as the term was commonly understood in the modernization tradition.) Anderson's assessment of the end of feudalism was also similar to Wallerstein's. But *Passages-Lineages* substantially departed from *The Modern World-System* in three key respects: the length and fixed nature of developmental stages; the cause and timing of capitalism's arrival; and the uniqueness of the West.

On the first, although Anderson's study also concentrated on societal stages of development, it applied those stages on a much larger scale. *Passages-Lineages'* open totalization covered the history of Europe from the Greco-Roman age to the modern world. Anderson saw links across successive, and overlapping, modes of production: slavery, in the ancient world; feudalism, in the middle ages; and modern capitalism. In other words, stages in history for Anderson meant something approaching, but falling just shy of, inevitability.

Anderson demonstrated his views by discussing the ancient origins of Europe's East-West divergence. It was the West that had driven the geographical expansion of the Roman Empire, erected a large ruling class, and constructed a slave economy (that was subsequently introduced in the East). By contrast, Roman political authority in the East was established on top of the prior Hellenistic civilization. The East's historically more complex social formation blunted the prevalence of slavery, at least insofar as it determined economic life.[85] The West was therefore more sensitive to contradictions in the mode of production. As slavery reached its internal limit, the West suffered the consequences.

One such limit was that slavery always needed an influx of laborers. Since female slaves were not a lucrative investment, there was no way to naturally expand the labor population. The acquisition of slaves was cheap in times of military expansion. Buying slaves in the absence of military conquest was more difficult. In times of peace, slave traders at the edge of the empire could not provide enough new slaves to keep prices from rising. This made each purchase a gamble for owners, who needed to see a return on their investment. As the pace of Rome's expansion slowed, its economy also slowed and political stability declined. For Anderson, this trend revealed a fundamental contradiction within the ancient world:

slavery required impressive geographical expansion, and yet, over time, the empire benefited less and less from expansion and was eventually hurt by it.[86] The empire became too big to manage.

Anderson noted that, by the fourth century, population decline in the West was more severe than in the East (whose cities retained large populations and commerce). Taxes were lower in the East as well as tax collectors' fees; in the West, taxes could be as much as sixty times greater.[87] Controlling classes were also different. Western emperors, unlike their Eastern counterparts, did not limit the political authority of lesser aristocrats. The West also did not block the revival of the senatorial aristocracy, an institution that added to the state's bureaucratic weight. Consequently, in the West, revolts came from two segments of society at once: the aristocracy and the peasantry. Weakened, the empire was unable to defend against Germanic invaders, who began to push into new territory in the early fifth century. Anderson saw the invasions' effects in dialectical terms. Germanic rule represented an antithesis to Rome (the thesis), a contradiction which would eventually be resolved (or, synthesized) with a new, feudal, mode of production.[88]

The West's relative weakness forced it to change *earlier* than the East, thus, strangely enough, placing the West developmentally *ahead* of the East. This paradoxical outcome would affect European social formations for centuries, for it was the West that would first develop feudalism and its successors. As Anderson saw it, feudalism was the product of colliding Roman and German social formations. Over the fifth century, juridical and political institutions and practices of the so-called barbarians developed alongside existing Roman institutions.[89] The new overlords converted to Christianity and preserved slavery. A pattern of external invasion, in addition to the simple passage of time, led to a genuine integration of what was Germanic and what was Roman.[90] A genuine synthesis, what emerged from this process was somehow both of its ancestors and yet also neither of them.

Feudal institutions came from a variety of sources: vassalage, from German or Gallo-Roman aristocracies; the manor, from Gallo-Roman estates; and two true hybrids, serfdom and the feudal legal systems. This odd combination thus made up the "feudal totality," which had what Anderson called "a deep double derivation."[91] In the West, labor shifted from slave to serf from the ninth to the fourteenth centuries. Enserfment meant that laborers were not property, but rather semi-free subjects with limited freedoms and a promise of physical protection in exchange for labor. Feudal relations were very much unlike wage labor of the modern world. Anderson characterized wage labor as a form of economic coercion because laborers were nominally free to live where they wished (and later, afforded some protections). He characterized serfdom as a form of extra-economic coercion because laborers, in many circumstances, did not have even the nominal freedom to move about if they wished.

At the other end of the social hierarchy, lesser nobles were vassals to the monarch, comprising a vertical division of authority spread out across a given territory. The monarch's reach had limits, too, in the form of communal lands under peasant control. Anderson called this form of political power, divided by lower authorities and geography, the *parcellization of sovereignty*. Moreover, because the monarch ruled exclusively through intermediaries, he was also limited by them. Nominally at the summit of the feudal hierarchy, the monarch was in practice restrained. In Anderson's interpretation, the prince in reality was "not a supreme sovereign" above all others; his power was limited "through innumerable layers of subinfeudation." The prince was further limited by a dominant cultural force. In fact, the size and strength of the Church (which, Anderson wrote, had survived the epochal transition only by its "sheer worldly bulk") meant that secular power could never be completely centralized.[92] Rather, in being restrained by other political, economic, and cultural forces, monarchical authority could also be described as the *decomposition of sovereignty*.[93]

By contrast, the development of feudalism happened much later in the East, with enserfment taking hold from the fifteenth to the eighteenth centuries. According to Anderson, there was no Western-style collision of economic and political structures. Instead, invasions by nomadic pastoral peoples limited the economic and political development of the East.[94]

Second, on the cause and timing of capitalism's arrival, Anderson agreed with Wallerstein that feudalism in the West met its demise due to a combination of ecological and economic crises. In *Passages-Lineages*, land exhaustion in the fourteenth century led to a decline in rural productivity, food shortfalls, and famine, effects that were exacerbated by the sudden arrival of the Black Death. Yet unlike Wallerstein, Anderson emphasized class conflict, not an emerging requirement for ceaseless accumulation. The key development for him was labor scarcity, which represented a first step toward capitalism. The crisis of feudalism, as he explained it, incentivized the replacement of service rents with monetary rents. But this was no peaceful process. Initially, the nobility tried doubling-down, shifting costs of production onto the peasantry. The nobility made no effort to disguise their abuses, which Anderson described as "among the most glacially explicit programmes of exploitation" in history.[95] A succession of peasant upheavals were almost universally suppressed. Still, the noble masters were enforcing an anachronism. History had passed them by. In the long run, feudal relations slowly came to an end in the West.

Moreover, Anderson also disagreed with Wallerstein's claim that capitalism began in the sixteenth century. Instead, he envisaged an intervening period. Absolutism, the attempt by secular rulers to centralize power, was for Anderson a "complex combination" of feudal and capitalist processes. (To be clear, it did not mean total authority in a single individual. Rather, absolutism was the overall "weight" of the monarchy on the "aristocratic order.")[96] As he saw it, just as the West was escaping serfdom in the fifteenth century, the East was imposing it. Peasants in the West entered modernity more as free laborers than as serfs, whereas peasants in the East entered modernity more as serfs than as free laborers. Thus, absolutism in the West was a way for the aristocracy to adjust to the end of serfdom and a growing urban economy. The East centralized authority at the same time, but for dramatically different reasons. In the East, absolutism, implemented in response to the threat of war from abroad, was a device for peasant enserfment in the countryside and to limit the independence of towns. Centuries later, the East was still far behind the development of the West.

Capitalism, for Anderson, did not arrive until the successive waves of bourgeois revolutions across the West. The result was the incremental implementation of explicitly capitalist institutions, procedures, and governance. The East developed capitalism much later and, like absolutism, it arrived largely by import from the West. In the case of Russia, the 1917 revolution did not overthrow a capitalist state but rather a feudal one, the most successful absolutist political structure in Europe.[97]

And, third, Anderson believed that only Europe's West could have produced capitalism. Whereas Wallerstein considered the early modern West to have had only a slight advantage over the East in the sixteenth century, Anderson considered the West to have had a massive advantage, rooted in antiquity. For him, capitalism was not the outcome of a series of historical accidents, just as it was not the necessary sequel to feudalism.

To reinforce his conclusions, Anderson offered Japan as a historical contrast. Though it was the only other region in the world to experience feudalism, Japan had had no earlier collision between slave and tribal modes of production. Without slavery, Anderson wrote, it thus had "no inherent drive within the feudal mode of production which inevitably compelled it to develop into the capitalist mode of production."[98] It also had no inherent drive toward absolutism. In fact, when Commodore Perry arrived in 1853, Japan was headed toward further political decentralization, as evidenced by its weakened military. Like the ruling institutions across Eastern Europe, Japan's new Meiji State centralized power when confronted with an external threat. But Japan was different in avoiding absolutism, its centralization accompanied by the introduction of citizenship, a single currency, and a market economy.[99] Japan, according to Anderson, only achieved capitalism because of nineteenth-century European imperialism. The consequences for international political economy were clear. Capitalism could only have come about from the antagonisms between slave and feudal modes of production. The results encompassed economics, politics, and culture. According to Anderson, from the Renaissance to the conquest and imposition of slavery in the New World, "the birth of capital also saw . . . the rebirth of antiquity."[100]

Like Wallerstein's, all of Anderson's efforts were aimed at changing the present. He was convinced that if socialists were to make any sense of their present condition, they needed to know the unique nature of capitalism. Yet in sharp contrast to Wallerstein, Anderson in the 1970s did not formulate specific recommendations for activists or policymakers. He preferred to state his and the NLR's intentions, and then let the ideas speak for themselves.

Assessing Totalities

However careful Anderson and Wallerstein tried to be, their methods were far from perfect. Three flaws stand out. First, Wallerstein's preference for closed totalities left him unable to explain the space immediately prior to the formation of the modern world-system. Second, Anderson's preference for open totalities forced him to simultaneously describe general rules and exceptions to those rules. And third, in covering such large geographical zones over long periods of time, each author risked minimizing the effects of princes, popes, and other personages on historical transformation.

On closed totalities, it proved daunting for Wallerstein to demarcate the temporal and spatial boundaries of the system. Some historians criticized Wallerstein for pointing to the "long" sixteenth century as the birth of capitalism. Even Wallerstein found his dating difficult to justify. Unhappy with his own account, he offered a revised explanation for the modern world-system's origins in the "long" sixteenth century.[101] But some intellectuals, otherwise sympathetic to world-systems analysis, did not find his dates realistic. They came to think that Europe did not change so fundamentally in the period 1450 to 1650. They thought there were elements of continuity in the centuries leading up to the modern world.[102] Writers such as Andre Gunder Frank, Janet Abu-Lughod, Barry K. Gills, and Robert A. Denemark traded closed totalities for open ones.[103] In a periodization reminiscent of, yet grander than, *Passages-Lineages*, they saw the entire Earth as a single system stretching back at least five thousand years.[104] It was not, however, that they saw no difference between the premodern and modern world, but rather that there were numerous continuities amid change. The accumulation and control of capital, they believed, always mattered in economic and social life in premodern world-systems. They acknowledged that capital did not always play a dominant role in the production of life necessities, but, on the other hand, they found the transition from feudalism to capitalism to be less profound than did Wallerstein.[105]

Wallerstein was unconvinced. He thought his contemporaries had sacrificed all utility in labeling a system capitalist or noncapitalist. Moreover, he stressed the limited nature of his argument. Whereas capital existed in prior epochs, the modern world-system was founded on the requirement that actors endlessly seek out more and more of it.[106] One of his letters to Frank was particularly revealing, for it questioned the nature of systems altogether. He wrote: "It can be demonstrated seriously that the fluttering of a leaf in my backyard will affect significantly the trajectory of Sirius. Ergo what? Shall we then lump all knowledge (and I do mean all knowledge) into one big stewpot? Of course a world system (as you have defined it) has existed since 2500 B.C. But why stop there? Go back to Australopithecus and it is also true. And then further back to the Pleistocene Age."[107]

The freedom and the burden of totalities was that there were no exact rules as to what constituted a social whole, when it began, or how far it extended. Wallerstein seemed to be searching for just such a rule, but, as his revisions and debates with others show, there was never widespread agreement as to what changed in the modern world. Almost all intellectuals who debated the origins of capitalism thought that *something* was different. But what? Over subsequent decades, Wallerstein, having discovered the concept of entropy from the physical sciences, would improve his answer with analogies to systems in the natural world. For the moment, his defense rested on the logic that temporal boundaries were necessary, not on the grounds that his particular dates were correct. It was easier to insist that his opponents were using flawed logic. For any scholar of closed totalities, it was a constant struggle to specify when and where a given totality began.

Unlike Wallerstein, Anderson did not have to justify his boundaries. But because his historical analysis was essentially without limits, Anderson was under sustained pressure to draw general conclusions and yet also note exceptions to those conclusions. *Passages-Lineages* compared two components of a complex totality, Europe's East and West, in a single totalizing analysis. He did not have the luxury of claiming that Scandinavia or the Byzantine Empire was simply outside the system at a given time. Within Europe (which he defined in the broadest possible terms) the system was always everywhere. Thus, Anderson had to simultaneously assert a generalization and also list exceptions to the rule. According to Theda Skocpol and Margaret Somers, Anderson's back-and-forth narrative made it difficult for readers to tell if he was describing a rule or an exception.[108]

Whereas Wallerstein's totalities suffered from being too closed, Anderson's totalities suffered from being too open. Both studies, however, fell victim to minimizing the role of individuals, institutions, and classes (or other collections of individuals). They tended to emphasize structures, which for them were economic and social forces that conditioned human behavior. Wallerstein's account, over a shorter time frame, was somewhat open to individual preferences, such as his account of Spain's Charles V, who almost pushed all of Europe under his control. Anderson's narrative, over a much longer time frame, almost completely avoided the role of individuals, and offered only a limited account of the actions of ruling groups. *Passages-Lineages* contextualized actions in such a way as to attribute their source to larger forces, conditioned by time and geography. According to Ira Katznelson, Anderson seemed to ignore human agency altogether.[109] When Anderson confronted agency, he limited the interests and actions of individuals through temporal barriers, that is, the period in which one lived. Strict periodization, for Katznelson, was unrealistic: the power of individuals was either sidelined or considered an expression of the historical era. Anderson subsumed individual interests into the mood of an age; human agency was really the agency of structures.[110]

Still, the difference between almost ignoring and completely ignoring the causal importance of individuals was slight: both Wallerstein and Anderson greatly downplayed the causal effects of individuals in their writings on early modernity. Katznelson advised those oriented to the long term to think of structures as outlining boundaries for human action. The solution for Katznelson was to link periodization (the structure-based temptation) with preferences (the agent-based temptation).[111]

Totalizing writers might also do well to imagine individuals operating within constraints. Some constraints, such as tariffs, sanctions, military blockades, might be created by other human beings. Others, like a nation-state's location in the world-economy or a region's stage of economic development, are larger forces beyond the immediate control of any human being. But even though structures constrain choices, individuals and their institutions still make decisions. There are very few, if any, structures that totally eliminate all individual preferences. Furthermore, some structures enable human action, such as public educational, environmental, or health institutions.

Ironically, such criticism of Wallerstein's and Anderson's scholarship may have been more in line with their own views. Neither scholar greatly downplayed human agency in later writings on twentieth-century politics. In the coming years, they would each confront questions of structures and agency, and, consequently, develop more generous interpretations of the power of collective action. Such confrontations were perhaps inevitable, however, given that Wallerstein and Anderson were spurred to action by global protests. They hoped, like so many before them, to change political reality in the world.

Intermission I

Immanuel Wallerstein's New Pair of Glasses

It may seem strange to think about a time when Immanuel Wallerstein was not associated with the world-systems tradition. In truth, his address to the Africa Studies Association in 1973 was likely the first public expression of world-systems analysis as it is understood today. This brief intermission discusses the evolution of Wallerstein's thought from 1968 to 1973, and will perhaps place in a clearer light the ideas expressed in *The Modern World-System I* and its methodological accompaniment, "The Rise and Future Demise of the World Capitalist System."[1]

The 1968 Columbia protests confirmed Wallerstein's doubts about the tools of social science, and in particular, its regard for the nation-state as the world's primary actor. Years later, Wallerstein reflected on how 1968 changed his thinking. That year, he said, "was certainly a major element in creating the ambiance in which world-systems analysis could come forward.... I certainly had many of those ideas earlier, but in a more confused way."[2] Motifs of colonialism, nationalism, race, ideology, as well as the structures of a world system and world economy (without hyphens) appeared throughout his writings in the 1960s, which in his expression, were "en route to world-systems analysis."[3] His description of understanding some sort of larger system was apt: Wallerstein frequently relied on variables originating outside the nation-state, but he did not have a systematic understanding of how those international variables related to domestic outcomes. The notion of a world-system as portrayed in the last chapter was a slow transition: the product of 1968, experiences in Africa, and a growing frustration with trends in social science research.

Wallerstein's transition from the state to the world-system can be seen through a series of snapshots, publications between 1967 and 1973 that discuss concepts and terminology of world-systems analysis. The first snapshot was an attempt to clarify terms within the state-centric framework. The second adopted a nascent world-systems framework. And the third drew on world-systems analysis (almost) in its present form.[4]

The first essay, authored with Terence K. Hopkins, advocated for state-based comparative scholarship. Hopkins and he proposed a typology of pluri-national studies, which they defined as research drawing on two or more nation-states. They identified three main types, compared in Table I.1: cross-national, multi-national, and international. They saw "nations" as distinct from "cultures," characterized by civilizations or religions. Although they wrote few words about this other category, *pluri-cultural studies* also apparently fell into three types: cross-cultural, multi-cultural, and inter-cultural.

In a typology reminiscent of Braudel and his notion of society as the set of sets, Hopkins and Wallerstein describe the *complex social unit* as appearing to scholars in various forms: "It is an entity in its own right; it is a context for its constituent members; and it, in turn, is a member of larger contexts."[5] In Hopkins and Wallerstein's typology, multi-national research involved comparisons of individuals and groups at the subnational level. They thought these studies were problematic, given the following contradiction: scholars studied specific locations, yet usually expressed their findings in universal terms (as if they knew about all societies everywhere).[6] International research, by contrast, was focused on the relationship among states, usually in the form of markets or regional associations. Hopkins and Wallerstein wrote the least about this type of pluri-national study. Still, their claim was that each type is a member of

Table I.1. Hopkins and Wallerstein's Typology of Pluri-National Studies

Type	Level	Comparison
Cross-national	Societal	National societies
Multi-national	Sub-national	Individuals and groups (national societies are the context, the 'setting'); hypotheses are devised and tested within society, yet stated as universally applicable
International	Supra-national	International networks or systems (national societies are "only 'members' of the larger-scale units being compared")

a larger context. In what context does international research appear? Of what larger analytical unit is it a member? Hopkins and Wallerstein did not say, though their statement esoterically hints at the existence of some grander conceptual unit of analysis.

Cross-national research, according to Hopkins and Wallerstein, differed substantially from the other types, for three reasons.[7] First, it focused on problems associated with development and modernization (that is, "of long term societal change in the modern world"). Next, cross-national research also looked to the experiences of nation-states and how established states affected the development of recently formed states. And last, in a foreshadowing use of terminology, Hopkins and Wallerstein wrote that cross-national techniques "are very different from those used in the study of other kinds of 'total' social units."[8] Social units, they contended, must be examined in terms of *all* the factors (including historical trajectories) that make up political systems. These characteristics made cross-national research unique. Therefore, to confuse cross-national studies with other types would unfairly neglect the former's distinctiveness.

Readers familiar with Wallerstein's writings may find it odd to see him advocate for the state as the preferred unit of analysis. Further still, Arend Lijphart cited their study favorably in an article that remains popular among political scientists, "Comparative Politics and the Comparative Method" (1971).[9] Yet, readers will also find a remarkable consistency in Wallerstein's research interests. Themes of development and relations between wealthy and poor states remained his empirical objects of study. Moreover, the use of *total* signified a sense of holism, and the reference to a *complex social unit* invited comparisons to the idea of a complex totality. The difference was that Wallerstein's holistic thinking was constrained within a nation-state paradigm. He nevertheless struggled with a simple question: What constitutes a social whole?

The transition Wallerstein underwent from 1967 to 1973 was not in research topic, but rather in historical imagination and measurement. In his writings of the late sixties, Wallerstein discussed extranational variables in terms of an unhyphenated *world system*. Undefined, the term appeared at crucial moments, with Wallerstein chalking up causation to extranational forces. Take, for example, the world system as barrier to the political development and success of newly independent African nations: "It is precisely because the dangers are so great to the existing world system that the obstacles to unity are so great."[10]

Alternatively, the world system was used to describe the difficulties of change within advanced industrial societies such as the United States. In one work, he wrote: "As long as the present world system guarantees the privileged position of these [middle class] groups . . . there is little reason to anticipate that arguments from the left will sway them politically."[11] In the same piece, he described the system as a kind of veto player (to borrow a term from contemporary social science): "A prerequisite to truly fundamental change . . . is a substantial change in the world system, in its division of labor and allocation of rewards."[12]

In these usages, the world system was treated as an independent variable, something not quite a unit of analysis. At times, however, it took on unit-like functions. Wallerstein primarily wrote about domestic factors causing varying levels of success in political development. But he so frequently invoked the extranational world system that its overall character seemed to be something more than a series of individual variables separately causing divergent developmental outcomes.

Wallerstein attempted to rectify state-based research with his frequent references to extranational variables. This brings us to a second snapshot, with Wallerstein jettisoning state-based and cross-national research altogether. In "Three Paths of National Development in Sixteenth Century Europe," from 1972, Wallerstein used an unhyphenated *world economy* as his unit of analysis.[13]

The argument in "Three Paths" is more sophisticated than its predecessors. Here, he refined the idea of a world system. Instead of general and brief references to a world system, now Wallerstein wrote about its functions. Through three case studies, on Poland, Venice, and England, he described both the uniqueness of modern capitalism and the various economic roles that states play within the world system. Readers also find a historically derived differentiation of the system into core, semiperiphery, and periphery over the "long" sixteenth century. On the division of labor, he summarized: "All this added up to a world economy in the sense that the various areas came to be dependent upon each other for their specialized roles. The profitability of specific economic activities became a function of the proper functioning of the system as a whole: profitability was generally served by increasing the overall productivity of the system."[14] The point for Wallerstein was that the states of the world system were interconnected in a historically contingent way. Yet the idea of a world economy in this sense proved problematic. It was simply too large. How could comparative work be done within a single, global, unit of analysis?

Moreover, how could a global system begin in sixteenth-century Europe? What was happening in China or Africa?

Wallerstein was well aware of these problems in 1972. The year prior, he began writing a history of the modern capitalist system,[15] and he had to wrestle with complications regarding the unit of analysis. By 1973 (at least), he had developed a solution in the form of a geographically modest, hyphenated, *world-system*.

In a third snapshot, Wallerstein discussed a familiar theme, African development, in terms of this new analytical perspective. As head of the Africa Studies Association for the 1972–73 year, he used his presidential address, "Africa in a Capitalist World," to draw connections between capitalism as a historical system and postcolonial Africa.[16] He did not use the occasion to describe his methods, but it was evident that he had fundamentally rethought the concept of development. Wallerstein later explained his rationale: "I wished to insist that we had to view Africa as an intrinsic part of the capitalist world in which we were living."[17]

Wallerstein's address surveyed recent writings on African development. Most studies were flawed, he said, because social science lacked a way to properly interpret data. He surmised that this error came from an inability among scholars, at least in the twentieth century, to think in larger terms, larger times and larger spaces.[18] Social scientists tended to limit their studies arbitrarily to a given territory, colonial authority, or state. But Africa in the fifties and sixties was a time of transition from one form of rule to another, with massive changes across varied settings. How could state-based studies survive their own spatial constraints? How can one write about issues of national liberation without expanding his or her analytical frames to include the colonial powers themselves? For Wallerstein, the answer had finally come into full focus: decolonization, he concluded, could not have been about both national liberation and class struggle unless one conceived, explicitly or implicitly, of a grander geographical plane.[19]

In his view, a new model would include international factors, often ignored or treated as mysterious extranational shocks to domestic politics. Africa was caught up in the history of the world. And for social science to systematically understand Africa or any part of the postcolonial world, researchers needed models capable of capturing the interaction between the state and external forces. Adopting a new model was not easy, he said. It involved rethinking the history of the world.

The call, Wallerstein clarified, was not just for a general attentiveness to the world stage. This had already been done, messily, without success.

What social science needed was a better unit of analysis. To continuously rely on improper or unspecified units seemed to him pointless for knowledge accumulation. He thus recommended that scholars use the world-system, a new analytical unit larger than the state but not necessarily encompassing the globe. In the modern world, this was the *capitalist world-economy*, born in sixteenth-century Europe, which since expanded to cover the earth. The world-economy, understood in terms of its long history and expansive geographic scope, ought to be a starting frame of reference for any study on Africa.

In inserting a hyphen into *world-system* and its main types—*mini-system, world-empire, world-economy*, and *world-government*—Wallerstein believed he had resolved a problem of translation. As he explained (and discussed previously in this work), Braudel wrote about "an economy *that is* a world" (*économie-monde*), not about "an economy *of the* world" (*économie mondiale*). Writing in French, one could make such distinctions straightforwardly. In English, special adjustments were required. Wallerstein's solution was to portray *world* and *system* (or *economy*) as inseparable.[20] "Hence the hyphen," he summarized, "since 'world' is not an attribute of the system. Rather the two words together constitute a single concept."[21]

It was in this speech that Wallerstein announced that the capitalist world-economy had a division of labor between the powerful developed core, the underdeveloped periphery, and the in-between semiperiphery. He noted that this division of labor created a vicious cycle, with core states becoming strong and weak states becoming weak through unequal exchange.[22] The concept of "unequal exchange" came from Polanyi, in addition to the language, discussed in chapter 2, of "reciprocity," "redistribution," and "exchange."[23]

In this new model, economic and political stagnation in newly independent African states could be understood in full view, against the historical legacy of colonialism. The model portrayed faltering development as the outcome of longstanding forces, which could not be overcome in the decade or so since independence. Yet as he explained, Wallerstein did not want those in Africa studies to treat world-systems as a bleak tradition. Rather, he thought the conditions of the world-economy "make possible certain political thrusts" of nationalism.[24]

By 1973, Wallerstein had changed his mind about the domestic and the international. He had concluded that it was the world-system, not the states, that went through stages of development. But he did not abandon one set of analytical tools suddenly or on a whim. From those early writings on Africa through his analysis of 1968, he grew dissatisfied with existing tools of social science that, he believed, led to incorrect conclusions. African nationalism and the protests at Columbia revealed that social science tools of the sixties could not explain the empirical world. Wallerstein's initial acceptance of state-based analysis, however reluctant, overturned into outright rebellion against much of social science. Content at first to typologize and redefine concepts, he eventually invented a new and larger unit. The three snapshots above display his shifting attitude. Wallerstein likened his methods to an unfinished lens: "I am not calling for intellectual supermen. I am merely asking that we wear a new pair of glasses, and that we wear these new glasses in the very process of grinding them."[25]

Chapter 5

There Is No Alternative

As the 1970s wore on, the excitement of 1968 faded. The radical tide turned. Many who had anticipated the advancement of workers' rights at home and newly independent states abroad saw the movement stall. Postwar economic prosperity turned into a global economic downturn. This was the beginning of a long period of slow growth, one in which the world-economy arguably remains.[1] By the early 1980s, North-South relations changed. Previously, international lending institutions such as the World Bank and International Monetary Fund were commonly associated with the liberalism of figures like Robert McNamara and Willy Brandt. These and other leaders saw their institutional role as one of improving, albeit slowly, economic and political well-being in the postcolonial world. In the 1980s, international lending institutions became associated with neoliberalism.[2] The new attitude, symbolized by Margaret Thatcher and Ronald Reagan, was one of reduced social welfare at home and open markets abroad. The Washington Consensus, as it became known in the sphere of international development, was defined by the belief that developing states should quickly integrate into the global capitalist economy. Regional development banks and global lending institutions collectively agreed on loan conditions, such as: currency devaluation, the cancellation of subsidies and tariffs, and the establishment of interest rates above the pace of inflation. Consequently, the development of the North continued to be financed by capital flows from the South.[3]

Wallerstein's and Anderson's post-1968 intellectual itineraries were already in motion as neoliberalism ascended in popularity. They responded to neoliberalism quite differently. Wallerstein's program at the Braudel

Center remained unchanged. Over the 1980s, Wallerstein came to see the very concepts of optimism and pessimism as irrelevant to the longevity of capitalism. It did not matter to him that the neoliberal ideology had taken positions of power, or, for that matter, if it were popular among everyday people. Wallerstein believed that the contradictions of capitalism were leading to a crisis of the system. Therefore, his prediction of capitalist demise was unaltered.

Anderson's reaction, by contrast, was personal. Already faced with the difficult task of writing a history of the bourgeois revolutions, the arrival of neoliberalism forced him to rethink his research goals. He wrote to influence a movement. Yet, it seemed as though he and the *New Left Review* were not having the effect they desired. By the early 1980s, Anderson doubted his ability to lead the NLR, and wondered if it was time for a new leader who would remake the *Review* into a more efficacious journal.

The decade, therefore, was transformative. For one scholar, it was the finalization of clinical rationality, a perspective set at a distance from political hopes or disappointments. For the other, it was recognition that social forces were moving in the wrong direction. In pursuing their divergent courses, however, both authors began to develop nuanced interpretations of the relative power of humans in comparison to structures. Wallerstein and Anderson were each known to emphasize long-term political and economic forces as agents of historical change. Though they held to this preference, Wallerstein and Anderson clarified their views in a way that suggested that humans might have considerable agency in the late twentieth and twenty-first centuries.

Capitalism Does Not Care About Your Passion

Surprisingly, given his adherence to the closed totality and its non-teleological vision of history, Wallerstein in the 1970s believed that capitalism would inevitably give way to socialism.[4] *The Modern World-System I* described capitalism as due to a series of historical accidents, yet he nonetheless thought that socialism was in our future. In the 1980s, these contradictory statements halted. He stopped making such predictions. At first, Wallerstein's tone wavered on the likelihood of socialism.[5] Then, by the end of the decade, he abandoned all predictions about the next historical system.[6] This was not because Wallerstein did not want to see global socialism realized; he simply no longer believed that the end of capitalism would automatically give way to socialism. There was nothing preordained, he concluded, about the rise of capitalism. Why should one expect one type of world-system to form out of another's collapse? World-systems, after all, were closed totalities, with self-contained processes. Consequently, one could not develop too many expectations about future world-systems based on past world-systems.[7]

One might think the diminution of socialism in Wallerstein's writings was the consequence of a newfound pessimism. One could reasonably assume that Wallerstein had lowered his expectations after concluding that revolutionaries were not likely to dismantle the capitalist system. To the contrary, his new attitude was a sign of serenity. Wallerstein's belief, simply, was that all systems end regardless of whether they were hated or loved.

This change in attitude can be attributed directly to Ilya Prigogine, whom Wallerstein met in 1980. Like anyone, Wallerstein had mentors who shaped his thinking during formative years, but this encounter was different in that by this point he was already a well-established scholar. Unlike those earlier introductions to Fanon or Braudel, meeting Prigogine was not unlike a political event, such as 1968. Born in Moscow a few months before the revolution, Prigogine spent his professional life in Brussels. In 1977, he won the Nobel Prize in Chemistry, the culmination of a career devoted to questioning traditional assumptions in the field of thermodynamics.[8] Wallerstein heard Prigogine speak at a conference and "found it truly brilliant."[9] He struck up a conversation with the Nobel laureate and discovered that they were thinking similar things about the nature of systems.

Prigogine's work in chemistry and physics took on three types of conventions in the hard sciences. These were assumptions about time, about predictability, and about stability. On time, Prigogine believed that many of his fellow scientists had adopted an inconsistent vision. On the one hand, modern physical science took for granted the Newtonian principle of *time-reversibility*, which contended that past and future were inseparable. The earth's rotation around the sun, for example, was a time-reversible phenomenon in the sense that the earth always rotated around the sun in the same manner.[10] Yet on the other hand, scientists also held views that presumed the *irreversibility* of time. Many ideas, such as the universe's "big bang" and the evolution of species, treated the passage of time to be more like an arrow, moving in a single direction. Prigogine often explained the distinction in terms of *entropy*, the notion that systems ultimately bend toward disorder. He wrote: "[I]rreversible processes produce entropy. In contrast, reversible processes leave the entropy constant."[11]

Despite acknowledging the presence of time-irreversible phenomena, many scientists in his view did not confront the consequences of their contradictory views on time. Time-reversibility also meant determinism, understood by Prigogine as predictability: the idea that the same initial conditions always caused the same outcomes. Modern science, having adopted a Newtonian perspective, had generally sought law-like regularities, applicable to all times and places. As such, Prigogine supposed that the ideology of science had divine aspirations. Scientists sought a unified field theory, a single law to read, in Stephen Hawking's description, the "mind of God."[12] But, Prigogine wondered, if time were evolutionary-dependent, how could the same conditions always yield the same result? What if the passage of time meant a different result? He adopted an anti-Newtonian view that conceived of phenomena, whether found in physics, chemistry, or biology, in terms of contingent regularities. Instead of looking for laws about, say, wetlands, gravity, or the sun's warmth, scientists, according to Prigogine, would be better off proposing their findings within spatial and temporal boundaries. He believed that scientific laws were only true at certain places and certain times. In other words, Prigogine thought in terms of historical systems.

Prigogine considered that there were moments in the lifespan of a system, any system, when it functioned with remarkable stability. He imagined stable systems to be like a pendulum: a slight change will have a slight effect; a big change will have a big effect. But, he noted, there were times when systems were unstable. He thought these systems were more like a pencil on its head: a slight change will have a considerable effect. Furthermore, unstable systems were not predictable: the same initial conditions might lead to dramatically different outcomes. Many systems, he claimed, manifested more like the analogy of the pencil than the pendulum. We cannot always determine with certainty that y_1 will happen under x conditions. But, we can make probabilistic predictions that y_1 or y_2 might happen under x conditions. Prigogine thought scientists would be better served if they embraced uncertainty as a central principle. "One can compare the universe . . . to a new-born baby, who could become an architect, a musician, or a bank clerk, but not all at the same time."[13] Instead, one can speak in probabilistic terms about a baby's future occupation, taking into account class, family life, and education. Conditions of predictability, he believed, should be thought of as the exception rather than the rule.

Prigogine did not wish to abandon scientific principles, but he did want to jettison the illusion of certainty. In doing so, he wished to make the following replacements:

Time reversibility	→	Time irreversibility
Determinism	→	Probability
Stability	→	Instability

In moving away from certainty, Prigogine wanted a new scientific paradigm. If successful, it meant that the age of Galileo and Newton would come to an end.[14] Attuned to unconventional ideas, Wallerstein was captivated. At age fifty, he arrived at what he called "something of an intellectual breakthrough."[15] He reflected: "I've had ideas very similar to those posed by Prigogine for many years, but I had never had the terms to express them until that moment, so now I had the language that allowed the expression of these ideas deep inside me."[16]

Yet Prigogine provided more than a vocabulary for talking about systems. Wallerstein came to think of natural systems, in addition to social systems, as historical. No system could be eternal. His assessment of the "future demise" of the capitalist world-economy was thus shielded from neoliberal pronouncements of capitalism's permanence. Thatcher, Reagan, the IMF, the World Bank, or other adherents to the ideology of neoliberalism could not make the capitalist world-economy survive beyond its natural lifespan. Nor could the actions of everyday people extend its life. Capitalism, according to Wallerstein, will end if anticapitalists are well organized and dedicated to their cause. Yet it will also end if anticapitalists suddenly embrace capitalism.

Wallerstein began writing about the nature of systemic collapse. From Prigogine, he took the concept of a *bifurcation* and applied it to social systems. To talk about bifurcations was to talk about the death of a system. All systems, Wallerstein believed, would reach a point in their histories whereby internal contradictions endanger the survival of the system. When systems were healthy and strong, he thought, any given event (such as war, currency collapse, or natural disaster) would not destabilize the survival of the system. But when the strength of a system declined, events and even the actions of individual people might lead to unexpected outcomes.[17]

The capitalist world-economy, according to Wallerstein, had reached such a point of weakness. For centuries, its success was predicated on geographic expansion. After capitalism formed (in the long sixteenth century), it underwent a period of consolidation (in the seventeenth), and then embarked on a great expansion (in the eighteenth and nineteenth). As laborers clamored for better pay and working conditions, and as natural resources were exhausted, owner-producers often looked to move. The lure of unspoiled lands and an unorganized labor force proved strong. Occasionally, owner-producers looked to zones outside of the world-economy. As of the late nineteenth century, the world-system had conquered the entire globe, and therefore, had lost the ability to "runaway" to new zones.[18] The system's greatest asset turned into its greatest liability. No previous world-system had become a global system, but, without any place to expand, capitalism in the twentieth century began to suffocate. Thus, internal contradictions had sent the capitalist world-economy into structural crisis.

He explained his position through an analysis of something called *long waves,* which were popularized in the 1920s by Russian economist Nikolai Kondratieff.[19] The concept of a long wave was controversial for Cold War social science, in part because of Kondratieff's nationality. American academics could more easily dismiss scholarship produced by a geopolitical adversary. Ironically, Kondratieff was persecuted in the Soviet Union because, in contrast to Moscow's claims, his writings suggested that capitalist growth would continue. In 1930, he was arrested, shipped to Siberia, and died a few years later.[20]

Wallerstein primarily paid attention to two types of long waves: the Kondratieff wave, which signified an economic trend of forty-five to sixty years, and, the logistical cycle, which signified an economic trend of 150 to 300 years. (Other economic cycles included: Kitchen, of two to three years; Juglar, of six to ten years; and Kuznets, of fifteen to twenty years.)[21] Wallerstein thought that there was a lack of attention paid to long waves by his fellow social scientists. This frustrated him because he believed that social science generally accepted the idea of short-term trends (up to a decade or so). In one undated essay, he noted that few intellectuals would have taken issue with the claim that food prices fluctuate over time. Nor would they have disagreed with the statement that ideological preferences may shift between elections. These short-term patterns were and remain easily accepted. "However," he wrote, "the minute we suggest that there are similar fluctuations over longer periods of time ('long waves') there is considerable controversy."[22] For him, a richer debate would be like that of physiologists who studied breathing in animals. Physiologists might disagree about how animals breathe, but, he wrote in a separate essay, they "do not argue about whether or not breathing occurs." And, Wallerstein contended, much like describing the life of an animal, it would be hard to describe the life of the world-economy without acknowledging that it breathes "repetitively and reasonably regularly."[23]

According to their proponents, long waves had periods of faster growth, called A-phases, and periods of slower growth, called B-phases. Wallerstein considered A- and B-phases to be like the world-economy taking in a breath and then letting it out. He thought Kondratieff waves were best signified by rising and falling profit-rates.[24] The logistical cycle, being over a much longer time frame, was the combined impact of three forces: population, prices (of wheat and cereal, in agrarian Europe), and economic activity. The latter was comprised of many factors, including commerce, land use and availability of lands, production of goods, and the value of monetary assets (which, in turn, were related to other things like urbanization and the political power those involved in production, such as guilds or, much later, unions).[25]

The long downturn of the seventeenth century, and long upswing of the eighteenth, were Wallerstein's subjects in the next two volumes of *The Modern World-System*, published in 1980 and 1989. Bookends to a decade, they were printed in rather different times, a period extending from neoliberalism's early days to its triumph. Yet the narrative's continuity, an Olympian perspective across two centuries, reflected the author's confidence. Volumes II and III showed why he believed the world-system had entered a point of bifurcation in his own time.

In *Mercantilism and the Consolidation of the European World-Economy, 1600–1750*, Wallerstein took on the common view among historians that the seventeenth century comprised the last convulsions of feudalism. Instead, he argued that following the creation and initial expansion of the world-system over roughly 150 years, the world-economy experienced a normal long-term downturn for another century and a half, until about 1750.[26]

The seventeenth century was, in Wallerstein's account, a time of consolidation for the capitalist world-economy.[27] Life was difficult throughout the world-system, though with uneven effects among the core, semiperiphery, and periphery. Core areas such as England and France limited the effects of the downturn via mercantilist policies, protecting domestic economic interests in agriculture, textiles, and (especially in England) shipbuilding. Strong state institutions also served to mitigate domestic class disputes, whether initiated by restless peasants and proletarians or by quarreling nobles and merchants. England, however, more cleverly navigated class antagonisms than did France. Both states taxed heavily, but England's plan was more concealed and thus met less resistance.[28] When monarchies were challenged in the second half of the 1600s, France preserved its social hierarchy, while competing classes in England reached an understanding. In England, members of the bourgeois class saw their interests best fulfilled through compromise with the nobility. The two groups, he explained, increasingly saw the lower strata as politically dangerous.[29] England's early resolution of this problem made for greater stability in the long run.

Semiperipheral states attempted mercantilism but found it vastly more difficult to manage domestic economic affairs than did England or France. Wallerstein noted that some historians called non-efficacious policies *pseudomercantilism,* whereby state policies only benefited a few local officials. Still, he thought it was significant that semiperipheral leaders could attempt mercantilism. Governments in the periphery could not.[30] Some semiperipheral areas, able to mimic the actions the core, saw their prestige increase. These included Sweden, Prussia, and northern Atlantic colonies in British North America.[31]

Others in the semiperiphery, however, were ineffective and saw their power decline, including: Spain, Portugal, western and southern Germanies, and northern Italy. Wallerstein described Spain's decline as "the most spectacular phenomenon of the seventeenth century—visible even to the men of the time."[32] In the previous century, Charles V had attempted to control the entire European world-economy, and thus form a world-empire, but failed. Imperial exhaustion increased during the seventeenth century. Crown expenses, wars, a restless lower nobility, and an obstinate merchant class (who favored Dutch-style free trade) blocked the successful application of mercantilism. Spain incrementally lost control of its colonies to core states, and where it did not lose possession, its ability to profit was undercut by English and French purchases of goods seized by buccaneers.[33] Spain steadily declined from 1600 to 1750, and became in Wallerstein's description, an instrument of the core, "a passive conveyor belt" to its own colonies.[34]

Portugal, too, attempted mercantilism, in this case to extract itself from its conveyor-belt position. After independence from Spain, Portugal made a strong attempt at advancement in the 1670s and 1680s, but ultimately failed. Portuguese officials modeled their actions after the French. They built industries and tried making bullion investments attractive.

But anti-mercantilist forces within Portugal triumphed. Owner-producers prevented the state from becoming too powerful at home and soured its partnerships with France by selling wine to North American colonies after French wine had been banned.[35]

Spain's slide from core to semiperiphery, as well as other shifts within the semiperiphery, served as a warning to core states that their positions were not guaranteed. But it was the periphery that suffered the worst effects of contraction. Unlike in the core (and to some extent the semiperiphery), the "upper strata" of the periphery, those who lived primarily off the labor of others, were not able to create strong states capable of minimizing internal conflicts. Seeing their prospects for profit diminished, members of the upper strata had few reasons to compromise. For Wallerstein, weak states had greater class antagonisms and political violence.[36] Owner-producers also turned to brutal and inhumane treatment of laborers. Their attempts at cost shifting meant a return to serfdom (or "coerced cash-crop labor") in Eastern Europe and the imposition of slavery in Hispanic America.[37] Such measures temporarily insulated the bourgeoisie and nobility from the effects of contraction.[38] In both areas, capitalist processes (in this case, the seventeenth-century downturn) meant that producers needed to cut costs, and thus turned to forms of forced labor. Wallerstein regarded the nobility and bourgeoisie in Eastern Europe as capitalist entrepreneurs, and peasant laborers as akin to semi-proletarians.[39] It seemed to him that producers and peasants behaved as entrepreneurs and proletarians even if they conceived of their roles in premodern terms. In the Americas, which he defined as the "extended Caribbean" (stretching from present-day Brazil to Maryland),[40] owner-producers turned to slavery because they could no long attract European settlers. Due to soil erosion and the declining availability of plots, the promise of good land at the end of the worker's term was no longer tenable.[41]

As Wallerstein told it, cost-shifting measures of the seventeenth century, especially in the periphery, could not be a permanent phenomenon. But why? If forced labor was more cost-effective, why not use it throughout the world-system in bust and boom times? Why pay a wage at all, even in times of faster growth? Wallerstein concluded that productivity under conditions of forced labor would diminish over time. He reasoned that owner-producers desired, in their ideal world, a moderate amount of forced labor: too much, and productivity declined; too little, and workers demanded better treatment.[42] For this reason, the nobility and bourgeoisie were typically quite happy with a moderate amount of non-waged laborers.

Wallerstein saw his interpretation as further disproving the idea that capitalism began much later than in the sixteenth century. But it also served another purpose: that of further disproving the idea that capitalism was a system of emancipation and political freedom. He may not have realized the necessity of this point when he planned his series on the modern world-system. By 1989, however, the year he published *The Modern World-System III: The Second Era of Great Expansion of the Capitalist World-Economy, 1730–1840s*, his earlier writings appeared prescient, foreshadowing the era of unrestricted markets in the name of political freedom. The third volume of his series, which dealt with a long-term phase of world-system expansion, also coincided with what has become known as the "parade of sovereignties" across the Soviet sphere and Gorbachev's subsequent attempts to save the Union.[43] By discussing expansion amid a moment of crisis, Wallerstein's book fit the times well.

In his history of the eighteenth century, which he defined as roughly 1730 to the 1840s, the logistical B-phase contraction shifted to a logistical A-phase expansion (marked by population, economic activity, and prices).[44] Functionally, this meant that the capitalist world-economy once again grew in size, expanding to new zones, with unruined lands, new resources, and cheaper labor.[45] In this period, the Indian region (labeled as the "Indian subcontinent"), along with the Ottoman Empire, Russian Empire, and West Africa all more or less followed the same pattern of incorporation. The process was not something external zones desired, and the benefits of incorporation were virtually nonexistent.[46] As a rule, incorporation meant peripheralization, though Russia proved to be the great exception. After holding off the European "wolves at the door,"[47] Russia incorporated into the semiperiphery. The tsars proved effective, first at delaying incorporation, and then at maintaining textile and beet sugar refining industries, as well as crude iron exports, once incorporation began.[48]

The process of incorporation is like that of a fly caught in a spider's web. Previously free, the fly becomes so caught up in the web that it cannot escape. The spider feeds, and the web expands. The image breaks down in the lengthy process of incorporation, often over a century, as was the case with the Indian, Ottoman, and Russian areas. And, external areas were also different than flies in that they had contact with the world-economy prior to being ensnared. Russia, for example, had trade relations and went to war against states in the European world-economy. But trade with external zones was different, Wallerstein thought, in that it consisted of luxury goods, not of staples. The luxury trade consisted of goods sent over great distances, usually in small shipments, and was consumed by the upper strata of society. The trade of staples consisted of things that were necessities, often in large shipments, and was consumed by all social levels.[49] Table 5.1 shows this expansion, adapted from Wallerstein's narrative.

Along with peripheralization, this phase of expansion usually involved deindustrialization and an increase in forced labor.[50] External zones also developed state institutions as part of the integration process.[51] Still, they did not resemble the Westphalian model. These states, though diplomatically linked to others, were neither strong nor weak. If states were too strong, Wallerstein hypothesized, they might wish to break from the world-system and adopt noncapitalist behaviors.[52] Conversely, states that were too weak could not protect capital flows in and out of their borders. States were needed not merely to establish order but to create a kind of order that served the interests of the core. In trading with West Africa, for example, merchants in core zones sought malleable (and in their view, impressionable) local governments that would facilitate incorporation.[53] In the Indian region, the Mughal Empire and surrounding political institutions were displaced by what Wallerstein called a "single (but complex) administrative unit, India, which was however nonsovereign."[54]

Table 5.1. The Capitalist World-Economy in 1750 and 1850

	Core	Semiperiphery	Periphery	External Areas
1750	Western Europe (France; Great Britain; United Provinces)	Austria; Brandenburg-Prussia; British North America (New England and Mid-Atlantic colonies); western Germanies; northern Italy; Portugal; Spain; Sweden; Switzerland	Christian Mediterranean (southern Italy); Denmark; east Elbia (eastern Germanies); Eastern Europe (Baltics, Czechia, Hungary, Poland); Hispanic America	Indian subcontinent; Ottoman empire; Russian empire; West Africa
1850	No change	Addition of: Russian empire	Addition of previous external areas: Indian subcontinent; Ottoman empire; West Africa	New: China; Fertile Crescent area (Middle East); Central Asia; West African savannah

An unfinished series, *The Modern World-System* did not cover more recent phases of expansion, including the incorporation of much of Africa and East Asia.[55] But one can nonetheless see where Wallerstein's narrative was headed: after expanding to cover the entire globe, the capitalist world-economy had no place left to go. Expansion had been its primary mechanism for resolving contradictions. Other mechanisms have included the creation of new technologies, new commodities, new contracts (such as those guaranteeing property rights), and the creation of the modern household.[56] Yet there is reason to believe that spatial expansion was more effective at relieving the pressures of entropy: external areas, by definition noncapitalist, had limitless possibilities from the standpoint of the world-system.

Wallerstein concluded that the modern world-system in the 1980s was showing signs of crisis. He calculated that the postwar period up until the crisis of 1968 or so was a Kondratieff A-phase of faster growth.[57] Then, starting in the early 1970s, the world-economy entered into a long B-phase of slower growth.[58] Some regions, he thought, would do well for a period of time, but the overall system had entered a long-term downturn.

Still, Wallerstein had not become the kind of ultrastructuralist one might think. For even though he thought individuals could do nothing to cause the world-system to fall apart earlier or later, he believed ordinary people might have a great impact on the character of future world-systems. In fact, it could even be said that Wallerstein believed human agency had increased. For if there was no inevitable successor to capitalism, then it would be people and their institutions who would create future systems. Unlike the eighteenth and nineteenth centuries, capitalism in the late twentieth century more closely resembled the analogy of the pencil than of the pendulum. Slight actions no longer seemed to have slight effects. In one interview from 2011, Wallerstein likened structural crisis to a condition of free will: "The situation changes when you get into structural crisis: instead of a lot of effort making a small amount of change, a little effort can make an enormous amount of change. The whole thing is so unstable, is so volatile, that a little effort pushes it in one direction or another. I sometimes say this is the historicization of the old Greek philosophical distinction between determinism and free will. When the system is relatively stable, it's a relatively determinist system in which we have relatively little free play. But when it's unstable, when it's going into structural crisis, free will comes into the picture. That is to say, your action and my action really matter in a way they didn't for 500 years."[59]

When a system was healthy, he explained, there was little that individual people could do to change the nature of their system. However, when a system was dying, there was a lot that individual people could do to change the system. The twenty-first century, therefore, was a historically unusual time of expanded human agency. Consequently, periods of time between world-systems were like Hobbesian states of nature, that is, without rules governing human action.[60]

Wallerstein's final verdict was straightforward: a more egalitarian would-system would exist if humans fashioned it. He, therefore, gave advice to activists. One suggestion was to encourage the de-commodification of goods and services. A key process of capitalism had been its propensity to turn services into commodities.[61] In the twentieth century, previously noncommodified services such as those provided by universities or hospitals, were transformed into profit-seeking enterprises in the name of efficiency. Wallerstein saw this rhetoric as rather duplicitous because such rhetoricians had little evidence that profit-seeking led to greater efficiency. In fact, he believed that all services could be best provided through nonprofit organizations. Why, he reasoned, should steel mills be less efficient or effective without profit maximization as their primary goal?[62] Universities survived for hundreds of years without this requirement. Organizations could accumulate modest amounts of capital and reinvest incidental profits in order to provide better services. Wallerstein could not imagine any fundamental need for organizations to be distracted by capitalist impulses.

How would such a system work? It would entail more than shedding the requisite for endless capital accumulation.[63] Feudalism had no such requirement and yet had great inequality. Wallerstein was reluctant to discuss his proposed system in specific terms. But if we were to name it for him, such a system might be called an *egalitarian world-system*. Wallerstein imagined this system to be a series of independent, nonmonopolistic, nonprofit organizations. A lack of centralization by states or other large organizations might enable nonprofits to operate with efficiency.[64] Wallerstein imagined it would be unnecessary to have the same autocratic system of management commonly found in capitalist businesses. Worker and managerial interests would likely remain at odds, but negotiation could keep the dealings between the two groups relatively fair. He also believed that lifetime benefits independent of occupation would allow for free movement of workers between jobs.[65]

Wallerstein's proposal may have surprised some readers. He did not think that government would need to exert a heavy hand over industry or plan production. Instead, genuine free market principles might keep various producers in check. He did not consider capitalism, with its tendency to produce monopolies, to be anything close to free market. Rather, government oversight in an egalitarian system might be "akin to traffic lights on a busy road." Agencies would be "limited to counteracting fraud, improving information flows, and sending up warning signals about over- and underproduction."[66] Wallerstein's vision, however, was far from the so-called libertarianism of the twenty-first century: he sought guaranteed worker benefits, extensive environmental protections, and a broad interpretation of what constituted fraud prevention.

It is worth noting that Wallerstein saw intellectuals aiding in the transition, certainly by encouraging activists, but also by commenting on the choices being offered. At times, he gave an inspirational message, in one talk telling leftists that their actions were "essential" for an egalitarian future. He said: "[I]n a chaotic world, every nano-action at every nano-moment on every nano-issue affects the outcome."[67] Yet he was not as rosy as he sometimes sounded. Wallerstein also acknowledged that reactionary forces could quite possibly implement a world-system with inequality and political violence greater than that of capitalism. For in a period of transition, groups hoping to maintain their privileged status would try several rhetorical tactics. He estimated that they might propose alternative systems, ostensibly to achieve greater equality, advanced in the name of ecology or women's rights. Intellectuals would have to sort out the genuine proposals from the disingenuous ones. He hoped, therefore, that his writings would contribute to a better understanding of our realities and our choices.[68]

Wallerstein's position on human agency was therefore dependent on the stability of the system in question. His writings on capitalism's seventeenth-century consolidation and eighteenth-century expansion were about the power of capitalism to determine the choices of individuals.[69] His writings on the structural crisis of capitalism were about the power of individuals to determine their future.[70] The one option unavailable to activists, he believed, was the perpetuation of the capitalist world-economy. Unlike Anderson, Wallerstein did not see human agency increasing in a linear fashion over time. To the contrary, following Wallerstein's logic, the ability of individuals to shape their futures would likely decline with the consolidation of the next world-system. On agency, therefore, he had discarded the concepts of pessimism and optimism. At conferences and public talks, he was frequently asked whether he was pessimistic or optimistic about the future. Wallerstein always gave the same answer. He put the odds at fifty-fifty.[71]

Our Dream Is Slipping Away

The 1980s were very different for Perry Anderson. Although it was a time of professional success, it was also a time of difficulty. The *New Left Review* was no longer on the precipice of financial failure. Sales were up. New Left Books and its publishing imprint, Verso, had earned a reputation for accurate translations and were now releasing original pieces with greater frequency.[72] Anderson published a three-part intellectual history of Western Marxism.[73] But unlike Wallerstein, Anderson's magnum opus did not move ahead as originally planned. In fact, he never published a formal sequel to *Passages-Lineages* (although his 2009 book, *The New Old World*, was a thematic continuation of his history of Europe). Anderson published on the bourgeois revolutions, but never finalized his thoughts in a systematic comparison of postabsolutist states. Moreover, Anderson grew discouraged by the rise of neoliberalism. Whereas Wallerstein's research was relatively detached from current events, neoliberalism caused Anderson to grow increasingly pessimistic about prospects for socialist revolution.

It was commonly thought that Anderson's project did not move ahead because of problems in writing about the bourgeois revolutions. Indeed, he was in new conceptual terrain: few historians had attempted a systematic study, perhaps because of the great difficulty in demonstrating a common trait across Europe. According to Wallerstein, Anderson, being "one of the most careful authors the world knows," was simply "too smart" to publish something that was not in final form.[74]

Some writers attributed Anderson's reluctance to publish to the work of Robert Brenner. Like Anderson's *Passages-Lineages*, Brenner's writings went beyond economic determinism to emphasize the causal effects of extra-economic variables such as the juridical standing of laborers. Brenner shared with Anderson an assumption that historical transitions were not caused exclusively by the economic base but also by political superstructures. But Brenner was different in thinking that the transition occurred at the societal level. He thought class conflict was about economic actors trying to reproduce themselves, by which he meant maintain their socioeconomic rank. Brenner reasoned that the dominance of the market came about under historically specific conditions, as a by-product of the contestation between peasants and lords. A fierce debate among social historians ensued.[75]

For Anderson, Brenner's perspective was something of a hurdle because it questioned the significance of the bourgeois revolutions. Brenner did not think that all class conflicts were equally important. He considered the struggle between aristocrats and peasants to have made bourgeois revolutions in many cases superfluous. He did not think that such upheavals were a necessary component in the transition to capitalism. According to Elliott, Anderson's "evident admiration" for Brenner's writings may have made it difficult to rebut critics who downplayed the bourgeois revolutions.[76]

On the other hand, Anderson did not recant his views. Nor did he behave as someone might who was questioning his argument. In fact, Anderson initially expressed doubts about Brenner's thesis.[77] By the early 1980s, he appeared to have general sense of a narrative for the period following absolutism.[78] True to form, his account of the bourgeois revolutions portrayed general characteristics as well as individual variation. As Anderson put it, "every one was a bastard birth."[79] Yet they shared the following common traits: an occasional alignment of aristocratic and bourgeois interests; the unpredictability of lower, laboring, classes; a diversity of objectives within the bourgeoisie; and, as one might expect from Anderson, the threat of war.[80]

He continued to publish on the subject as late as 1992. Therefore, it is unlikely that Brenner's alternative vision of the transition was by itself sufficient to derail Anderson's project. But the strenuous task of writing about bourgeois revolutions in the neoliberal conjuncture may have been insurmountable. In the third installment of his genealogy of Marxism (what he called an "unpremeditated trilogy"), Anderson recognized the surprising political turn. He wrote: "the flow of theory in these [recent] years did not run in the direction I had envisaged."[81] He had expected to see, in the late 1970s, popular movements to take up Marxist theory. He had expected a resurgence of revolutionary spirit in theorists and activists. Yet the opposite happened. Instead of Left advancement, the Right gained ground. Neoliberalism had become, in Anderson's opinion, "the most successful ideology in world history."[82]

The rise of neoliberalism was all the more disconcerting because, in sharp contrast to Wallerstein, Anderson considered revolutionaries necessary to the demise of capitalism. Furthermore, the post-1968 world was one in which humans had great potential to change their circumstances.

He believed that unlike the transitions of centuries past, historical developments had reduced the power of structures and increased the power of revolutionary classes.

It should be noted that for all transitions prior to the one *away* from capitalism, Anderson remained an outspoken proponent of economic and political structures of the largest scale (that is, at a level all but completely removed from what individuals said or did). Thus, he maintained a hard line against intellectuals such as his onetime comrade E. P. Thompson,[83] who, according to Anderson, greatly exaggerated the role of humans in the creation of social classes.[84] But, buried in a polemic against the agent-oriented Thompson, the normally structure-oriented Anderson explained his paradoxical views. For him, the near past was fundamentally different than the distant past. Whereas the transition away from feudalism was a class struggle actuated primarily by forces within the mode of production, class struggles of the nineteenth and twentieth centuries had shifted somewhat. These later struggles were fought by *conscious* classes, albeit still spurred to action by processes related to the mode of production.[85] By consciousness, Anderson meant collective awareness of common experience, social standing, and self-identification.[86] He also considered class consciousness to be a recent development, a product of the nineteenth century.[87] With self-identification, lower classes of the 1800s and 1900s were in a better position to alter their surroundings. According to Anderson, industrial workers were unlike feudal serfs because they self-identified as, and drew solidarity from, being part of a class. The development of class consciousness meant that transformative agency was now shared, split unevenly between the mode of production and revolutionaries. In short, human agency had increased with an awareness of class-based injustice.

Anderson believed, in fact, that it was the job of social historians to study the past in order to expand human agency.[88] Their goal was to create a world with *"real popular self-determination for the first time in history."*[89] Yet despite a favorable conjuncture, Anderson and the *Review* had been unable to have an impact. Their commitment to activists after 1968 had not yielded results. They were far from being part of the vanguard. But that was not all. The problem for Anderson was not merely that the Right seemed to be winning, but that socialist movements had yielded such disastrous results. The Left was still no closer to understanding how a socialist system should operate. The historical record of anticapitalist states, he acknowledged, had been dismal: across the world, anticapitalist movements had turned into perversions of Left principles.[90] Anderson's verdict on the Soviet Union, for example, was that it had abandoned its ethos: "Marxism was largely reduced to a memento in Russia, as Stalin's rule reached its apogee. The most advanced country in the world in the development of historical materialism, which had outdone all Europe by the variety and vigour of its theorists, was turned within a decade into a semi-literate backwater, formidable only by the weight of its censorship and the crudity of its propaganda."[91]

Not only facing defeat from without, the Left was facing defeat from within. Anderson was like Wallerstein in that he strongly believed that the Left needed to reflect on what a noncapitalist world would look like. And he agreed that there was no historical model from which intellectuals could draw. The emancipation of labor could not come from past experience. Political theorists would have to imagine a noncapitalist yet egalitarian social order that had never before existed.[92] Thus, the Left needed to think through some crucial questions, including: the abolishment of classes, attainment of complete gender equality,[93] humanity's relationship to the ecological world, and, perhaps most urgently, the threat of global nuclear destruction.[94]

Yet Anderson's view on the end of capitalism was not totally opposed to Wallerstein's. For as much as Anderson expressed the need for the Left to be organized, he nonetheless believed there were objective limits to capital accumulation. He did not place as much stock in Kondratieff waves as did Wallerstein or Eric Hobsbawm.[95] (Anderson preferred Brenner's alternative terminology of a Long Downswing in place of a B-phase wave.)[96] Instead, Anderson emphasized another limit favored by Wallerstein: capitalism's propensity for ecological exhaustion. Ecology and its effects, he thought, contradicted the assumption of unlimited capitalist growth. The earth's resources imposed a limit on consumption. And, even if consumption of resources were to somehow continue, ecological degradation would ultimately harm the human species. If the third world were to adopt the automobiles, food consumption, and household comforts of the first world, humans could not continue to live on the earth. The only way that advanced states could maintain their lifestyles would be if there remained a wealth and income gap between the first and third worlds. But this would only buy a small amount of time for the capitalists: the rate of ecological exploitation would still ultimately cause the destruction of the species: the climate, the ozone, the oceans, and forests would deteriorate, making the planet unlivable.[97] Though Anderson knew capitalism could not march on forever, he saw no fixed timetable for its end. Moreover, this grisly death of capitalism only heightened the urgency for Left organizations.

Given the rise of neoliberalism, in addition to the need for socialist activism, it was logical that Anderson admired those who could somehow escape feelings of pessimism. He praised figures such as his comrade Fredric Jameson, whose Hegelian heritage, Anderson thought, enabled a circumvention of cynicism. The result was a realism with "utopian longings," capable of dreaming of the impossible while also avoiding false reassurance for disaffected Leftists.[98]

Anderson's conclusions had personal ramifications. Instead of the *New Left Review* serving as part of the vanguard, Anderson's writings and editorship had, to him, proven inconsequential. The NLR's post-1968 recommitment to unifying socialist theory and practice was not enough. Thus, he contemplated his tenure as the *New Left Review*'s principal editor.

Anderson had always been a paradoxical captain. Although he admired activist Marxists who wrote for the working class and who never retreated into obscure debates, his own writings were far from plainspoken.[99] Moreover, the NLR under Anderson's editorship remained a forum for ideas, not a center of activism. In the 1960s, it seemed best for the *New Left Review* to withdraw from popular politics and live in isolation to think about the long-term intellectual needs of the Left.[100] With the advancement of the Right and the failure of the Left, Anderson questioned whether his style of leadership was right for the political climate of the 1980s. Other committee members, he noted, embraced popular issues of the day. Comrades such as Tom Nairn, Robin Blackburn, Anthony Barnett, and Fred Halliday wrote popular pieces for periodicals like the *New Statesman*, *Times Higher Educational Supplement*, *Marxism Today*, *Socialist Challenge*, and the *London Review of Books* (LRB). The *New Left Review*, Anderson believed, should become a bit more like these journals in terms of their popular orientation. And he mused that the NLR should seek out essays written in a warmer and more passionate style.[101] The journal should also publish writings by participants in the British socialist movement, including New Left activists, leaders from the Communist Party, and the Left wing of the Labour Party.[102] Far from keeping culture and politics at a distance, Anderson supposed that the journal should become participatory once again. This task, however, required a different editor.[103]

It was perhaps easier for Anderson to leave given disunity among editorial committee members. Internal documents show Anderson repeatedly placed much of the blame on himself.[104] He attributed divisiveness to his unnecessary meddling in editorial processes.[105]

In addition, Anderson was unhappy with the internal structure of the journal.[106] In the early 1960s, NLR had no professional staff. By 1975, the journal had a professional staff and New Left Books had branched out from translating to publishing original research.[107] Prosperity meant that meetings were now more administrative than political. Increased sales caused an increase in submissions requiring review, even though committee members were often engrossed in independent research. It fell to the editor to maintain the journal's cohesion. Yet conflict resolution was ad hoc: when disagreements arose over manuscripts, there was no mechanism for resolving them.[108] (Strangely enough, Anderson also wondered if the NLR's professionalization had made lead editorship unnecessary.)

As he contemplated what to do at the NLR, he tried academic life. Immanuel Wallerstein recruited Anderson to teach at Binghamton University, offering him any position he wished, options which ranged from an annual adjunct appointment to a tenured professorship in sociology.[109] He opted for a more flexible schedule, teaching for six weeks in the springs of 1978, 1979, and 1980.[110] His duties included one undergraduate and one graduate course of his choosing; with the latter came advising doctoral students in sociology.[111] One year, he taught on "Western Marxism" and "Bourgeois Revolutions." He assigned books by writers who had inspired his own intellectual development, including Lukács, Sartre, and Althusser, as well as thinkers with whom he disagreed, such as Gramsci. Anderson also assigned works by notable contemporaries, such as Jameson.[112] Despite his popularity with graduate students, the tradition did not last. Late in the summer of 1980, Anderson informed Wallerstein and Binghamton that he would not be able to renew for another three-year appointment. He had decided to take a Simon Fellowship at the University of Manchester, a post that gave him the freedom to leave the NLR if he so chose.[113]

Anderson remained principal editor for another three years as the *Review* prepared for a transition. During that time, the journal deepened its connections with the New Left's elders, including Thompson, Raymond Williams, and Ralph Miliband. These increased ties delighted Anderson. His ongoing debate with Thompson was becoming something more than a polemic, though it was never truly resolved.[114] More importantly, Anderson judged that NLR had produced some of its finest work in the early 1980s, such as Anthony Barnett's timely analysis of the Falklands War.[115] Anderson praised its accessible style.[116] The journal also tried to be involved in current events. In early 1982, Robin Blackburn launched an organization on behalf of NLR. The "Socialist Society" has been described as the most public way the journal reconnected with the activists and the old guard of the New Left.[117] Because this new organization was so foreign to the usual activities of the NLR, it was not universally supported by the editorial committee.[118]

In 1983, Anderson handed editorship over to Blackburn, who stayed in that role for seventeen years.[119] One account called this handoff the relinquishment of "titular editorship," since Anderson remained an influential force at the *Review*.[120] (He remained financially connected to the journal and stayed on the editorial board.) The change was significant, however, because it represented an attempt to adjust to a new political climate. Unlike Wallerstein, Anderson's professional activities shifted with political trends. In 1989, he accepted a professorship at UCLA, where he would teach for nearly three decades.

Conclusion

The age of neoliberalism was an opportunity to contemplate research and prospects for the future. Anderson's reflections on neoliberalism and his subsequent decision to move on from the NLR stood in sharp contrast to Wallerstein's doubling-down and decision to push forward with the Braudel Center's agenda. For Anderson, the Left's retreat and Right's advancement, in addition to internal disputes, meant it was time to step down as editor. Neoliberalism was more than a distraction from research. It also signaled to Anderson that his counternarrative was not taking hold among socialists. Wallerstein, however, was just getting started as director of his own institute and its journal, *Review*. Furthermore, Prigogine taught Wallerstein that capitalist demise was a forgone conclusion.

Wallerstein and Anderson each advanced more sophisticated interpretations of the relationship between structures and individuals. They both envisioned an increase in human agency. For Anderson, the increase was due to the development of class consciousness in the nineteenth century. For Wallerstein, the increase was due to the relative weakness of the capitalist world-economy. Yet there was a clear difference: whereas Anderson saw people and their organizations as capable of overthrowing capitalism and implementing socialism, Wallerstein asserted that capitalism would fall apart on its own and humans would create the next world-system.

Consequently, the former reflected on the role of activists in the death of capitalism; the latter reflected on the role of activists in the birth of a postcapitalist system.

They wrote about human beings and the future of capitalism against the backdrop of neoliberalism. After the fall of the Berlin Wall, their divergence would increase. Whereas Anderson was willing to adjust his course amid a series of political disappointments, Wallerstein, seeing one storm after another, kept his hand on the tiller.

Chapter 6

Shed a Tear for East European Communism?

For many observers, the fall of one-party communism in Eastern Europe was empirical proof of the vitality of neoliberal programs. The year 1989 has come to symbolize a revolt against the status quo. But what was the status quo? The nationalists of the late eighties and early nineties desired sovereign statehood and a form of government unlike the repressive Soviet apparatus. Some saw the battle in binary terms: to be anti-Soviet meant to be pro-Western and pro-capitalist. They did not know that their experience would be more like the fiscal doldrums of Latin America than the prosperity of North America.[1] Years of turbulence and social unrest led to Gorbachev's resignation on December 25, 1991. The Soviet Union was no more.

For many leftists, the astonishing development was not the end of Soviet tyranny but the fall of the Union and speed by which free market principles took hold. Moscow sold assets at an incredible pace. The shock, however, proved to be too much: Russia's gross domestic product shrank throughout the 1990s, sometimes by double digits.[2] A new billionaire class emerged while many others suffered during the transition. Still, neoliberals in the West promoted free market principles. For them, 1989 was a revolt against rule of one-party communism (and Left ideas in general). After all, capitalism, according to its promoters, was a superior economic system, especially when paired with a Western-style democratic government.

Radicals reacted in diverse ways. Immanuel Wallerstein was not swayed by the end of what he called the Communism of the Parties. In his opinion, 1989 represented the fall of the liberal Center and a sign of capitalism in crisis. Perry Anderson's impression of global capitalism continued to change. He recognized 1989 as a decisive victory for the Right and for capital. Although both thinkers understood the twentieth century as a time of fierce ideological combat, they differed on who was winning.

Beware of the Liberal Chameleon

It was hardly surprising that Wallerstein failed to conclude that 1989 signaled the demise of the Left. He, after all, believed that the vitality or sickness of a system (at least a system that survived its infancy) had nothing to do with what people thought or did. But readers might be surprised that he saw 1989 as a sign of the capitalist system in crisis. After the end of the Soviet Union, he determined that it was global capitalism, not its rivals, that was endangered.[3] Two points might clarify Wallerstein's position. One, for him, Moscow did not personify an alternative world-system. The end of Soviet rule was the end of a state contained within the capitalist world-economy. And two, he conceived of centrist liberalism as an ideological defense of the modern world-system. The late-twentieth-century resurgence of extreme ideologies threatened the dominance of the liberal Center.

In Wallerstein's assessment, the Soviet Union was noncapitalist only in attitude, having been part of the modern world-system for hundreds of years. The old Russian Empire was incorporated in the eighteenth century.[4] And, contrary to the common Western narrative, Wallerstein did not believe the 1917 revolution led to an exit from the capitalist world-economy. In the history of the modern world-system, no region, once the process of incorporation began, ever left the system. The Soviets, in fact, sacrificed to preserve the order of the world-system in World War II. Likewise, though the postwar years are generally understood to be a time of great conflict, Wallerstein did not consider the Cold War to be terribly cold. He thought of the great rivalry between the United States and the Soviet Union as more of a symbiotic relationship than a contested one. The summit at Yalta divided the world-system into two spheres, one Soviet (roughly one-third of the world) and one American (roughly two-thirds of the world). This division was subsequently reinforced by nuclear weapons, which prevented outright war between the two nations.[5] For Wallerstein, the balance of terror not only secured fair play in their tacit agreement but supplied a useful fear that could be deployed to prod reluctant partners on each side. It was a success in that many nations around the world perceived of foreign policy in terms of a grander contest. Yalta thus worked well, ensuring a "Cold War."

Wallerstein found many Cold War incidents—the Berlin airlift of 1948, the rebellions of Eastern Europe in the 1950s, and the Polish uprising in 1980—where the United States and the Soviet Union stayed true to their agreement: no shooting, and no attempt to change their respective zones.[6] Still, the Soviet Union and the United States occasionally came close to war, or fought proxy wars, such as in Cuba or in Vietnam. These cases, for him, were less of a West-East struggle and more of a North-South struggle. Developing nations in the Global South, especially in Asia, mostly refused to acknowledge the separation of the world into Soviet and American zones and defied orders of the great powers. The Communist Party of China (CPC), for example, ignored Stalin's directive to forge a deal with their chief rival, the Kuomintang (KMT), and pushed to take over the country.[7] In Wallerstein's reading, it was the Global South's rejection of Yalta that tended to pull Moscow and Washington toward war.[8] It was the Soviets and the Americans who resisted.

Wallerstein kept returning to one year. Yalta, he thought, began to break down after 1968. Moscow and Washington were still committed to the agreement, but many other countries as well as everyday people, in both the Global North and South, were increasingly defiant. He saw four main changes:

1. *Great powers had a diminished ability to dominant the Third World*. Difficulties in Vietnam and Afghanistan, despite the superpowers' vast military superiority, had only reproduced the *balance of terror* between the United States and the Soviet Union.[9]

2. *Low-ranking groups became more defiant*.[10] By the late twentieth century, low-ranking groups had become much less likely to follow the commands of their economic and social superiors. Even after the 1968 movements had ended, low-ranking groups (which consisted of workers, younger professionals, women, and ethnic minorities) were less likely to conform to the expectations of high-ranking status groups (which consisted of older professionals, men, and ethnic majorities).[11]

3. *Workers broke from merchants.* An extension of the first two, labor insubordination increased.[12]

4. *Civil society broke from the state.* Wallerstein noticed more combative state-society relations across the world. He singled out the "so-called dictatorships of the proletariat" as being especially problematic. Social insurgencies in the communist party states in Eastern Europe and Asia had reached a point whereby repression became ineffective. Soviet officials now lacked confidence in their ability to restore party dominance over society.[13]

Wallerstein and his colleagues at the Braudel Center interpreted 1989 as a "continuation of 1968."[14] Both periods contained widespread social uprisings that, collectively, amounted to votes of no confidence in the operations of the world-system. Wallerstein came to refer to these and other similar years of widespread uprisings as *antisystemic movements*. He saw such moments as repudiations of the modern world-system itself. Sometimes they appeared as class movements, while other times they appeared as nationalist movements. Class movements (also known as social or labor movements) typically formed in industrial centers and sought to liberate the proletariat (urban, landless, wage workers) from the bourgeoisie (merchants). National movements typically formed in the semiperiphery and sought liberation from foreign powers.[15] Many used a vocabulary of progress and human rights. And although they have often been unsuccessful, powerful figures in the world-system have always viewed them as dangerous. In the years following the French Revolution, for example, Great Britain repressed its own lower classes when it noticed growing sympathy for French proletarians.[16]

Such movements had happened several times before the late twentieth century, in 1789, 1848, 1917, and 1945. Now, they seemed to be happening with greater frequency. The 1970s and 1980s were restless times. Labor had broken from capital, and, without new zones to incorporate, the capitalist world-economy lacked a sufficient fix for reform. Antisystemic forces attempted to change the system, while establishment forces sought to maintain it.[17]

The problem for beneficiaries of the modern world-system was that they were less and less able to convince everyday people of the virtues of capitalism. According to Wallerstein, unlike previous world-systems, the capitalist world-economy depended on the promise of a better life. He explained the paradox in this way: "Inequality is a fundamental reality of the modern world-system, as it has been of every known historical system. What is different, what is particular to historical capitalism, is that equality has been proclaimed as its objective (and indeed as its achievement)—equality in the marketplace, equality before the law, the fundamental social equality of all individuals endowed with equal rights."[18] Capitalism's promise was the slow and steady improvement in the treatment of ordinary people. The promise was a better economic life (in the form of wages) and better political life (in the form of participation in the political process). The promise was never that a better life would be created overnight, or even over a lifetime. The promise was that each successive generation would see real-world improvement over previous generations. For Wallerstein, the delayed realization of rewards served the upper classes well (at least from the perspective of the system) because it allowed them to continue to exclude segments of society—namely, workers, ethnic minorities, and women—from equal treatment as citizens as long as mild progress was made toward their inclusion.

Wallerstein identified this slow and steady attitude as centrist liberalism. It was liberal because it proclaimed the values of equality and democracy. It was centrist because it advocated for neither a fast nor slow pace of reform. To its right was conservatism, which advocated for as slow a rate of social change as possible. To its left was radicalism (and later, socialism) because it advocated for as fast a rate of social change as possible.

For Wallerstein, these modern ideologies were born out of the French Revolution. The year 1789 was significant for him because it symbolized the arrival of two new norms. The first was that people came to think of power transfers as routine; what previously had been a once- or twice-in-a-lifetime experience was accepted as a regular occurrence.[19] And second, the people came to believe that ultimate political authority resided in themselves; they were no longer subjects but citizens.

In Wallerstein's interpretation, the old aristocracy adopted conservatism in response to 1789. The bourgeoisie adopted liberalism. Initially, the lower classes (peasants, and later, proletarians) also adopted liberalism. Over time, however, many in the upper classes, which Wallerstein labeled the *notables,* realized that they had closely aligned interests. The upper classes wanted to ensure that the lower classes did not successfully exercise the full force of their potential power. The lower, *dangerous classes* had the weight of a vast numerical majority that, if actuated, could undo the entire class structure from within. The notables wanted to always appear to represent the interest of the wider citizenry.[20] Thus, they found it in their interests to grant limited political rights and economic welfare to the lower classes as long as such changes did not dismantle the power structure.[21] Beginning with Louis Napoleon, forward-looking conservatives adopted a liberal tone. By the end of the nineteenth century, leaders of powerful nation-states such as Great Britain and France adopted, at least in rhetoric, liberal principles. Slowly, liberalism became a tool not only of the bourgeois merchant, but of the "enlightened conservative" as well.[22] Hopeful about the future, many in the lower classes also embraced liberalism because it promised some immediate reforms and held out the option for more to come.[23] Others in the dangerous classes, feeling betrayed, chucked their support for liberalism in favor of radicalism and socialism. But by this point, centrist liberalism was victorious. It won because it could seem to represent the interests of anyone.

The *liberal-imperial* state, as Wallerstein called it,[24] turned to a new project in the twentieth century. If the century before World War I had been about diminishing the power of dangerous classes in core zones, the period afterward had been about diminishing the power of the periphery. This was the establishment of liberalism on a world scale.[25] In principle, liberals were opposed to the subjugation of other human beings, but, in practice, they could support imperial policies abroad as long as there was some perceived benefit to the project of emancipation at home.

Liberalism achieved unrivaled dominance in the early twentieth century. A sign of its command, for Wallerstein, was the ideology of Leninism, which he considered was far from a "great ideological opponent" to Wilsonism.[26] Rather than cultivating a world revolution by the working classes, the Soviet Union sought great power status through rapid industrialization. It claimed that the fight for socialism in one country would in the long term lead to global socialism. In the name of anti-imperialism, the Soviet Union encouraged national self-determination and economic development for peoples around the world. For Wallerstein, Lenin's tone was strikingly similar to Wilson's. It was phrased a little differently, but, at heart, anti-imperialism and socialism meant the promotion of national economic development.[27]

Liberal principles, Wallerstein explained, were also used by leaders of communist parties across Eastern Europe. Marx had envisioned a dictatorship of the proletariat, whereby the will of the working class would dominate. But party officials lived very different lives from that of everyday workers. When imbued with power and privilege, Wallerstein wrote, youthful radicalism often transformed into a bourgeois existence.[28] And, like their Western counterparts, communist party states also promised delayed rewards through gradual reform. Thus, the antisystemic movement of 1989 was not against a communist ideology at all. It was against a centrist liberal ideology masquerading as representation for the lower classes. In reality, it still stood for the interests of the notables.

The expiration of the Soviet Union was, for Wallerstein, a convulsion in an unsteady world-system. Moscow had been part of the world capitalist system and a defender of centrist liberalism. The separatist movements that shattered the Soviet federal system into fifteen states exposed weaknesses of the notables and of liberalism as a tool for pacification.

According to Wallerstein, the collapse of the Soviet Union was not the first sign of trouble for centrist liberalism. The first sign of trouble was 1968 and its rebellious publics that reinvigorated potent ideologies. After that momentous year, he contended, "[c]onservatives would again become conservatives, and radicals, radicals. The centrist liberals did not disappear, but they were cut down to size."[29] From this point, Left groups and Right groups became resurgent. Centrist liberalism, which was the ideology of many Western policymakers, had to compete once again.[30]

The decline of the Center posed problems for the liberal-imperial state. Washington, for example, faced ferocious resistance not only from the Vietnamese, but from the American Left back home. It became harder for the United States to persuade other countries, as well as its own people, to toe the ideological line. Decades after students occupied buildings at Columbia, the meaning of those protests had finally come into full view. The historical moments of 1968 and 1989, as Wallerstein saw them, were more than symbolic. They signaled a loss of faith in a system that had entered a time of crisis.

But like the moment of 1968, 1989 was no victory party for the Left. Wallerstein did not think that radicals and conservatives were equal beneficiaries of recent changes. In the United States, the Left all but disappeared in the decades leading up to 2016. As far as American dialogue was concerned, he said, anyone left of the Center might as well be "from the moon."[31] Far Right ideologies, characterized by "uncaring self-interestedness," became quite popular.[32] Wallerstein, therefore, agreed with Anderson that the 1990s saw a resurgence of the Right. What distinguished the former, however, was that he did not interpret the return of the Right as a sign of capitalism's stability.

Wallerstein concluded that what ended in the historical moment of 1989 was not a war between Moscow and Washington, but a political pact between mutual beneficiaries. Furthermore, though he concurred that the collapse of communist parties signaled the death of an ideology, what died in 1989 was not a challenger but the guarantor of the capitalist world-economy.

Wallerstein's conception of centrist liberalism was reminiscent of a theme from chapter 2, albeit on a world scale. According to Gramsci (at least Anderson's interpretation of Gramsci), hegemony meant the dominance of a social class, reinforced culturally.[33] Indeed, centrist liberalism served as an ideological accompaniment for the dominance of the upper strata, located in the core. In the Gramscian sense, centrist liberalism served the hegemonic power of the privileged. Yet Wallerstein defined hegemony narrowly, reflective of the world-systemic context and its alternative expressions of dominance (beyond the national society). Neither neo- nor anti-Gramscian, Wallerstein conceived of hegemony as unrivaled dominance within the world-system, with ideological reinforcement.[34]

He believed that only states (not classes or transnational interests) could rise to hegemony, marked by the disproportionate concentration of power. Hegemony meant influence, Wallerstein wrote, "so unbalanced that one power can largely impose its rules and its wishes . . . in the economic, political, military, diplomatic, and even cultural arenas."[35] Hegemony was fueled by the convergence of economic superiority in agro-industrial production, in commerce, and in finance.

The first case of hegemony in the capitalist world-economy demonstrated a pattern. In the mid-1600s, the Dutch gained advantages in fisheries, hemp, flaxseed, textiles, sugar refining, and timber-related industrial technologies used to produce windmills, ships, paper, and of course, books. In turn, the United Provinces could move more goods at a lower cost than other European nations. Dutch companies could ship supplies efficiently, first in the European North Atlantic, then the Americas, and on to the Mediterranean and the Indian Ocean. The East India Company and the West India Company, separately and significantly, moved spices, cotton, tea, tobacco—and slaves—across the world. In a sign of strength, dominance in production and commerce led to dominance in finance.

The Amsterdam stock exchange was, in effect, the Wall Street of the seventeenth century.³⁶

Three centuries later, the city of Wallerstein's birth was the capital of the world-economy. The city was not merely symbolic of American power. It was the center of finance for the capitalist world-economy, the third in long-term sequence, shifting from Amsterdam to London to New York. The hegemonic power of the United Provinces lasted from 1625 to about 1672, with a slow decline. As Wallerstein noted: "As late as 1728, Daniel Defoe was still referring to the Dutch as 'the Carryers of the World, the middle Persons in Trade, the Factors and Brokers of Europe.'"³⁷ By this point, England and France were in the midst of a long-term struggle for supremacy in the modern world-system. State behavior certainly mattered for great power status (such as a naval investment in England that paid off far greater than a land-force investment in France.)³⁸ Nevertheless, in Wallerstein's judgment, hegemony only occurred under specific structural conditions. The rise to hegemonic status corresponded with the peak of a logistical cycle (explored in the previous chapter), and after a period of geopolitical turmoil: in the first instance, the Thirty Years' War, and the defeat of the Hapsburg alliance; in the second, the Napoleonic Wars at the turn of the nineteenth century. In prevailing over France, the United Kingdom emerged as the hegemonic power, lasting from 1815 to about 1873. Likewise, in prevailing over Germany (in a long struggle, encompassing two global wars), U.S. hegemony lasted from 1945 until about 1967.³⁹

Like Gramsci, Wallerstein thought hegemonic power required ideological support. The governments of the United Provinces, the United Kingdom, and the United States all promoted the ideology of liberalism throughout the world-system. For the Dutch, liberalism was mostly the liberalism of free trade. As the center of power shifted westward, liberal promises intensified, embodying conceptions of citizenship. All three utilized mercantilism, of course, but nevertheless spoke the language of liberalism.⁴⁰ Rather than invent new justifications of their disproportionate power, rising states employed variations on a theme. Thus, liberalism served two overlapping purposes, defending capitalist processes and the interests of hegemonic powers (or those aspiring to hegemony).

In the late twentieth century, as U.S. power continued to decline, aspiring states ran into a problem. With liberalism in doubt, there was no longer an easily accepted, appealing cultural narrative with which to justify the great split between core and peripheral zones. For Wallerstein, the fall of the Soviet Union meant that the United States lost more than its great Other, a way to corral two-thirds of the world. Washington also lost its cultural rationalization. And the world-system as a whole was confronted with the fact that many populations were increasingly unconvinced of the virtues of capitalism.

We Must Change Our Expectations, Not Give In

Anderson was unlike Wallerstein in that his thoughts on the relative stability of global capitalism depended on the strength of anticapitalist organizations. Whether such groups came in the form of nationalist revolutionaries, political parties, or other anticapitalist organizations, Anderson believed that people were necessary for the dismantling of capitalism (at least in the near term). Though not a supporter of the one-party regimes in Eastern Europe, Anderson became more pessimistic after the fall of the communist parties. He watched as the free market swept over Eastern Europe virtually overnight. He did not share Wallerstein's sentiment that Moscow had been part of the capitalist system all along. The following decade of capitalist advancement—geographically, culturally, ideologically—only cemented his pessimism about the future. For him, the greatest disappointment of the 1990s, however, was that too many of his fellow intellectuals seemed to have given up.

The Right's great asset was that it had developed a portrait of the world that was accessible to the wider public. Right intellectuals such as Zbigniew Brzezinski, Thomas Friedman, and Francis Fukuyama, expressed their views in a confident and readable style.[41] Inspired by the likes of Michael Oakeshott, Leo Strauss, Carl Schmitt, and Friedrich von Hayek, conservatives wrote about the benefits of social order, supported neoliberal economics, and desired to slow the spread of popular sovereignty.[42] Anderson did not think much of the quality of their ideas. (Of his conservative contemporaries, only Fukuyama was difficult to take on.)[43] Nonetheless, these intellectuals, Anderson warned, were not marginal thinkers: even though they received less academic attention than centrists (or even some leftists), the Right had the ear of power.[44]

Furthermore, in Anderson's opinion, the Right had a willing and captive audience ready to devour its message. The culture of uncritical consumerism, spread via television and computers, primed the public for promotions of free market capitalism.[45] He believed consumerism was dangerous because it was promoted as a form of utopianism, with no room for thinking about noncapitalist utopias or realities. The utopia of consumerism, or "virtualized utopia,"[46] told the public that the current reality was the best of all possible realities, a message easily summarized:

Capitalism = Utopia

In the age of ultracapitalism, Anderson remarked, we no longer imagine social change. We can only imagine biological change, such as that from prosthetics, plastic surgery, or science fiction. Perversely, biology seemed more in flux than society. As Fredric Jameson famously wrote, the postmodern mind found it "easier to imagine the end of the world than to imagine the end of capitalism."[47] To this, Anderson added that it was also easier to imagine the "end of identity, or mortality."[48] Traditional visual arts, which had long been critical of capitalism, simply could not compete. And the great advantage of promoting free market capitalism, he supposed, was that it gave the illusion of freedom. Illusion was more useful than reality.[49]

He believed the strength of Right intellectualism was only matched by the weakness of Left intellectualism. While the Right developed a coherent explanation of world politics, the Left had no singular program. The Left, after shifting into the academy, had grown inaccessible to lower classes.[50] To make matters worse, many leftists seemed to have either surrendered their radical credentials or lost touch with reality.

Of course, it was not as if there was some a shortage of radical minds. Anderson noted that some intellectuals continued to be prolific, such as his brother Benedict, along with Jameson, Eric Hobsbawm, Robert Brenner, Giovanni Arrighi, and Tom Nairn. But, Anderson lamented, radicals did not have a common agenda.[51] This was even truer among non-Marxist leftists and centrists. Jürgen Habermas, Jacques Derrida, Michael Mann, Joseph Stiglitz, and Amartya Sen were individually productive (even if they did not possess the political commitments of their forebears, such as Weber or Keynes). Still, their collective output came up short. Of the Center and Center-Left, Anderson wrote of "a spectacle of impressive theoretical energy and productivity, whose social sum is significantly less than its intellectual parts."[52]

Out of the conjuncture of the 1990s, Anderson saw leftists moving in at least three directions: *resignation, accommodation,* or *consolation.* The first amounted to simply giving up, moving to the Center, and eliminating all hope for a noncapitalist future.[53] The second was a recognition of the dominance of capitalism and an attempt to adapt.[54] This meant taking uncritical positions toward private property or NATO's role in the world, which would previously have been unthinkable. Consolation was a ferocious doubling-down.[55] Regardless, he believed leftists should avoid self-deception, exaggerating the importance of anticapitalist forces that had no real chance of success.

Anderson had little tolerance for resignation. In one essay, he indicted the likes of John Rawls and Jürgen Habermas (and, to a lesser extent, Noberto Bobbio) for joining the Center. He considered centrists "adjustable" because they took contradictory and duplicitous positions on war and peace.[56] On Western intervention, for example, Anderson saw a pattern to the views of Habermas and Bobbio. Their opinions adjusted in the following steps: one, justify intervention (in the name of rights, law, or national liberation); two, condemn the violence used by the great powers; then, three, acknowledge that the world is better off, even in light of the violence. Anderson found their shared argument incomprehensible. It was as if the centrists thought any intervention was acceptable as long as it was expressed in the name of peace.[57] For all their emphasis on Kant, Anderson remarked, they seemed to forget that a distrust of human nature ran throughout his writings on a world state.[58] It was Kant, after all, who took into account human nature in describing a historical endpoint.

Pure consolation, Anderson thought, was also the wrong direction for Leftists. Consolation stemmed from an inability to see capitalism's dominance in the late twentieth century. Although Anderson respected Hobsbawm,[59] he believed that the elder historian had an "inability to take the enemy seriously,"[60] downplaying not only the strength of Thatcherism, but the force of U.S. hegemony and the ideological appeal of neoliberalism.[61] Unlike his writings on the nineteenth century,[62] Hobsbawm dropped any analysis of the bourgeoisie when examining the twentieth century. He made virtually no mention of neoliberalism. At times, according to Anderson, Hobsbawm's prose seemed more "like a radical version of a normally conservative discourse."[63] Anderson sympathized, but concluded that personal disappointment should not substitute for serious analysis. In fact, he noticed a contradiction. On the one hand, Hobsbawm knew that the Cold War ideological divide was, in terms of its historical significance, overblown. But on the other hand, Hobsbawm's own recollections registered the weight of being devoted to a cause that went down in defeat.[64] Given Hobsbawm's pessimism after the crisis of 2008, Anderson's evaluation may have been overstated.

The correct direction for the post–Cold War Left, in Anderson's estimation, was a stance between accommodation and consolation. He thought leftists should stand firmly against capitalism while also recognizing the limited impact of their actions.[65] In 2000, Anderson announced that such an oppositional stance would be the new direction of the *New Left Review*. From 2000 to 2003, he resumed chief editorship, duties he shared with Susan Watkins, and took the journal in a new direction. The NLR's "second series" was focused more on critique from a Left perspective and concentrated less a singular point of view. In a controversial editorial, Anderson wrote that the NLR was responding to the global triumph of capitalism in the twentieth century: "The only starting-point for a realistic Left today is a lucid registration of historical defeat."[66] It was up to the Left to confront and criticize power, yet remain realistic about the slim prospects for a socialist reality in the foreseeable future.

In Anderson's opinion, it was imperative that the Left avoid self-deception. The NLR should "calmly shock readers by calling a spade a spade."[67] By doing so, leftists might be in a better position to effect change, pushing institutions toward behaviors that better matched their rhetoric. One thing the Left did well was criticism of establishment hypocrisy (governmental or otherwise).[68] The NLR ought to provide a meeting place for all of the various voices on the Left. Thus, the goals of the new *New Left Review* were threefold: taking a realistic view of the world, criticizing the establishment, and promoting a Left perspective from multiple and diverse voices.

Debate over the new NLR ensued. One writer for the *Times Literary Supplement* expressed relief that contributors to NLR did not share Anderson's pessimism: "*NLR* is worth reading because the majority of its contributors have chosen to disregard the alleged 'historic defeat.'"[69] Other observers, however, were less sanguine. In *International Socialism*, Boris Kagarlitsky's essay, "The Suicide of *New Left Review*," was an intellectual death certificate.[70] Kagarlitsky had not previously supported the journal and what he called its "superficial radicalism" and "toothless moderation." But he acknowledged that the NLR had been the definitive outlet for English-speaking international Marxists. The journal's new direction was a dramatic betrayal of those Leftists who looked to the journal for guidance. Kagarlitsky passionately wrote: "A familiar, well loved journal no longer exists. It has died, or more precisely, its own parents have killed it."[71]

In Kagarlitsky's opinion, leftists around the world had relied on the NLR for interpretations of the past, summations of resistance movements, and prospects for the future. To declare this project a failure, without levying any self-criticism, seemed disingenuous. What did Anderson, who lived in a world of personal comfort and political stability, have to lose? What had he sacrificed? It must have been easy, Kagarlitsky surmised, to abandon the project: "Have Western intellectuals really lost anything, apart from their principles? No one has been thrown in prison or put in front of a firing squad. Their homes have not been blown up, nor their cities bombed. They are not tear-gassed on the streets, they have no problems making ends meet, and they need not stoop to begging publishers to give them free copies of books they cannot afford to buy."[72] According to Kagarlitsky, Anderson's socialism was about the history of ideas, which could be discarded when they were no longer fashionable.

The editors of *Monthly Review* had similar reactions. In their opinion, Anderson and the NLR seemed to think that since the socialist movement was dead, "all we can and should do is wait and hope for capitalism to create the conditions for change." This was unsatisfactory: "Do the billions of people on this planet who live in misery, hunger, untreated diseases, and unnecessary early deaths have to wait . . . ?"[73] A third critical view shared Anderson's pessimism, but thought he had overstated the power of the capitalists: "What is particularly striking is that Perry Anderson seems more convinced of the omnipotence of neo-liberalism than most of its supporters."[74]

Some scholars approved of the NLR's second series. Gregory Elliott, for example, believed that the new NLR was merely coming to terms with historical reality.[75] Anderson's assessment must have been hard to state given the ambitious agenda of the NLR's first series. But, Elliott wrote, the returning editor had little choice: "For of socialist future there is no new beginning, and of capitalist history no final end, currently in sight."[76]

Unhappy readers implied that Anderson and the NLR had conceded a permanent capitalist victory. This was certainly the view of the capitalists! It was not the *Review*'s position. Anderson did not suggest that capitalism, by winning the twentieth century, was humanity's permanent condition. He, like Wallerstein, held out some hope for the future. Yet Anderson, who acknowledged the end of East European communism as a setback for the Left, developed a nuanced response.

In "The Ends of History," Anderson assessed the long-term implications of the collapse of the Soviet Union. The essay took on Francis Fukuyama's contention that the end of history had arrived in the form of a liberal capitalist states system.[77] The piece is worth recounting in detail:

Anderson found Fukuyama's thesis highly original, difficult to refute, and an opportunity to consider the future of socialism.

In advancing an end of history argument, Fukuyama combined the interpretations of Hegel and Kojève, unifying the realm of thought (the ideational) and the realm of practice (the empirical). The argument's strength came from its realism. Fukuyama put critics in the difficult position of having to demonstrate the viability of alternatives; it would not be enough to merely describe the moral deficiencies of capitalism. Some critics of Fukuyma, Anderson explained, merely highlighted tensions within Hegelian thought, such as on the questions of war, inequality, and culture.[78] He considered most assessments to have fallen short because they did not address the argument on its own terms. Fukuyama never claimed that the end of history entailed social improvement, only the end of competition between the supreme system and its rivals.[79] Anderson cut to the chase: "What the end of history means, above all, is the end of socialism."[80]

Still, Fukuyama's end of history was not without problems. His understanding of a historical endpoint contradicted others who addressed the subject. Of those who thought about some type of historical endpoint, most did not think of the *end* in terms of Fukuyama's capitalist constitutionalism. For many, the end of history was not an exact stage of sociohistorical development.[81] Anderson agreed. Hegel, who arguably began the tradition of historical ends, thought more about philosophical and religious ends than political ones. His sense of finality was in terms of ideas, not institutions. In fact, Hegel seemed to conclude the *opposite* of what Fukuyama had assumed: there would be no condition of perpetual political stability.[82]

As explained by Anderson, Antoine-Augustin Cournot's sense of historical closure could be found through market equilibrium, whereby rational market regularities would dominate prices.[83] This was far from a utopia, however, since the unrestricted market was not a guarantor of morality or justice. But Cournot's vision of order, like many of his contemporaries, was not one of individual liberty. After living through three revolutions in France, he discounted stability through popular rule. Hegel, of course, had not supported representative democracy, but Cournot went a step farther: "Freedom was no longer the central ideal of human life."[84]

It was not until the third iteration of the end of history, from Alexandre Kojève, that something close to the vision promoted by Fukuyama appeared. Anderson found Kojève's interpretation somewhat representative of Hegel, but one that failed to mirror the emphases of his predecessors.[85] According to Anderson, Kojève's infatuation with desire and satisfaction led to a new view of social change. He associated historical developments with the fight for recognition, which was an acknowledgment of superiority. Kojève's account went as follows: humans desire the desire of others, and the individual, desiring recognition, struggles against others, and achieves satisfaction from recognition. History thus was a dialectic of the struggle for recognition. In Anderson's interpretation, Kojève did not intend for the end of history to mean the liberation of all citizens. To the contrary only the executive could be truly satisfied (and the rest of society falls short of complete recognition from others). He explained: "[T]he citizenry could nevertheless be *potentially* satisfied since . . . all might aspire to head the state."[86]

What did the final historical era look like to Kojève? Fukuyama may have been confident about capitalism, but Kojève's own view shifted over time. Initially, he believed that Hegel was wrong to announce that a final epoch began with Napoleon Bonaparte; the makings of the end of history were to be found in the Soviet Union.[87] But by the late 1950s, Kojève's attitude had shifted, and it now seemed as though Western Europe embodied the end of history. Moreover, instead of war, it was capital that brought humanity to its final epoch.[88] The idea had taken an ideological turn to the right.

Anderson's lengthy investigation demonstrated that the notion of historical closure, for most intellectuals, *did not* mean capitalist neoliberalism within the modern democratic state. Such a break from the idea's lineage raised questions about Fukuyama's argument, but did not nullify it. Innovative thinkers, after all, often defy their intellectual heritage. Nonetheless, it seemed to Anderson highly unlikely that capitalism could persist forever. For in inverting the original meaning of the end of history, Fukuyama placed himself in an untenable position: the promise of a lasting capitalist democracy.

Fukuyama's argument was strongest, according to Anderson, when one thought of the collapse of communism. But the thesis broke down when one thought of the strength of capitalism.[89] How could one expect the world's developing regions to replicate the economic growth patterns of advanced capitalist states? As discussed in chapter 5, Anderson, Wallerstein, and many other radicals posited that unlimited capital accumulation (what many understand as "growth") cannot continue forever.

Moreover, to take the argument on its own terms, Fukuyama was unrealistic about the global balance of power. He apparently expected that great powers would successfully watch over the rest of the world. In reality, Anderson supposed, they would not even be able to prevent nuclear weapons from spreading.[90] He also found Fukuyama's emphasis on democratic constitutionalism problematic. In the West, voter turnout remained low, well-financed campaigns dominated elections, women remained in a subordinate social position, and parties often failed to represent divergent views. In Anderson's opinion, the Western democratic model fell far short of any meaningful end of history.[91] It was farcical to think that the removal of rivals had somehow ushered in the end of history for capitalist democracy. Not only had Fukuyama departed from others who wrote about historical ends, but, according to Anderson, his assumptions—on capital accumulation, the global balance of power, and democracy—bordered on the absurd. Given trends in the twenty-first century, Anderson's conclusions proved prescient.

In intervening years, historical developments led Fukuyama to rethink some of his opinions, which, though significant, did not for Anderson amount to a fundamental departure. In 2004, Fukuyama broke from his fellow neoconservatives (and in fact abandoned neoconservatism altogether) over the exercise of U.S. power.[92] For him, the straining of relationships during the Iraq War meant that American power was not automatically synonymous with global liberty. Such a change of heart, Anderson assumed, was due to Fukuyama's attachment to Kojève rather than Strauss: whereas the former was concerned with global projects (such the universalizing force of international capitalism), the latter was concerned with national projects (such as the American founding). Many of Fukuyama's Straussian contemporaries, such as Charles Krauthammer, saw the global good as indistinct from American interests.[93]

Fukuyama also shifted to frame *The End of History and the Last Man* as work of modernization theory, emphasizing economic development as a road to political stability and peace. Consequently, according to Anderson, Fukuyama reached for generic conclusions (of "desolating predictability") about listening to allies and turning to soft power.[94] Mystified, Anderson reminded readers that Kojève (and Fukuyama) mostly wrote about a world of politics and the desire for recognition. The economic route, albeit safer, misrepresented Fukuyama's earlier work: "The mental universe of Alexandre Kojève was a long way from that of the Daniel Lerners, Gabriel Almonds, and their kind."[95] Still, Anderson understood that it was easier to advise cautious economic policies rather than the principal tool familiar to Hegel and Kojève: unrelenting war.

Out of his assessment of Fukuyama, Anderson's own preliminary interpretation on the future of capitalism comes into focus. Whereas Wallerstein consistently claimed that capitalism was in crisis, Anderson found himself in the position of claiming (1) that capitalism had won the twentieth century, but (2) that it could not last forever. Yet the interpretation was not contradictory: socialism (as a symbolic alternative to capitalism) had suffered a severe setback with the collapse of East European communism, but it may not be gone forever.

Anderson imagined four possible models for socialism in the future. He recalled the trampling of egalitarian systems in early modern Paraguay, England, and France. In each case, old orders reversed social advancement. In Paraguay, the Jesuits established in the early 1600s an egalitarian system that abolished money, collectivized most agriculture, and yet preserved native languages and traditions. It lasted for 150 years, until Spain revoked the Jesuit Order's mission and ruined the society it created. Natives in this case ultimately experienced the same brutality as others in the Americas, and the social experiment was remembered by many as a kind of brief abnormality. Like the Jesuit Order's society, socialism in the future may be remembered as a peculiarity that simply died out.[96]

Or socialism could follow the path of the Leveller democratic movement in England. After the monarchy was overthrown in the 1640s, Levellers made religious-based arguments to demand democratic political rights, such as civil liberties, male suffrage, and a written constitution. The English Revolution was unsuccessful, and in 1660, aristocratic rule returned.[97] When similar demands resurfaced in the French Revolution, they did so without the theological framework of the Levellers. Thus, while the notion of rights was in some ways a rebirth of ideas from the English Revolution, their secular orientation meant that they came from an alternative intellectual lineage. Likewise, Anderson mused, the return of socialist ideas may be devoid of the socialist vocabulary. He thought this return might happen in an ecological program, not based on the rights of workers, but nonetheless committed to a collectivist economic sensibility and what Anderson called "equal life-chances for all humanity."[98]

A third model might be that of the French Revolution. In Anderson's description, Jacobinism and socialism emerged nearly simultaneously.

Shared political interests meant for practical alliances at times. Yet the socialists desired something beyond the "bourgeois-democratic matrix" of 1789. For Anderson, socialism's formation was not an extension of Jacobinism but amounted to a "genuine mutation" into a "different species."[99] Perhaps, he thought, socialism in the future would mutate once again. The new movement would acknowledge an intellectual debt but defy its heritage in places. For example, socialism was often found in feminist thought, but feminists, like Simone de Beauvoir, also departed from their male forebears.[100]

Or, alternatively, the future of socialism could resemble that of liberalism. In the decade after World War I, liberalism seemed to be imploding, but by the 1950s it entered a triumphant period. Liberalism survived, gaining appeal by expanding political rights and establishing welfare systems. Such measures helped vanquish socialism, which had been tarnished by Stalin. By the 1990s, Anderson thought liberalism had a more difficult task ahead because its proponents had no plan of action to combat the problems of capitalism. Noting steadily declining profit rates, he concluded that growth could be sustained only by expanding credit. Further deceleration would alter the political relationship within the OECD zone and move the struggles of the South into the North. If socialism could devise a solution to these problems, it could be rehabilitated in the minds of the public.[101]

In summary, Anderson looked to four futures: socialism may be forgotten; socialism may return, following a different intellectual lineage; new socialists may acknowledge the trajectory of thought but modify it in important respects; or socialism may make a triumphant return. He did not anticipate a decline in the dominance of capitalism, nor did he foreclose on socialist advancement in the future. Today, the partial resurgence of Left parties and political figures is too recent to determine which, if any, of Anderson's futures indeed occurred (or if socialism's revival will last).

Critics accused Anderson of conceding to the inevitability of capitalism. Some of these criticisms were merited; the NLR could no longer serve as a beacon for revolutionaries. But there was also a consistency to Anderson's behavior. His activism, which had always been located in the pages of intellectual publications, had taken the form of uncompromising criticism. In his opinion: *Yes, capitalism has, for the time being, won. This is a terrible fact. But we do not have to celebrate its righteousness or promote it as the culmination of historical progress. We can, instead, hold its promoters accountable for their actions.*

Conclusion

Anderson and Wallerstein had opposite reactions to the end of the Warsaw zone. In Wallerstein's opinion, Leninism and Wilsonism were separate articulations of liberalism; thus, the fall of the Berlin wall symbolized a threat to the stability of the modern world-system. Anderson, by contrast, saw East European communism as a flawed but nonetheless noncapitalist area of the world. As free market capitalism stormed the region, he witnessed a victorious Right push a coherent and triumphalist message; many leftists, at least the ones who did not become capitalists, appeared to do nothing at all.

Part of Anderson's assessment in the 1990s rested on the observation that Western culture had embraced capitalist principles. Wallerstein would no doubt have agreed. The big difference was that he could not be convinced that it mattered if people supported capitalism. He believed the system had entered a structural crisis. Yet, oddly, their diverging interpretations of capitalism at the end of the twentieth century would give way to similar assessments of Western power in the twenty-first.

Intermission II

Perry Anderson's Clear-Headed Radicalism

As the years passed, Anderson did not waver from his, and the *New Left Review*'s, adjustments inaugurated in the journal's second series.[1] Not one to soothe radical feelings, even to inspire activism, Anderson saw signs of the triumph of capital in multiple domains: in geopolitics, in neoliberal economics, in art, even in the minds of once-formidable radicals.[2] Yet his writings did not have a tone of surrender, of succumbing to defeat. Instead, his pessimism was matched by defiance, certainly of capitalism, but also of the capitalist ideology that had penetrated academia. With diminished objectives came a more pragmatic perspective: an opposition to capitalist advancement, though without socialist strategy. Embodying these unusual characteristics was *The H-Word: The Peripeteia of Hegemony*.[3] This intermission, unlike its companion on Immanuel Wallerstein, does not show Anderson's changing views in light of the passage of time—nearly two decades after "Renewals"—but rather a confirmation and doubling-down on an earlier judgment.

Aptly titled, his intellectual history of hegemony was concise and expansive, covering more time and more geography than did *Passages-Lineages*.[4] In roughly two hundred pages, Anderson hardly wasted a word, exploring views of hegemony in North America, Europe, Eurasia, Asia, and South Asia, extending at its farthest point to the age of Homer. In all of these usages, however, Anderson found a persistent debate: the relative weight of force versus consent. All hegemons, however described by observers, have relied on power and violence. But they have also relied on some element of persuasion. As Anderson put it: "Classically, it has always implied something more than simple might. That surplus has often become detached, as if exhausting its meaning."[5]

For Thucydides, *hēgemonia* meant "attachment," "guide," or "lead," whereas *arkhē* meant "authority" or "coercion." Yet for many others, including Xenophon, the two words were interchangeable.[6] There was a similar, though far from identical, pattern in China. In the classical age, there existed a threefold understanding of political leadership: the king, who acquired the "right men"; the hegemon, who acquired "allies"; and, the strongman, who acquired "territory."[7] Here, terms also became indistinguishable, first merging to a singular "the way of the sovereign," then further changing over the centuries to a purely negative connotation, synonymous with bullying or acts of evil.[8] In both cases, the slide in meaning demonstrated the genuine interlinkage of domination via might or permission.

Anderson found applications of the term in divergent contexts. The Chinese thought of hegemony as an internal style of rule, whereas for the Greeks it meant building a league of alliances. In addition to within-group and between-group applications, Anderson located one more: across groups. For ease of discussion, yet at the risk of oversimplification and anachronism, we can think of these separate pathways as national, international, and transnational visions of hegemony.

The central figure of *The H-Word* was Antonio Gramsci,[9] who expanded the Russian revolutionary concept of proletarian rule by consent (as opposed to force, the "dictatorship of the proletariat") into a general concept, denoting the rule of a social class.[10] Gramsci's theory of hegemony fused the elements of violence with persuasion, revealing how hegemonic power worked in democracies: force backed by the majority vote.[11] In the decades after his death, Gramscianism came to mean many things. Gramsci became infinitely malleable for officials of the Italian Communist Party (PCI) and related institutions, whose most absurd claims associated Gramsci with U.S. leadership, free trade, and liberal democracy.[12] Anderson was also unconvinced by Ernesto Laclau and Chantal Mouffe's collaborative project on hegemony, which so expanded the concept (into a mostly discursive act) that it ceased to have any description of social control. Anderson found other applications more respectable, such as Stuart Hall's descriptions of the United Kingdom, and Ranajit Guha's analysis of India.[13] After Guha, Anderson was most impressed by Giovanni Arrighi's international conceptualization.[14] Like Wallerstein, Arrighi conceived of hegemony as arising from world-economic trends; unlike Wallerstein, Arrighi thought of his work as building upon the ideas of Gramsci.[15]

One place seemingly immune to Gramsci was the United States, which mostly took to defending hegemony in the form of American "leadership" in the world. Anderson agreed with Susan Strange's critique of U.S. liberal scholarship, especially that of Robert Keohane and Joseph Nye, who seemed eager to downplay notions of hegemony. In her indictment, the liberal turn to "regimes"—those international linkages that created posthegemonic rules for global conduct—was a misplaced attempt to alleviate fears of American decline. Anderson summarized: "The real America was not falling, but it was one they preferred not to see: a global empire achieved by a combination of military pacts and open markets."[16] It was only after the fall of the Soviet Union that liberal scholars realized U.S. power was secure. (Here, Anderson's and Wallerstein's impressions sharply contrast.) Then, after 1991, figures such as Nye turned to inventing friendlier terms for the word, such as "soft power." By attracting others to follow its lead, according to this logic, the United States would not need to use coercive force. Anderson turned sarcastic: "Happily, along with its other, firmer means of enforcing its will, no country in the world was blessed with so much soft power as the United States."[17] Yet he also believed that such justifications of power were natural. China, whose thinkers had long regarded hegemony as a negative concept in both the domestic and international contexts, began in the late twentieth century to mimic American claims of the necessity of moral leadership and international norms. After Mao stressed that China should "never seek hegemony," the idea returned in the form of morality and internationalism. Today, China's diplomats talk of humane behavior from "a new kind of hegemon."[18]

The transnational element was added late in *The H-Word*. Though complex, transnational hegemony was inspired by the work of Gramsci, Arrighi, and Robert Cox. Its writers identified a nonstate hegemonic class of owner-producers who had limited the power of labor in many parts of the world.[19] Consent arrived via consumerism, situated above the twin functions of consumption and production (work). The effect on regular people, Anderson wrote, was that of "deadening their energies and abilities to imagine any other and better order of the world."[20]

In distinguishing among national, international, and transnational hegemonies, Anderson drew upon a more inclusive definition than Wallerstein. The latter's three modern hegemonies had been swapped for limitless hegemonies. They also seemed to disagree on the balance of dominance and persuasion. Wallerstein thought of hegemony primarily in terms of dominance, coinciding with a logistical peak and an extended conflict. Yet as the discussion in the previous chapter shows, he identified a role for liberalism, which sought to gain the support of the lower strata and peripheral states. In the domestic and transnational contexts, Anderson thought there could be no hegemony without consent. In the international context, he regarded dominance as outweighing persuasion.[21]

Two puzzling questions emerged from *The H-Word*—one about Anderson's radicalism, the other having to do with agency. The first question had to do with the possibility of adaptation in politics. In emphasizing continuity across millennia, did Anderson's totalization become so grand that he, in effect, no longer registered world-historical change? Writing in *The Nation*, Bruce Robbins found it curious that mainstays of Marxism such as class or the mode of production seemed to have fallen by the wayside in Anderson's book.[22] Robbins also noted the high praise that Anderson bestowed on realists in the field of international relations (IR). Realist writers stressed continuity in world politics, based on the interests of great powers in a zero-sum environment, competitive and conflictual.[23] In remaining centered on might, the "stoic" Anderson went too far for Robbins, who wrote that the elder Marxist set aside his duties as a historian, a "vocation . . . which demands an interpretive plunge beneath the frothy surface of events, the seizing of a structure that is more solid than violence."[24]

Robbins's claims were reminiscent of comments Anderson had levied at comrades from time to time. He once noted how odd it was that Eric Hobsbawm's work on the twentieth century jettisoned any mention of class, and took Thompson to task for supposedly neglecting causal forces beyond human experience (that is, simply recording what people did and when).[25] Yet in taking on *The Age of Extremes* and *The Making of the English Working Class*, Anderson addressed works that accounted for periods of momentous historical change. *The H-Word* explored something far narrower, an enduring concept across time, its meaning only partially altered.

Furthermore, Anderson praised realists, a trait found in other works as well.[26] He found realist accounts appealing, not as a theory of international relations, but because they remained critical of liberal interventionists. Though not immune to impulse or national cheerleading, the judgments of realists came through as refreshingly honest antidotes (to use a favorite word of Anderson's) to the conclusions of liberals. Here, scholarly admiration was fueled by common disdain for the pronouncements of ideologues. Anderson's sober radicalism, infused by praise for realism, remained one of attitude rather than a renunciation of radical thought.

A more perplexing feature of *The H-Word* concerned conditions of hegemony. Unlike Wallerstein, Anderson often attributed hegemony to the actions of social classes or powerful individuals. In defining hegemony as more than dominance, he distinguished between those leaders that were merely coercive and those that also effectively garnered support for their leadership. There was thus an element of choice in Anderson's narrative. Hegemons decided whether to become hegemons. Take, for example, the discussion of Ranajit Guha, who sought to correct ambiguities within Gramsci's thought by developing a typology of power. Hegemony, for Guha, occurred under conditions of dominance if persuasion exceeded coercion. Anderson believed Guha had rightly identified British colonial rule in India as dominance without hegemony: Raj power rested more on coercion than persuasion.[27] A counterfactual takes this logic to its conclusion: if the British had been more persuasive than coercive, then they would have followed the path of hegemony. The rationale was not faulty. It was merely surprising that such words came from a thinker who once penned a book-length defense of Althusser.[28]

Anderson's attention to the decisions of leaders revealed his most pressing concern, the twenty-first-century behavior of the world's hegemonic power. Obama's Nobel Peace Prize, awarded at the start of his tenure, symbolized the combined military and cultural power of the United States. Obama was unique among American executives in presiding "over uninterrupted military campaigns abroad across two full terms."[29] In portraying American hegemony as more than the product of logistical waves, Anderson demonstrated a rationale for his defiance. Sober yet unyielding, his twenty-first-century compositions might, paradoxically, encourage such acts of resistance among fellow radicals.

Chapter 7

Do Not Believe What Great Powers Say

The twenty-first century began, and remains, in turbulence. At the start of the century, terrorist attacks and subsequent Western interventions, supported by cable commentary and theme music, sparked a public debate over the exercise of power. Radicals became part of this conversation, too, and offered interpretations on the usefulness of labels such as "terrorism."[1] And with the economic crisis of 2008, the neoliberal order was once again called into question. Still, neoliberalism had proven remarkably adept at survival. With each successive crisis, many policymakers in the developed world have proposed market fundamentalism as their solution.[2] As Perry Anderson put it, economic reforms of the last thirty years brought ever "more ruthless styles of exploitation and neglect."[3] Yet in light of anti-Western sentiment in the postcolonial world, accompanied by a restless citizenry within the great powers, the promise of a liberal capitalist peace appeared untenable. Radicalism experienced something of a resurgence in the public sphere.

For their part, Anderson and Immanuel Wallerstein once again turned to critical accounts of great power narratives. In doing so, they also continued the macrohistorical projects they began in the 1970s. Much of the interim Wallerstein spent writing about knowledge accumulation and the division of the disciplines, subjects he regarded as intimately connected to the condition of twentieth-century capitalism.[4] In the twenty-first century, however, he returned to *The Modern World-System*. Twenty-two years had passed between publishing the third (in 1989) and fourth (in 2011) volumes of his series. He initially planned four volumes but ultimately concluded an additional two or three were needed. Though the fourth would be his last, Wallerstein never abandoned his biography of capitalism. He continued to publish essays on the nineteenth and twentieth centuries, the proposed subject of his sequels.[5]

While this work has addressed the argument of that final volume, an analysis of liberalism, its political context has not yet been examined. The 2003 U.S. invasion of Iraq exemplified for Wallerstein the hectoring rhetoric of liberal-imperial states. In exposing the American narrative, a story common among many intervening powers over the centuries, he returned to a theme from early in his career. Once again, Wallerstein resisted justifications of dominance over political subordinates.

Anderson's return, on the other hand, was more surprising. Most of his writings in the 1980s and 1990s had to do with Marxist historiography and the evolution of Left scholarship, along with a comparison of notable conservatives, liberals, and socialists.[6] After the end of the Soviet Union, Anderson published commentaries on various regions of the world, including: Europe, Russia, China, Brazil, India, and the Arab world.[7] They appeared to be merely assessments of regions or nations. Then, in 2009, he published *The New Old World*. It was a collection of writings on the European Union along with some new material that placed Europe in a wider historical context.

Thematically, Anderson's writings converged with Wallerstein's once again, this time on the self-proclaimed values of great powers. Each found that under capitalism powerful states justified behavior in terms of religious principles, or secular ideals of *civilization* or *rights*. They noticed that these pronouncements often happened to coincide with the material interests of Western Europe and the United States. Furthermore, such rhetorical overtures were applied inconsistently and often rested upon contradictory or dubious logics. Wallerstein elaborated on how core states justified their interventions into the periphery, and how they used the same language to suppress groups at home. Anderson wrote about how elites in great powers wrapped their self-serving policies in popular narratives. Both called attention to how the notion of human progress concealed a desire for maintaining, or even rolling back, the status quo.

All this Moralizing and the Bombs Keep Falling

In the rhetoric of powerful states, Wallerstein saw feigned sincerity and subtle forms of repression at work. His writings on liberalism (reviewed in chapter 6) explored how core states delayed domestic progress—namely, the expansion of active citizenship; they argued that equality should be realized not immediately but at a slow and steady pace. However, the modern political spectrum was not the only ideological program at work in the capitalist world-economy. At least since meeting Fanon, Wallerstein regarded the promotion of values to be a weapon of the world-system's power brokers. And, following Fanon, Wallerstein had always found it curious that espoused values were expressed in universal terms, despite changing over time. The hypocrisy of great powers was never greater than in times of military intervention: core states used morality to justify armed intervention into the periphery and, afterward, described their behavior in terms of self-sacrifice.

In the early days of the modern world-system, according to Wallerstein, powerful states expressed their sense of morality in terms of Christianity. Violations of divine law, they said, could necessitate intervention. Over time, morality became secularized and articulated in terms of protecting human rights. But, Wallerstein thought, the specific moral standard invoked by great powers actually mattered very little. What mattered was that great powers acted as if they, and only they, possessed true knowledge. Wallerstein called this tendency *European universalism*. It was universal because it pretended to be a moral truth enshrined in divine or natural law. And it was European because such truths were not universal at all, but *particularist*, by which Wallerstein meant that they were actually expressions of European values and truths. In other words, European universalism was a regionally specific moral code that posed as a set of rules for all humanity.[8]

In the fall of 2004, Wallerstein gave a series of lectures at the University of British Columbia on the narratives of powerful states.[9] European universalism had a permissive attitude toward intervening in the non-European world. The roles of intervener and intervened, as well as the perceived moral violation, changed over time. But the rationale for intervention did not. To convey this point, Wallerstein began with an extended discussion of Spain and the enslavement of native Amerindians in the early days of the capitalist world-economy. He took up the arguments of two theologians who, at the behest of Charles V, formally debated in 1550 before a panel comprised of secular and spiritual figures.[10] Wallerstein thought, simply, that the logic of domination remained consistent: "If I have spent so much time spelling out the arguments of two sixteenth-century theologians, it is because nothing that has been said since has added anything essential to the debate."[11]

Wallerstein labeled the pro-intervention narrative the Sepúlveda argument. Named for one participant, Juan Ginés de Sepúlveda, this narrative described the Amerindians as uneducated, brutish, and in need of punishment for violating divine law. Thus, Spaniards were obligated (also by divine law) to protect innocent Amerindians from harm; and, moreover, Spanish conquest would ensure the safety of priests bringing Christianity to the barbarians.[12] Therefore, according to the Sepúlveda argument, great powers had the duty to intervene in order to prevent atrocities waged by barbarians against the defenseless.

The other participant, Bartolomé de Las Casas, represented the anti-intervention narrative. His was a systematic dismantling of pro-intervention logic. We can think of the Las Casas argument in terms of critical questions, which exposed the intervening power's true motives.

1. *What does it mean to be barbarian?* People could behave like savages in all parts of the world. More often, the kind of behavior indicted by Sepúlveda was the product of a few individuals, not an entire people. There was certainly such savage behavior in Spain. In fact, Las Casas noted, the Roman Empire once perceived the region that would become Spain as barbaric.[13]

2. *In whose jurisdiction do the barbarians reside?* Under what authority was Spain capable of enforcing religious codes? For example, Jews and Muslims in Spain were required to obey Spanish law, but they did not have to convert to Catholicism. It seemed wrong to Las Casas (and Wallerstein) that the Church could fault native peoples for disobeying Catholic doctrine when they had no prior knowledge of Catholicism.[14]

3. *Are barbarians converted through their own free will?* Sepúlveda and Las Casas agreed that conversion to Christianity should happen out of free will. But Las Casas noted that violence was used to "convert" Amerindians to Catholicism. There was, he thought, very little free will involved.

4. *How much harm is caused by intervention?* As portrayed by Wallerstein, Las Casas was not unconcerned about those

who suffered under barbaric leaders and their practices. Instead, he wondered whether powerful states were the best liberators of oppressed peoples. In many cases of intervention, the result was more harmful than helpful. Often, more innocents were lost than without intervention.[15] In light of the sum total of their cruelty, did the Spaniards really think they understood God? Did they actually believe they had done more good than harm?[16]

Las Casas, however, had a virtually impossible task. To be against intervention, Wallerstein explained, meant that one "had to argue simultaneously against both beliefs and interests."[17] As we know from history, it was the Sepúlveda argument that won over the Spanish monarchy because it was a moral argument that aligned with Spain's material desires. Thus, the weaker philosophical-theological argument became dominant, not for only for Spain, but for all great powers in the history of the modern world-system.

Interventions of the twentieth and twenty-first centuries seemed hardly different to Wallerstein than the actions of Spanish imperialists. For example, the United States's invasion of Iraq, like many invasions, was argued (at least in part) along humanitarian lines. But, he explained, even if one were to take Washington's logic at face value, it was never clear just which groups were the innocents and which groups were the barbarians (other than Saddam Hussein's inner circle). The thinking seemed to be: intervene now, and the good guys and bad guys can be sorted out later. The result for Wallerstein was a moral mess: intervening parties invoked distinct understandings of who was an innocent and who was a barbarian.[18]

Wallerstein opposed more recent interventions, too. He was against the United States's 2011 intervention in Libya, as well as France's 2013 commitment of troops to Mali.[19] Though he trusted the consciences of Obama and Hollande, Wallerstein did not think they appropriately weighed short-term outcomes against long-term outcomes. In the short term, a great power could most likely prevent slaughter. Yet the long-term outcome was often worse. Wallerstein challenged readers to think of the Iraq invasion, and asked: "Have fewer people been slaughtered as a result over a ten-year period? It doesn't seem so."[20]

Thus, Wallerstein's issue with humanitarian intervention was simple: with any given intervention, he was "never sure it [was] humanitarian."[21]

He suspected others had the same assessment, which was why he believed that proponents of intervention found it easier to point to the Rwandan genocide and other times great powers declined to intervene than to successful interventions. In these instances, those favoring intervention often branded their opponents as naive and complicit in enabling bad deeds. But, Wallerstein urged, we would do well to listen to reticent interveners, who might teach the rest of society, not only about our limited efficacy, but "some humility about our righteousness" as well.[22]

Although Wallerstein disregarded European universalism as a moral code, which he called "morally ambiguous," he did not think that European universalism should be replaced by another, regionally specific, set of values that also supposedly applied to all humans across the globe. Some scholars, for example, have hoped that European universalism could be replaced by an Asia-based moral code. Others proposed that indigenous groups serve as a model for behavior in the future. Wallerstein, in some controversy, rejected both of these alternatives outright. He referred to these proposals as forms of *anti-Eurocentric Eurocentricism* because they took the existing fabric of European universalism and made a cosmetic alteration.[23] Instead of challenging its logic, adherents to anti-Eurocentric Eurocentricism often merely wished to elevate a new region.[24]

But neither was Wallerstein arguing for the end of universalism: he did not comprehensively reject the existence of universal values or truths. In other words, he disagreed with those who, in jettisoning European universalism, adopted *radical relativism*. He considered radical relativists to be those who let go not only of European values, but the notion of values altogether.[25]

In place of these opposing vices—at one extreme, some form of (Eurocentric or anti-Eurocentric) particularist universalism, and, at the other, radical relativism—Wallerstein recommended that we adopt some elements of each extreme. He therefore proposed a third option, which he interchangeably called *global universalism* or *universal universalism*. Though he did not have a specific moral code in mind, he had some ideas as to how others might create one. The process, he thought, meant *universalizing particulars* and *particularizing universals* in what he called "a kind of constant dialectical exchange."[26] He called upon intellectuals, especially those whose research covered the domains of politics and society, to develop such a global universalism.[27] In preparing his lectures, he must have been reminded of Fanon, who, as Wallerstein once observed, strove to be both particular and universal.

Wallerstein had long believed that such a shift toward universal universalism would require a change in our vocabulary. Policymakers, writers, television personalities, and everyday people would have to change how they thought about others. The concept of the Other historically enabled subtle and not-so-subtle forms of domination. On occasion, in fact, Wallerstein had asked *The New York Times* to address what might be called an Othering bias in its articles. He thought the paper served to reinforce prejudices held by government as well as society. Two such exchanges illustrate this point.

The first, from 1972, concerned a *Times* factsheet on Ghana. A dismayed Wallerstein wrote to the news editor regarding the paper's "tone of prejudice and condescension."[28] He took issue with several item listed about Ghana, its history, and its people. He thought articles about Africans differed from articles about Europeans. The *Times* described Ghanaians as being "of black Sudanese stock," which, Wallerstein scolded, was "a term best reserved for cattle."[29] Would the *Times* refer to Britons or French people of being from a certain stock? Such language was reserved for African peoples.[30] In response, the foreign editor assured Wallerstein that while the paper would recheck for accuracy, the article did not have a tone of prejudice because the piece was written for generalists and not specialists.[31] It would not have been possible, he added, for such a level of detail. Undeterred, Wallerstein replied that, of course, he was not suggesting that the *Times* write a scholarly piece. "I was merely suggesting that you be accurate."[32]

The second case, from 1974, concerned the paper's unwillingness to capitalize "Black" when referring to African Americans. He found it odd that Blacks seemed to be the only group that the *Times* would *not* capitalize. In his letter to the editor, Wallerstein referred to one *Times* piece listing several such categories. In apparent reference to the diversity of New York's newsstands, the article noted one stand that "carried thick piles of Jewish, Hebrew, West Indian, black, Spanish and Chinese newspapers."[33] Wallerstein wondered how this omission did not raise a red flag to the paper. He added: "In 1900, the Times styles rules would have required 'negro.' By 1950, the rules required 'Negro.' Today these rules call for 'black.' How long do we have to wait until the Times accords equality of capitalization to 'Black?' "[34]

In the newspaper's response, George Palmer, assistant to the managing editor, disagreed: "The New York Times lower-cases the 'b' in black in its general news coverage on the ground that it is a common noun, just as white is a common noun."³⁵ Wallerstein responded that Palmer's letter only further illustrated the problem: "Elementary linguistic theory tells us that whether a noun is common or proper is determined by context and not by fiat (certainly not that of the New York Times). . . . Elementary social theory tells us that . . . use of a common noun symbolism for a proper noun is regarded as an affront. Elementary political theory tells us that when a newspaper declines to discuss its deliberate affronts in public, it is somewhat ashamed of its position."³⁶ In short, he saw the *Times*'s unwillingness to discuss the issues as indicative of its guilt. This was not some minor issue for him. It was part of capitalism's history and legacy, a subtle yet powerful reinforcement of inequality within the system. Today, the paper still does not capitalize "black." It has made progress on discussing the issue in public, as evidenced by a 2014 op-ed.³⁷

Until we have achieved a universal universalism, if such a morality ever arises, Wallerstein advised scholars and citizens not to give in to the prepackaged moral codes offered by core zones. The self-satisfied tone of European universalism, which distinguished between whose who were righteous and those who were sinners, or between civilized peoples and barbarians, pervaded all discussions of race and peoplehood. This vocabulary was at work not only for discussing foreign places, but at home too.

When It's Convenient, We Always Stand for Human Advancement

Like Wallerstein, Anderson distrusted the values championed by great powers. He, too, found their ideological proclamations to have little to do with their actions. In his twenty-first-century writings, Anderson took to task intellectuals and policymakers who promoted European integration. In his opinion, many of these writers and public figures sought to cover up their regressive programs with a progressive mask. Though he supported the initial intellectual thrust behind integration—that is, the establishment of a European federal state—Anderson had great disdain for the outcome, which he believed had been hijacked by neoliberals. Promoters of the European Union in the twenty-first century, he explained, spoke on maximizing human potential, rights, and living standards even as they undercut the real gains in those very areas over the last century. Europe's future looked more and more like a revival of its past.

He expressed many of these views in *The New Old World*, an informal sequel to *Passages-Lineages*. On this claim, some elaboration may be necessary. Anderson, after all, remarked that its chapters—many of them originally published as stand-alone essays[38]—were "reworked . . . relatively little," and that he preferred to "let them stand as testimonies of the time."[39] In the *New Left Review*, he later acknowledged an indirect connection to *Passages-Lineages* by referring to "two earlier works on Europe."[40] The NLR's editors, in introducing a symposium on Anderson's book, went much farther: "One attempt in this field [of historicizing the Eurozone] has been Perry Anderson's [*The*] *New Old World*, which follows a comparative survey of pre-capitalist Europe in two much earlier works, *Passages from Antiquity to Feudalism* and *Lineages of the Absolutist State*, with reflections on the continent at a high point of bourgeois rule, on the eve of the crisis that now grips the EU."[41]

Still, the most compelling evidence for treating the *The New Old World* as an original work and as an extension of *Passages-Lineages* came from Anderson's own prose. In his criticism of Alan Milward, to whom the book is dedicated, Anderson wrote that too many of the former's works created a "historical richness" that surpassed their "theoretical scheme."[42] For a time, Anderson's own research fit this description. His writings on Europe positioned contemporary events within longer historical developments, but only in fragments, without a compelling theory or narrative of Europe in the modern world.[43] Thus, by compiling the book in the way that he did, he finally produced a work about Europe whose sum was more than its parts.

Hinted in the title yet buried in the text, the thesis of Anderson's book was that aspects of Europe's distant past had reemerged in Europe's present. After nearly one hundred pages, readers learn Anderson's main contention: "Entailed, if never stated, is only one plausible outcome: that ultimately, the Old World is likely to be compacted into the shapes of the New."[44] What he meant was that Europe experienced periods of unification prior to postwar integration. He used *New World* to refer to Europe of the twentieth and twenty-first centuries, and *Old World* to refer to Europe before the early modern world, loosely defined. Anderson never directly compared aspects of these worlds, something unsurprising for his regular readers but nonetheless strange in light of his expressed desire to reach ordinary citizens. Nonetheless, we can identify the following three such worlds that have returned in contemporary Europe: economics,

Table 7.1. Old World Born Anew

Realm	Old World	Period
Economics	Deregulation (Americanization)	Early modernity
Civilization	Historical nostalgia	Feudalism
Culture	Ethno-religious tensions	Antiquity

civilization, and culture (compared in Table 7.1). Although Anderson did not use these labels, such conveniences may be useful for understanding his interpretation of the Union today.

Old World economics was the rollback of business regulation. This took form as a kind of Americanization of Europe. The original plan for a united Europe had been Jean Monnet's vision of a federal system that both united national markets and equitably redistributed wealth.[45] At the time, Monnet's proposal competed against a less unified intergovernmentalist plan of connected sovereign states. What ultimately emerged was quite different from either of these plans. The dominant mode of integration, Anderson thought, was hardly integration at all: a neoliberal, anticentralist, and antiwelfare association of states inspired by the writings of Friedrich Hayek.[46] According to Anderson, many early proponents of unification would have thought this to be the least likely outcome.

Far from federalism, the new system became ultra-confederalism, unified only by trade relations reminiscent of Europe prior to the welfare state. Thus, the first way in which the Old World returned was in the dismantling of the welfare state. France's thirty-five-hour workweek came under attack, and Sweden kept raising its pension collection age. The E.U. bureaucracy, Anderson explained, became the ultimate form of minimalism, "less even than the dream of a nightwatchman."[47] Originally envisioned as a way to stand up to the United States,[48] the European Union transformed into a kind of "deputy empire."[49] He noted that, today, "this Union is not about democracy, and not welfare, but capital."[50] Thus, the Old World reawakened in the undoing of social provisions, this time in the form of business deregulation found prior to the twentieth century. The new Americanized Europe attracted a surge in European studies within the United States university system, or, what Anderson called "a new ideological affinity between subject and object."[51]

In terms of the European civilization, the Old World had come back in the form of nostalgia.[52] The Union's own official Museum of Europe, Anderson noticed, described unification as a civilizational project that spanned a thousand years. It can be divided into three eras. Europe's first phase of unification, which took form under Christianity, amounted to a homogenization of religion, culture, and institutions. Still, this was a Christian consciousness, not a European one. The idea of Europe was developed later, Anderson explained. "For contemporaries, their world was Christendom. The concept of 'Europe' did not exist for them, and to attribute it to such forebears is an anachronism."[53]

A second era of unification occurred, what Anderson called a "single ambience," after the Reformation and Wars of Religion. During this period, European elites adopted Enlightenment ideas.[54] This unification was undone, first by the French Revolution, then the "Wars of Ideology" in the twentieth century.[55]

Unlike the others, the third unification became a deliberate process of integration, not for any purpose, but for the sake of integration itself. Between World War II and the end of the Cold War, elites intentionally pulled Europe together. Its planners had recent memories of the defeat of fascism and the end of colonialism, as well as beliefs about the processes of modernization. But, Anderson observed, this third formation could not have been possible without its predecessors: the current project was informed by the Enlightenment, just as the Enlightenment was informed by Christianity.[56]

Yet Anderson did not think that all civilization unifications were the same (compared in Table 7.2). The first formed without a sense of Europe that, in Hegelian terms, Anderson called a "totality in-itself." The first unification included all Europeans, but it did not provide a *European* identity; there was only the label of Christianity. (In other words, the totality was Christianity, not Europe.) Anderson called the second unification "selectivity for-itself," by which he meant that the European identity existed only for a small portion of society and served only the interests of a few people. (The totality in this case was selective in its representation.)

By contrast, Anderson called the third project of unification a "totality in-itself-for-itself." He wrote: "the Community claims both the conscious allegiance and factual inclusion of all citizens."[57] It was a synthesis of the two prior cultural forms of unifications. But the problem, as he saw it, was that unification *was* the founding goal, nothing more. This Europe encompassed all Europeans, possessed a European identity, but nonetheless did not serve the masses. The creation of European institutions was a monumental but unsatisfying achievement.[58] Europe's aim was a goal-less goal of still further integration.[59]

No longer about democracy or peace, unification became subject to momentum. Yet as Anderson pointed out, an inversion of principles did not stop political elites and intellectuals from promoting the Union in terms of ideals such as human rights and democracy. Like Wallerstein, Anderson detested duplicity. Therefore, he also pointed out disingenuous or inconsistent justifications of political action. He took political elites and intellectuals to task for what he considered to be their disingenuous support of the European Union. Pro-integration intellectuals, in his description, touted the EU as the "light of the world." Among its supporters have been Mark Leonard, Jeremy Rifkin, Jürgen Habermas,[60] Ulrich Beck, and Marcel Gauchet. In different ways, they expressed what Anderson called "an apparently illimitable narcissism" and a high degree of "political vanity."[61] He thought such exaggerations took away from whatever had been genuinely achieved by unification.[62]

To Anderson, claims of Europe as a beacon for the world seemed especially strange in light of popular dissatisfaction with the process of integration. Enthusiasm among citizens was much less than the enthusiasm expressed by their leaders. In 2004, the European Constitution was promoted with such political fanfare, favorable media coverage, and elite support (especially from Habermas) that hardly anyone thought the constitution would not be adopted. But, Anderson wrote, "voters made short work of it."[63] The constitution was long, bureaucratically cumbersome, and

Table 7.2. European Civilization as Hegelian Triad

Order	Duration	Summary	Motivating End	Impact on Europeans
1st	c. 1000–c. 1500	Totality in-itself	Christianity	Factual inclusion
2nd	c. 1600–1789	Selectivity for-itself	Enlightenment beliefs	European consciousness
3rd	1945–	Totality in-itself-for-itself	Becoming "increasingly obscure"	Factual inclusion and European consciousness

disproportionately favored the United Kingdom, France, Germany, and Italy. Since the process of integration began, the public repeatedly voted against it.[64] The gap, Anderson remarked, was astounding: "The contrast between such realities and the placards of the touts for the new Europe could scarcely be starker. The truth is that the light of the world, role-model for humanity at large, cannot even count on the consent of its populations at home."[65]

Political defeat must have come as a shock for elites, who had for some time been successful at minimizing lower-class power. Much like Wallerstein's account of modern liberalism, an ideology which effectively forced subordinate groups to fight separately for political inclusion, Anderson found that Europe's elite encouraged divisions among the lower classes. As a result, a third, cultural, Old World had been reborn in the form of ethnic and religious conflicts that, at times, appeared stronger than class divisions. This became apparent in light of the rise of inequality and simultaneous decline of the workers' movement. He reflected: "Europe might finally have achieved unity, only to find that its post-classical identity was beginning to dissolve, towards something closer to Antiquity."[66] During the second half of the twentieth century, communist parties in Western Europe were virtually eradicated, and, with the Far Left gone, the Center Left began to erode too. The steady loss of genuine Left intellectuals, activists, and policymakers has led to new social divisions based upon older forms of identification. Older ethno-religious conflict slowly displaced working-class solidarity. This, Anderson noted, was not due solely to "false consciousness." Immigration had increased competition for jobs, strained social welfare programs, and motivated wage reductions.[67]

The problem of immigration arose from and contributed to inequality, both within Europe and between Europe and its former colonies. Global inequality had prompted mass immigration and increased inequality on the continent. In Anderson's assessment, Europe was to blame: international aid was exported with strings attached, while migrant laborers were imported to serve the needs of business.[68]

The Union's failure to pursue more than neoliberal profit maximization led to cultural undoing from within. In this, Anderson found "historical irony." Historically, Christian Europe was defined and contained by Islamic cultures to the south. Now, it was being transformed from the inside out. Culturally, the New Europe was reverting back to demographic and political divisions of the Greco-Roman world.[69] Left intellectuals and parties should have channeled lower-class hostility toward the elite. Anderson lamented their "abdication" of responsibility, a consequence of which was that political options were limited.[70] In his opinion, this trend increased after publication of *The New Old World*. Political groups on the Left and Right grew in popularity, though the latter outmaneuvered the former. The Right had a compelling program that the Left could not match: an anti-immigration platform in the name of welfare state protections.[71] The problem for the Left, he concluded, was that its proposed reforms were less radical than the Right's. Moreover, there was a logic as to why everyday people were drawn to Far Right parties: lower classes, long suffering the pain of neoliberalism, had reached a point where desperation exceeded their apprehension.[72]

In showing the return of the Old within the New, Anderson revealed the hypocrisy of integration. However sincere the original architects may have been about peace, stability, and the protection of rights, the passage of time transformed the project into something different. Now more Old than New, the Union as he saw it had become a zone for free trade and the interests of upper classes, both of which were guaranteed by displacing lower-class solidarity with ethno-religious divisiveness. Proponents, of course, continued to speak in terms of rights and human potential, but Anderson did not believe they meant it.

Anderson's assessment of the Union was perhaps best illustrated with his analysis of Cyprus and Turkey. These cases contradicted the Union's pronounced commitments to peace and multiculturalism and, in the Turkish case, even symbolized American dominance in the region.[73] For all its talk of inclusion, he wrote, the European Union failed to confront abuses of its past and present.

Cyprus endured occupation by a Union partner, the United Kingdom, as well as a candidate for accession, Turkey. The UK possessed in Cyprus a military base larger than Guantánamo.[74] Turkey brutally overtook the northern part of Cyprus in June 1974. More than political occupation, Anderson observed, the aggressor engaged in ethnic cleansing in an invasion unchecked by Britain and the United States.[75] Ankara then created and diplomatically recognized the Turkish Republic of Northern Cyprus.

Unlike other recent candidates for accession, Turkey's past was one of national suppression and extermination. Anderson's history went back to the late Ottoman period, an empire long in decline. In 1908, the Young Turks seized power, and promoted a Turkish nationalism they intended to replace other allegiances, including the Muslim identification of the Ottomans.[76] The ruling organization of the Young Turks, the Committee of Union and Progress (CUP), feared during World War I that a rival nationalist group, the Armenians, would side with Russia (where a quarter of them lived).[77] In January 1915, the CUP ordered that Armenian soldiers be disarmed. In the spring, the state took more severe measures. Although ethnic expulsions and killings were not uncommon in the region's history, the Armenian genocide was without precedent: "systematic, state-organized murder of an entire community."[78] Between 1.2 and 1.4 million Armenians, about two-thirds of the total population, were exterminated. The international community immediately denounced the killings, but Turkish leaders "scarcely bothered even to deny it" when confronted by the United States.[79]

Kemal Atatürk completed the march to secularism in the 1920s. He suppressed religious institutions, dress, and customs. Secularism was accompanied by the forceful maintenance of class relations: strikes and demonstrations were swiftly put down. The ruling ideology of Turkey, Kemalism, was nationalist and statist, conveyed to the masses in what Anderson called "crypto-religious" trappings.[80] Kemal excluded Christians, Greeks, and Armenians. He originally promised autonomy for the Kurds, but shifted course in the 1920s. Kurdish names and symbols were eliminated, and predominantly Kurdish regions were militarized with Turkish troops. Rebellions were forcefully and brutally squashed. Anderson wrote that by the 1930s, the Kurds officially "ceased to exist." According to Kemalism, only Turks lived in Turkey, and for decades the Kurds had no legal existence. Reportedly, Kemal never publicly said the word *Kurd* after 1925.[81]

Like Wallerstein, Anderson thought that Otherness, mixed with civilization and, indeed, rights, amounted to a self-defeating series of concepts. Furthermore, their inconsistent application demonstrated the insincerity of Western leaders. He pointed to the United States, which pushed for Turkey to join the EU: Washington wanted to promote Ankara as a symbol of secular liberalism in the Muslim world.[82] Twice this century, the U.S. House took up a resolution condemning the Armenian genocide. It was defeated each time. In 2000, President Bill Clinton successfully lobbied to prevent a floor vote. In 2007, House leaders reversed themselves after former secretary of state Madeleine Albright and several other Democrats lobbied against it.[83] Existing relations were not to be disturbed.

Admitted to the Union in 2004, Cyprus possessed veto power over Turkey.[84] A concerned European Commission, aware that no candidate for accession had ever been denied, suggested that Cyprus forget past injustices. And if Turkey were to be admitted, Brussels and Washington would announce a triumph of multiculturalism as a Muslim democracy joined the European Union. But who would benefit? For Anderson, Union elites would benefit, at least from a public relations standpoint. Cyprus would suffer. And Turkey may not be better off, as Anderson wrote in 2009: "Turkish dreams of a better life in Europe are to be respected. But emancipation rarely just arrives from abroad."[85] Since then, Turkey has become increasingly authoritarian. Cyprus has maintained its opposition. In 2019, the Union admitted defeat, suspending accession talks.

The crises of the Union—economic, political, cultural—intervened in the planned march toward progress. Yet the case of Turkey remains symbolic of the problems within Europe. Contradictions in Turkish nationalism, namely, the promotion of a nation at the expense of minority ethnicities, mirror the contradictions of the European Union: a rhetorical multinationalism that barely conceals its neoliberal transnational reality.

The New Old World remains timely in its conclusion: the Union in deed far removed from the Union in speech. European (and American) economic interests played a far greater role in unification than desires to preserve peace, behave morally, or serve as a role model for humanity. Yet despite widespread dissatisfaction with the Union, Anderson later cautioned, centrist forces (pro-Union elites) remain strong; Left radicals ought to become as resilient as forces on the Right. By 2017, he concluded that the Union's neoliberal character was impossible to reform, and that Leftists should seek its destruction.[86] For him, two truths about the European Union required acknowledgment: it did not align with its original plan; it was not what elites purported it to be. Far from being a federal supra-state gargantuan capable of rivaling U.S. political and economic hegemony, Europe became a lesser associate of the United States, altered to reflect American neoliberal values.[87]

In subsequent writings, Anderson turned his attention to a similar sequence in the United States: an elite neoliberalism followed by populist anti-neoliberalism. The neoliberalism of the Union, which for some time benefited the United States, produced a populist backlash capable of crossing the Atlantic. Though the electoral system of the United States, like Britain, ensured that major parties retained their dominance, public feelings of fear and desperation combined to support unconventional politics and nonestablishment candidates. And, as in Europe, the American Right had more electoral success than the Left: in 2016, the populism of Trump and Brexit leaders proved greater than the populism of Sanders and Corbyn.[88]

Conclusion

Whereas Wallerstein demonstrated the contradictions of so-called humanitarian intervention, Anderson showed how easily powerful states could ignore atrocities. Theirs were separate articulations of the same argument. Although great powers often spoke in lofty tones, such proclamations were tools for the pursuit of their interests. If Western leaders really were committed to universal values, policymakers would pursue them even when it came at a political or material cost. With a parade of policymakers and intellectuals promoting post–Cold War liberal capitalist peace, it likely seemed necessary to expose the hypocrisy of Western rhetoric. What Wallerstein and Anderson revealed about morality was something closer to Nietzsche than to Kant. Neither Wallerstein nor Anderson denied the possibility of universal truth, yet each was skeptical about the universalizing claims he heard. If universal values and truths did exist, one could be sure that the great powers did not advocate for them. Once the ideological mask was ripped away, the only truth underneath was, at least for the powerful, that morality was infinitely malleable.

Conclusion

The Point Is to Interpret,
and Then Change, the World

At the intersection of political events and intellectual life, practitioners of radical political economy think about world politics from a sociohistorical perspective. As such, they are activist intellectuals who believe their research exists for a purpose. They side with underdeveloped zones and peripheral actors. They tend to think in terms of how events are interconnected, historically and geographically. Perry Anderson and Immanuel Wallerstein represent this group of thinkers. In the postwar years, they were outraged by injustice and desired a more egalitarian world. Thus, they took up methods and embarked on projects they believed were important for political circumstances. Yet as we reflect on their (mostly) twentieth-century experiences, we cannot help but think about ultra-capitalism in the twenty-first century, with both economic and political characteristics. Economically, unpredictability in markets and dwindling material resources have everyday people uneasy in underdeveloped and advanced zones alike. Politically, the reactionary Right and the proletarian Left are both experiencing a resurgence. These conditions are no longer confined to developing zones of the globe.

The world today bears a resemblance to the tumultuous times of Wallerstein's and Anderson's early years. The 1930s was like the present age in its market unpredictability, volatility in monetary policy, and high levels of income and wealth inequality. Moreover, with American hegemony in doubt, other great powers are becoming more assertive in pursuing their foreign policy goals. Wallerstein and Anderson, born eight years and an ocean apart, experienced the same interwar milieu: a global slump and fierce ideological battles. Then came global war and the subsequent Moscow-Washington rivalry. Wallerstein's New York childhood and well-traveled family caused him to think about underprivileged peoples in the world. Anderson's childhood travels also led him to develop similar political sympathies. Both were curious about nationalism (though Anderson considered himself particularly resistant to nationalist sympathies).

Both Wallerstein and Anderson have reflected on their youthful curiosity in politics and their lifelong sensitivity to current events. Their intellectual lives, therefore, have become a kind of biography of changing times. In fact, Anderson has said as much about a fellow British Marxist, Eric Hobsbawm, calling the twentieth century "The Age of EJH."[1] This work has not attempted to impose a singularity of thought upon its subjects. An interesting writer will change his or her thinking over the decades, a point Anderson made about Antonio Gramsci: "[T]he thought of a genuinely original mind will typically exhibit—not randomly but intelligibly—significant structural contradictions, inseparable from its creativity."[2]

In this narrative, the experiences of Wallerstein and Anderson have been of planned paths shifted by circumstance. This normality of human experience is analogous to the lives of totalities, which also take unexpected twists and turns. For Wallerstein, world-systems have no predetermined track but rather function as the outcome of complex internal processes. The behavior of individuals, firms, states, and other actors send what we might call *inputs* into the system, which, collectively, lead to systemic outcomes or *outputs*. During the routine functioning of a system, according to him, small inputs lead to small outputs, and large inputs lead to large outputs. These outcomes provide the context for future actions, in effect limiting certain kinds of behavior. The actions of people and their institutions are restrained not because activities are made to be impossible, but rather because they become highly improbable.

Another way to consider inputs and outputs is from a medical perspective. At the risk of mixed imagery, some inputs can function like viruses that, if virulent, endanger the lives of world-systems. In Georgi Derluguian's recollection, Wallerstein's friend Terence Hopkins in fact used to remark that the closest "kindred spirit [to world-systems analysis] must be epidemiology because it traces mutating microbes back to their origins across biological macro-environments."[3] Take for example, the case of Charles V, the Spanish king who tried to push all of Europe under his control. The still young capitalist world-economy managed to fight off the virus, but, as Wallerstein noted, the system almost succumbed. Four centuries later, the world-system once again fought off an illness. This time it was a German alliance that sought to conquer Europe, the United States, and Western colonial possessions. In both cases, the capitalist world-economy managed to avoid transforming into a world-empire (or fracture into several world-systems). Yet these were rare occurrences. Most states sought to maximize their positions without transforming the world-system.

In Wallerstein's opinion, world-systems were not guaranteed to survive. Indeed, he regarded imperial Spain as very nearly a mortal disease for capitalism. This precedent may have been on his mind when he testified before Congress, appealing for the United States to create a more egalitarian world-system. He believed the world's hegemonic power could destroy the system from within.

Anderson's sense of history was more rigid in that he saw much of economic and political development undisturbed by circumstance over the long term. Whereas humans can be impulsive or irregular in their behavior, modes of production in *Passages-Lineages* generally took more predictable paths. Still, he did find an element of surprise in his history of Europe. For example, the sudden and widespread strike of the Black Death in the fourteenth century forced changes in social relations all across Europe. (Paradoxically, the changes were in opposite directions: whereas the West trended towards nonserf labor, enserfment became more widespread in the East.)

Wallerstein's and Anderson's intellectual commitments were shaped by formative experiences. For Wallerstein, it was McCarthyism at home and decolonization abroad that led him to criticize U.S. foreign policy. American xenophobia, he noticed, contained an odd combination of isolationism and interventionism, a mix that allowed McCarthy and his acolytes to oppose decolonization. Wallerstein found this characteristic of the Far Right disconcerting in light of American hegemony. Though his primary focus was international development, he never lost his appreciation for ideological narratives, paying attention to how notions of human freedom can also be weapons for the powerful. Regarding development, Wallerstein was not encouraged by the methods of mainstream social scientists, even though many favored decolonization. Social science had falsely associated economic growth with political development. To the contrary, it appeared to him as though continued interaction with the West led to the underdevelopment (that is, economic immiseration) of newly independent states. Development in his view seemed neither progressive nor inevitable.

Whereas Wallerstein's early writings were a response to general trends in the world, Anderson was spurred to action by two specific events in the fall of 1956, his first year at Oxford. Within weeks of the start of the school year came the Soviet suppression of Hungary and Western intervention in Suez. Although Anderson had always been a leftist, he and his peers considered 1956 to be a turning point. These events taught him that the Left needed to develop a rival narrative capable of challenging the dominant framing of the Cold War. Neither the capitalist West, nor the communist parties of Eastern Europe, nor the socialist government in France stayed true to their espoused principles. Cold War rhetoric proclaimed that human freedom was at stake. But in truth, Anderson believed it was domestic order, economic growth, and geopolitical interest driving decisions in London, Moscow, and Paris. Furthermore, even though a vast majority of leftists had long ago abandoned their support for East European communist parties, Western governments for the most part continued to lump noncapitalists together. Thus, Anderson believed it was necessary to create new explanations of the present that corrected these misconceptions.

The early 1960s were nonetheless a time of optimism. Wallerstein was encouraged by African nationalist movements, and Anderson hoped that under Harold Wilson the Labour Party might finally become a genuine Left party. But neither was a fool. Wallerstein worried about the prospects for postindependence stability, and Anderson wondered if Wilson might be more of a centrist than he led on. Both proved to be true, and by the late 1960s, the young scholars had grown discouraged.

The world-revolution of 1968 brought renewed optimism. They came to think that capitalism was vulnerable and that socialism was not far away. They were convinced that the major problem was a lack of public and scholarly understanding of the historical processes that gave rise to the international order. Wallerstein thought universities might become zones of honest debate about American hegemony as well as places where radical intellectuals could aid nationalist movements in the third world. Anderson understood 1968 as the year independence movements spilled over into the developed world. Now that the revolution had been brought home, so to speak, activists needed intellectual guidance. The *New Left Review*, Anderson believed, could be part of the vanguard for socialist revolution.

Both scholars sought to influence the wider social conversation about the origins of Cold War politics, and how the Left could chart a new course. They hoped that new terms and new ways of thinking would catch on, in scholarship and in society. Today, social scientists describe this as a process of *multiplicity*, referring to the way that narratives are repeated and altered in public discussions.[4] Wallerstein and Anderson wanted to spread new narratives about capitalism and socialism.

As observers, we are reminded of how Wallerstein and Anderson were political actors trying to affect the outside world. In this sense, they were similar to Cold War diplomats, who often struggled to understand the potential consequences of decisions. They were required to act based on available information, however imperfect, and possibly without ever fully grasping the effects of their actions.[5] The revolt of 1968 gave Wallerstein and Anderson reason to think socialism was possible and perhaps not far away. This outcome may have seemed unlikely to Western political leaders, though sudden world-historical change frequently takes the powerful by surprise.

Renewed optimism led to Wallerstein's and Anderson's most famous intellectual projects. They thought that ideas of historical change could grow in nourishing institutional environments. And by the mid-1970s, they each led cultural institutions too: the Braudel Center and the *New Left Review* were places where comrades could wage debates about capitalism in historical perspective.

The key to their efforts in the 1970s can be summarized in a word: totality. They embraced a holistic methodology, and, by publishing histories of capitalism, offered a commentary on the present. The use of totalities enabled Wallerstein and Anderson to write about macrohistorical trends, drawing conclusions from the passing of centuries. Unlike Anderson's history of capitalism, Wallerstein's account mostly avoided the ancient or medieval worlds. As a proponent of closed totalities, he thought the evolution of each system was more important than the succession of systems that preceded it. Anderson, who preferred open totalities, offered a historical dialectic that attributed modern capitalism to the slave and feudal modes of production before it. Modernity, for him, was produced by the sequence of forms beginning in antiquity. Each approach carried obligations. Wallerstein's closed totalities meant that he had to constantly explain the geographic and temporal boundaries of world-systems. Why was the system here, not there? Why now, not then? And Anderson's open totalities meant that he needed to always follow his general narrative with cases that exemplified and departed from the historical trend. How does this case fit? How is this case exceptional?

For Wallerstein, Anderson, and many other social historians, totalities have been a useful way to present research from a holistic perspective. Yet those who adopt totalities should be prepared for some debate on the unit of analysis. Much of social scientific and historical research is based on a world divided into nation-states; thus, for most writers the terms *exogenous* and *endogenous* refer to what is outside and inside of nation-states. But if the totality is the unit of analysis, then the terms refer to what is inside and outside of the totality. In this case, the unit of analysis is often something larger than the nation-state, occupying entire continents or even the globe.

Perhaps due to his focus on closed totalities, Wallerstein has debated the unit of analysis on many occasions. One of the more interesting exchanges, with Robert Brenner, occured in 1973 just as *The Modern World-System I* was about to appear in print.[6] Brenner thought of himself as continuing in the tradition of Maurice Dobb and Ernesto Laclau in that he saw domestic factors, and class conflict in particular, as causing the transition to and away from feudalism. He believed Wallerstein was continuing a line of thought from Paul Sweezy that emphasized international market forces as causing domestic class positions and conflicts.[7] Brenner, who was preparing his own work on the development of capitalism in Europe,[8] thought this "external" conception was ahistorical, ignoring "internal" class forces. He believed that Wallerstein's perspective was "Smithian," for two reasons: one, by focusing on international trade; and two, for apparently portraying capitalism as the natural condition, waiting to be released in the modern world.[9]

Wallerstein forcefully rejected Brenner's categorization. The former did not think of himself as continuing the domestic versus international transition that Marxists had argued about for some time. He reasoned: "The immediate question is, internal or external to what?"[10] Brenner and Wallerstein could not agree on the meaning of terms underlying their arguments. Thus, the discussion stopped before it really began. Wallerstein refused to move past Brenner's starting premise about the unit of analysis, and Brenner never did address Wallerstein's use of totalities as opposed to nation-states.[11]

Despite intractability, their true views aligned more than readers may have realized. Both thinkers conceived of capitalism as an accident, an arrangement that was neither the natural economic formation nor guaranteed to happen. Nonetheless, the debate was beneficial in that it prompted other social historians to continue a conversation about the nature of world-historical change.¹² In fact, the "transition debate" has experienced a resurgence in recent years.¹³

The most significant disagreement between Anderson and Wallerstein, however, was not on exogenous versus endogenous factors but on how to define capitalism. Their diverging interpretations on the origins of capitalism were influenced by the separate meanings they imparted to the term. Anderson did not advocate for a single definition, but his writings suggested that wage labor was a necessary component of capitalism. Furthermore, Anderson believed that for capitalism to take hold, a society (or social formation, as he preferred to call it) would need to undergo bourgeois revolution. Wallerstein rejected any correlation between capitalism and labor-type, to a large extent because he saw core production and peripheral production as interconnected, with a mix of labor for profit maximization. He asserted that the modern world-system functioned according to a requirement for the ceaseless accumulation of capital (by which he meant stored value). Consequently, Wallerstein dated the development of capitalism in Western Europe and part of the Americas to the period 1450–1640. Anderson saw capitalism as beginning later, with the first bourgeois revolution in seventeenth-century England and spreading through Western Europe at a much slower pace. Theirs was no small divergence. For example, whereas Wallerstein claimed Moscow was incorporated into the capitalist world-economy in the late eighteenth century, Anderson contended that Tsarist Russia remained feudal until the revolution in 1917 and did not become truly capitalist until the 1990s.

Ironically, Wallerstein's and Anderson's preference for structures did not deter them from believing, at least through the 1970s, that the lower classes would create socialism at some point in the future. Wallerstein's typology of world-systems listed a *socialist world-government* as a future likelihood, even though he acknowledged that such a system had never before existed. Wallerstein's attitude reflected his hopefulness about the future after 1968. Anderson's vision of human agency was more puzzling. How could structures determine the past but not the future? This question was at the heart of his extended debate with a member of the NLR's "old guard"¹⁴ (explored in chapters 2 and 5).

Unlike the Brenner-Wallerstein debate, Anderson's dispute with E. P. Thompson lasted twenty years, from the early 1960s to the 1980s. It also had a personal tone. After Anderson became editor of the NLR in 1962 (in what Thompson reportedly called a "coup"),¹⁵ one of the main objectives for the journal was to bring continental Marxism home to Britain through translations and analysis of European Marxists. Anderson's NLR all but ignored the role of Thompson and other English Marxists of an earlier generation. An astonished Thompson penned a polemic against the new NLR,[16] to which Anderson responded with a polemic of his own.[17] The substance of Anderson's and Thompson's extended dispute, however, was on the notion of historical change. In 1963, Thompson's *The Making of the English Working Class* asserted that the "working class did not rise like the sun at an appointed time. It was present at its own making." Its formation "owes as much to agency as to conditioning."[18] The idea was that experiences of exploitation caused workers to see a collective interest, opposed to others, which brought the working class into existence. Anderson's view was the opposite: a class exists even if its members are not aware of its existence.[19] This element of Anderson's vision of history clarified (at least according to him) apparent contradictions of structures and agents. Structures, in his view, did not have to determine the future as they did the past because human agency had increased over time. With the emergence of workers' organizations and writings on historical materialism, lower classes of the industrial age were self-aware in a way that their predecessors may not have been. The advent of conscious classes meant that humans had an increased capacity to dismantle capitalism. He believed the *New Left Review* could potentially serve as part of the vanguard for socialist revolution.

The Thompson-Anderson debate also stopped short, though not for lack of time. In addition to their personal reconciliation,[20] global politics perhaps redirected their attention. The years 1979 and 1981, respectively, mark the ascendancy of Thatcher and Reagan. This was the age of neoliberalism. Expectations for socialism had to be put on hold.

Like many popular ideologies, neoliberalism promoted human freedom. Yet unlike socialists, social democrats, New Dealers, Keynesians, and others who sought human freedom via governmental restrictions on corporations, neoliberals conceived of human freedom as market freedom. The individual was thought to be free if markets and trade were free. But what did it mean to be free? And, more importantly, *who* was free? Neoliberalism did not exist to serve all people equally. Its promoters did not, for example, consider it necessary to guarantee wages or prices, nor did they seek to promote safety in the workplace. Instead, neoliberal policies benefited elites—that is, the upper classes whose interests were served via opportunities for increased capital accumulation.[21] According to one account, neoliberalism was freedom from governmental limitations:

"from the demands of social justice, from environmental constraints, from collective bargaining and from the taxation that funds public services."[22] Thus, neoliberalism was far from market fundamentalism in a literal sense: instead of a diminished state apparatus or a state that stays away from markets, the neoliberal state was envisioned to guarantee open markets and private property rights. In truth, neoliberalization meant undoing the twentieth-century liberal state.

By this time, Anderson and Wallerstein each had 1968-influenced intellectual and institutional plans already in motion at the NLR and the Braudel Center. It may not have been clear early on that this moment would be a turning point, but, as years passed, radicals realized that global socialism was not nearly as close as it had seemed in 1968. Today, scholars can look at Wallerstein's and Anderson's decisions with the benefit of hindsight, knowing how history would proceed. Their choices, amid unfolding events, reveal how they processed new information and adjusted to changing times. When all turns out as expected, the historical narrative is assumed to be correct, and there is little incentive to develop new concepts. But when events move in the other direction, soul-searching is warranted. Some radical citizens and writers forged ahead as if nothing had happened, as if it were still 1968 and protesters had stayed in the streets. Others simply shifted course, adopting liberal or conservative viewpoints. But another group pressed forward, albeit aware of the difficult road ahead. They reflected on the new milieu, and contemplated what it meant to be radical in a time of ultracapitalism.

For such "resisters," as Razmig Keucheyan called them, the rise of neoliberalism meant downgrading expectations.[23] Molly Andrews met many citizen resisters in the 1980s when she studied lifelong English socialists. Andrews found that her respondents, confronting the rollbacks of Thatcher's government, often imagined the passage of time like a spiral, progressing, moving backward, and then progressing again.[24] The French philosopher Alain Badiou took a similar stance, describing political failure as part of the expected path toward communism. For Badiou, communism would take time, only emerging after repeated attempts; only the capitalists would have people believe that failure was the same thing as impossibility.[25]

Though they were both resisters,[26] Wallerstein's and Anderson's reactions to Thatcherism-Reaganism were rather different than those who still anticipated an egalitarian postcapitalist future. Wallerstein, who met Ilya Prigogine early in the decade, came to see pro-capitalist passions (or, for that matter, anticapitalist passions) as irrelevant for the survival of the system. Prigogine's research in chemistry and physics led to him question scientific assumptions about time, about predictability in the physical world, and about the stability of systems. He found that scientists generally should think of the natural world as possessing a lifespan, having no predetermined course of events. Wallerstein embraced Prigogine's perspective and adopted the principle of uncertainty in his writings. Most notably, he stopped predicting the arrival of socialism as capitalism's heir.

Anderson, by contrast, believed that capitalism needed committed revolutionaries to be overthrown, at least in the decades ahead. Neoliberalism in his view signaled capitalism's increasing dominance. He was greatly disappointed by the lack of socialist advancement and doubted his ability to lead the *New Left Review*. Thus, as Wallerstein grew more committed to a detached analysis of the operations of capitalism, Anderson saw socialism slipping away.

From this point on, they had opposing interpretations of what was happening on the world scene. Wallerstein saw the collapse of communist party states in Eastern Europe as a sign of capitalism's instability. He, therefore, concluded that the modern world-system's days were numbered. Anderson in the 1990s saw the demise of the Warsaw zone to be a victory for the capitalists and a sign of capitalism's strength. He concluded it was the Right that won the twentieth century, and that the best the Left could do would be to remain anticapitalist and not give in to the Center.

In this century, Wallerstein and Anderson both wrote about U.S. foreign policy. Wallerstein retired from SUNY Binghamton in 1999 and moved to a research post at Yale. Anderson continued in his position at UCLA for an additional two decades. Time in the United States, combined with their longstanding interest in hegemony, steered both toward writing about American politics and its role in the world. But here, too, Wallerstein and Anderson diverged: whereas the former saw decline, the latter considered American hegemony to be intact.

Remarkably, Wallerstein and Anderson continued to express similar positions on human agency. Wallerstein believed that the relative power of activists increased greatly during times of systemic crisis. When the capitalist world-economy was healthy, there was very little that humans could do to dislodge the system (though some great powers have tried). But as the system became increasingly unstable, Wallerstein thought that the actions of humans could have a considerable impact. People could not save capitalism. But, he surmised, they could determine what kind of system would replace it—namely, whether such a system will be more egalitarian or more inegalitarian. He imagined times of transition to be like states of nature: without rules, unpredictable, and often violent. In Anderson's interpretation, capitalism remained robust as a system. Still, he also believed that anticapitalists of the twentieth and twenty-first centuries were armed with knowledge that workers of previous centuries did not have: they had achieved class consciousness, they understood their role in an exploitative process, and they had some practice in organizational strategies and tactics. Yet, understanding the appeal of right-wing populism, both writers also realized that people would not be automatically drawn to Left organizations. In Wallerstein's opinion, voters who turned to the Far Right, to candidates who worked against the economic interests of the lower classes, were not suffering from "false consciousness." Instead, reasoning that establishment policymakers had not served them well, such voters turned to unconventional candidates for a different mode of governing. Wallerstein asked: "Is this so implausible?"[27] Anderson reached a similar conclusion. In his view, Far Right parties and candidates did well when voter desperation exceeded voter apprehension, that is, when citizens felt they had nothing left to lose.[28] For Wallerstein and Anderson, the Left once again needed to develop a compelling social narrative, an explanation for the present that took stock of the past. They also saw an opportunity. People were unconvinced by the promises of those in power. Thus, Wallerstein and Anderson thought socialist organizations could potentially make a real difference in the twenty-first century.

Perhaps as a consequence of their stances on human agency, Wallerstein and Anderson returned in the twenty-first century to the projects they had begun in 1974. Anderson wrote about the disingenuous narratives of political elites in the project of European unification, drawing connections to the distant past. Wallerstein wrote about the rhetorical justifications of power, deployed by core states to rationalize their exploitation of the periphery. He continued his series on *The Modern World-System*, but his ambitions exceeded available time. On August 31, 2019, Immanuel Wallerstein died at his home in Connecticut. In his final years, he remained confident in his assessment of the structural crisis of capitalism.

For both thinkers, this century was fundamentally different than its predecessor. Reinvigoration of a theme did not mean the restoration of optimism. The hopefulness of 1968 was gone. Confidence in future socialism diminished in the neoliberal pandemic. What replaced it was something tempered by disappointment. Wallerstein, who had come to believe that all systems had lives, was, to a certain extent, inoculated from the frustrating news of the late twentieth century. Optimism vanished, of course, but what replaced it was something altogether beyond the categories of optimism and pessimism. What replaced it was a serene assurance that capitalism could not recover and that a successor was yet to be born. No amount of information, he thought, could help scholars figure out what would replace capitalism, because the outcome had not been determined. Thus, he put the odds of future egalitarianism (or, for that matter, new forms of exploitation) at fifty-fifty. By contrast, Anderson had no such inoculation. He wanted to be like his comrade Fredric Jameson, who, in a resemblance to Wallerstein, had a more dispassionate attitude. But Anderson's Marxism was intimately connected to the activism of everyday people. He placed too much historical importance on the transition to socialism in movements and in activists not to have his hopes rise and fall with their successes and failures.

The absence of optimism in the writings of Wallerstein, Anderson, and other authors of radical political economy was disheartening for some fellow radicals. But Wallerstein's and Anderson's intellectual productivity did not suffer. In fact, they continued their previous intellectual projects (at least to the extent that they thought continuation was possible), and they began new ones under new circumstances. The question for radicals today may not be whether one should have optimism, but how one can adjust to changing times.

One such issue facing radicals is how to conceptualize the nation-state system. Like Wallerstein and Anderson before them, many radicals have complicated relationships to the state and doubt the stability of the Westphalian system. Wallerstein initially used the nation-state as his unit of analysis. After some time, however, he became convinced that the distinction between the national and the extranational was a false one: to talk of development was to talk of the development of the world-system. Yet Wallerstein never denied the importance of the nation-state. In fact, he thought the creation of the interstate system was part of the modern world-system's formation,[29] and consequently, that failures of nation-state efficacy were indicative of structural crisis.

Anderson at times appeared to use the state as his unit of analysis. But his comparative cross-national research was embedded within the larger complex totality that, like Wallerstein's world-system, contained multiple nation-states. Thus, Anderson's comparative perspective was often about interconnected cases within a larger system (though he rarely used the term). In truth, his detachment from the state was more personal than

Wallerstein's. Anderson attributed his lack of national attachment to his childhood: moving frequently, he later thought, had ensured that he did not develop the kind of patriotism common for others.

In moving beyond the state as their unit of analysis, Wallerstein and Anderson provided a model for research during potential periods of international transformation. For some time, scholars of international relations have wondered whether the modern interstate system is giving way to some other form of political organization.[30] Previously, it may have mattered less if social scientists placed too much efficacy in the nation-state: indeed, states were prominent players on the world stage. But, in a time of systemic uncertainty, it is now possible to falsely prop up the state in academic discourse even as its effectual power declines.

It could be that all of this questioning is for nothing. There are two possible outcomes to the current crisis: either the capitalist nation-state system will continue on as usual, or, it will transform into another kind of system. The crisis of 2008 could be, as the prevailing explanation teaches, part of the normal rhythms of capitalism. In this outcome, the state system and the capitalist economy might persist for some time. But the crisis of 2008 could also be, as the unconventional explanation teaches, a crisis of the system itself. If this case, then two pillars of the modern world may be crumbling. A shift away from states will aid social science in either outcome.

There may also be a kind of existentialist lesson from discovering (or rediscovering) the lives of Immanuel Wallerstein and Perry Anderson. According to Sarah Bakewell, we might think about biography as the search for turning points, "those moments in which a person makes a choice about some situation, and thus changes everything."[31] In such periods of creativity, we, the observers, "catch a person in the very act of turning existence into essence."[32] We are influenced by our circumstances—biological, cultural, political, and economic. Wallerstein and Anderson adopted a similar attitude about their own lives as well as writing about the lives of others, thinking of essence in terms of crucial turning points. Anderson emphasized conjunctures, points in time when history shifts course. As we have seen, his political coming of age occurred with the events of 1956, and shifted once again in 1968. Though he avoided the term *conjuncture*, Wallerstein also stressed the importance of crucial turning points and the realizations that came about in those moments. For him, the year 1968 was the most important of the century. Wallerstein, Anderson, and other radicals used particular years as expressions of social trends, extending three to five years (though Anderson's time frames were frequently shorter).

More generally, the radical perspective offers something that other traditions of political economy do not. The radical obsession with the just society, even if pursued by cautious intellectuals, may provide a kind of moral sustenance for which writers of international political economy have been looking. Classical liberal international relations theorists, after all, believed in the postwar age that their writings could contribute to a more peaceful world. Radical writers of the twenty-first century believe their writings can contribute to a more just world. They could very well be wrong. It is nonetheless worth the effort.

Notes

Introduction

1. For a transcript see, "President Bush's Speech to the Nation on the Economic Crisis," *The New York Times*, September 24, 2008: https://nyti.ms/2ow5DdD.

2. See, for example, Daniel Drezner, *The System Worked* (Oxford: Oxford University Press, 2014); Timothy F. Geithner, *Stress Test* (New York: Crown, 2014); Stephen C. Nelson and Peter J. Katzenstein, "Uncertainty, Risk, and the Financial Crisis of 2008," *International Organization* 68, no. 2 (2014): 361–92.

3. Definitions of capitalism vary. Typically, though not always, one means an economic system specific to the modern world that relies on at least two of the following characteristics: private ownership of production, wage labor, profit maximization, and the endless accumulation of capital (by which one means stored value).

4. See, for example: Samir Amin, *The Implosion of Contemporary Capitalism* (New York: Monthly Review, 2013); Benjamin Kunkel, *Utopia or Bust* (London: Verso, 2014); Wolfgang Streeck, "How Will Capitalism End?" *New Left Review* II/87 (2014): 35–64; Martin Wolf, *The Shifts and the Shocks* (New York: Penguin, 2014).

5. Benjamin J. Cohen, *International Political Economy: An Intellectual History* (Princeton: Princeton University Press, 2008).

6. Subsequent generations of IPE have classified their forebears into an "American School" and a "British School" (Cohen 2008). Others, however, have used dichotomies such as *Positivist vs. Critical, Rationalist vs. Continental*, or *Orthodox vs. Heterodox* (Murphy and Nelson 2001). More recently, scholars called attention to other splits, such as *Mainstream vs. Critical* (Cafruny et al. 2016) and *Traditional IPE vs. Cultural Political Economy* (Best and Paterson 2010). Craig N. Murphy and Douglas R. Nelson, "International Political Economy: A Tale of Two Heterodoxies," *British Journal of Politics and International Relations* 3, no. 3 (2001): 393–412. Alan Cafruny, Leila Simona Talani, and Gonzalo Pozo Martin, eds., *The Palgrave Handbook of Critical International Political Economy* (London:

Palgrave, 2016). Jacqueline Best and Matthew Paterson, *Cultural Political Economy* (London: Routledge, 2010).

7. Murphy and Nelson 2001, 398.

8. Cohen 2008, 66–94.

9. In place of "school," this work uses a less fixed label of *tradition*, which it defines as a group of scholars with similar beliefs but without a dogmatic or rigid adherence to a single set of principles.

10. Craig N. Murphy, "Do the Left-Out Matter?" *New Political Economy* 14, no. 3 (2009): 357–65.

11. Cafruny et al. 2016.

12. It should be noted that categories are intellectual convinces that can help make sense of a complicated world, and, as such, cannot account for all cases. Robert Cox comes to mind as a syncretic thinker who might be especially resistant to typologies.

13. Stanley Aronowitz, *Taking it Big: C. Wright Mills and the Making of Political Intellectuals* (New York: Columbia University Press, 2012), 189.

14. Over the last several decades, many political intellectuals have moved into universities, and, consequently, relinquished their popular orientation. According to Russell Jacoby, whereas intellectuals used to write for the public, many today choose to write for other academics. *The Last Intellectuals: American Culture in the Age of Academe* (New York: Basic Books, [1987] 2000).

15. See, for example, two seminal works: E. H. Carr, *What Is History?* (New York: Random House, 1961); John A. Garraty, *The Nature of Biography* (New York: Alfred A. Knopf, 1957).

16. Quoted in Jan Willem Stutje, *Ernest Mandel: A Rebel's Dream Deferred*, trans. Christopher Beck and Peter Drucker (London: Verso, 2009), 254.

17. This is the category of scientific history that Nietzsche rejects outright in *On the Advantage and Disadvantage of History for Life*, trans. Peter Preuss (Indianapolis: Hackett [1874] 1980), 13–14.

18. Ibid., 21–22.

19. Many intellectuals pair their vision of history with a vision of morality. Those who adhere to Nietzsche's category of critical history are also often concerned with historical injustices (that is, correcting inequalities, such as those based on class, gender, or race). For a pairing of Nietzsche's historical categories with the moral codes of social movement scholars, see Cyrus Ernesto Zirakzadeh, "For What Do We Cheer? Nietzsche, Moral Stands, and Social Movement Research," *New Political Science* 35, no. 3 (2013): 492–506.

20. James N. Rosenau, "Mapping and Organizing the Journeys," in *Journeys through World Politics: Autobiographical Reflections of Thirty-Four Academic Travelers*, ed. Joseph Kruzel and James N. Rosenau (Lexington, MA: Lexington Books, 1989), 3.

21. Perry Anderson, "Renewals," *New Left Review* II/1 (2000): 5–24.

22. This position was most famously articulated by Francis Fukuyama, "The End of History?" *The National Interest*, summer issue (1989): 3–18.

23. Hobsbawm interview by Jeremy Paxman, "Newsnight," *BBC News*, January 19, 2012: http://news.bbc.co.uk/2/hi/programmes/newsnight/96826.

24. Slavoj Žižek is one such figure urging restraint, though his views are substantially different than the protagonists of this work. But an insight may be applicable. He believed that the record of communist parties has been so dismal, an outright betrayal of their rhetoric, that anticapitalists should put their plans on hold. In his opinion, if the mantra of the twentieth century was that the time for thinking was over and the time for acting had begun, the mantra of the twenty-first century should be that the time for acting should be paused and the time for thinking should take priority. For an interview, see "Don't Act. Just Think," *Big Think*, August 28, 2012: http://bigthink.com/videos/dont-act-just-think. See also: Stanley Aronowitz, *Left Turn* (Boulder: Paradigm, 2006); Nick Srnicek and Alex Williams, *Inventing the Future* (London: Verso, 2015); and, Roberto Mangabeira Unger, *The Left Alternative* (London: Verso, 2009).

25. Some readers may find "human agency" a redundant and strange term. Here, I borrow from Perry Anderson, who drew a distinction between the agent as "active initiator" and agent as "passive instrument." The latter brings to mind "phrases like 'agents of a foreign power' and 'agents for a merchant bank'" (1980, 18). Thus, his use of "human agency" (e.g., 1980, 3, 52, 125, 144 fn25) distinguished the agency of individual humans from the agency of institutions (such as banks or foreign powers), or even from the agency of structures. Admittedly, institutions and structures are comprised of individuals, but with different mechanisms for initiating change. See *Arguments Within English Marxism* (London: Verso, 1980).

26. In fact, in 2010, the International Studies Association organized a conference in New Orleans on the gap between scholarship and policymaking. Thomas G. Weiss and Elizabeth R. DeSombre, Call for Papers: "Theory vs. Policy? Connecting Scholars and Practitioners," International Studies Association (2010): www.isanet.org.

27. Joseph S. Nye, "Bridging the Gap between Theory and Policy," *Political Psychology* 29, no. 4 (2008): 593–603; Joseph S. Nye, "Scholars on the Sidelines," op-ed for *The Washington Post*, April 13, 2009: http://www.washingtonpost.com/wp-dyn/content/article/2009/04/12/AR2009041202260.html; Robert Jervis, "Bridges, Barriers, and Gaps: Research and Policy," *Political Psychology* 29, no. 4 (2008): 571–92; Alexander George, *Bridging the Gap: Theory and Practice in Foreign Policy* (Washington, DC: United States Institute of Peace, 1993).

28. Stephen M. Walt, "The Relationship between Theory and Policy in International Relations," *Annual Review of Political Science* 8 (2005): 23–48, 42. Also see his blog post for *Foreign Policy*, "The Cult of Irrelevance," April 15, 2009: http://walt.foreignpolicy.com/posts/2009/04/15/the_cult_of_irrelevance.

29. Of course, there are risks in searching for lessons from pioneers. Biographical portraits often take on a sympathetic tone. The goal of this book is not to be uncritical. Hagiography would be a disservice to the radical tradition. Thus, this work also examines flaws and contradictions in their work. It is necessary to expose imperfections. Like Stephen H. Marshall, who wanted to avoid "nostalgic veneration" of prophetic African American intellectuals, I too hope to reveal both the advancements and limitations of an intellectual tradition. Stephen H. Marshall, *The City on the Hill from Below: The Crisis of Prophetic Black Politics* (Philadelphia: Temple University Press, 2011).

30. This work relies on many sources of information. The data analyzed in this piece consist of published and unpublished documents. Over nearly seven decades, Anderson and Wallerstein wrote dozens of books and hundreds of articles. My research was aided by archival documents held at Binghamton University (cited as the Wallerstein Papers), Columbia University, and the *New Left Review*. I have cited the original source whenever possible. Internal *New Left Review* documents, however, were acquired on the condition of anonymity. I organized the data chronologically and thematically. Comparing numerous pieces helped substantiate the validity of the findings. I also interviewed Wallerstein at his Yale office. We spoke for more than an hour, with no topics prohibited from discussion. Citations are to the published version: Interview with Immanuel Wallerstein by Gregory P. Williams, "Retrospective on the Origins of World-Systems Analysis," *Journal of World-Systems Research* 19, no. 2 (2013): 202–10.

31. For an overview, see Peregrine Schwartz-Shea and Dvora Yanow, *Interpretive Research Design* (New York: Routledge, 2012).

32. Shaul R. Shenhav, *Analyzing Social Narratives* (London: Routledge, 2015).

33. This was one of Carr's (1961) main points. Robert E. Goodin and Charles Tilly also express this dual conceptualization of political context in their introduction to the edited volume, *The Oxford Handbook of Contextual Political Analysis* (Oxford: Oxford University Press, 2006).

34. Schwartz-Shea and Yanow 2012, 52.

35. Ibid., 100–104.

36. Carr 1961, 51.

37. Following recent memoirs by Stuart Hall and Benedict Anderson, and keeping with biographical practice, this work prioritizes the chronologically expressed narrative. Thomas Barfield stated this idea well in his history of Afghanistan. The point, he wrote, was to address theoretical models as well as historical events, but in a way that holds the reader's interest (2010, 15). I hope I have done the same. Stuart Hall, *Familiar Stranger: A Life between Two Islands*, with Bill Schwarz (Durham: Duke University Press, 2017); Benedict Anderson, *A Life Beyond Boundaries* (London: Verso, 2016); and Thomas Barfield, *Afghanistan: A Cultural and Political History* (Princeton: Princeton University Press, 2010).

Citations for Benedict Anderson are noted as "B. Anderson," while citations for Perry are listed as "Anderson."

38. George Monbiot, *How Did We Get into This Mess? Politics, Equality, Nature* (London: Verso, 2016), 1.

39. In chronological order: Gregory Elliott, *Perry Anderson: The Merciless Laboratory of History* (Minneapolis: University of Minnesota Press, 1998); Paul Blackledge, *Perry Anderson, Marxism, and the New Left* (London: Merlin Press, 2004); and Duncan Thompson, *Pessimism of the Intellect? A History of* New Left Review (London: Merlin Press, 2007), hereafter cited as D. Thompson.

40. See, most notably, Walter Goldfrank's writings, including: "Paradigm Regained? The Rules of Wallerstein's World-System Method," *Journal of World-Systems Research* 6, no. 2 (2000): 150–95; "Wallerstein's World-System: Roots and Contributions," in *Routledge Handbook of World-Systems Analysis*, ed. Salvatore J. Babones and Christopher Chase-Dunn (London: Routledge, 2012). See also: Charles Ragin and Daniel Chirot, "The World System of Immanuel Wallerstein: Sociology and Politics as History," in *Vision and Method in Historical Sociology*, ed. Theda Skocpol (Cambridge: Cambridge University Press, 1984), 276–312.

Chapter 1

1. Wallerstein interview by Carlos Antonio Aguirre Rojas, "The World-Systems Analysis Perspective," in *Uncertain Worlds: World-Systems Analysis in Changing Times* (Boulder: Paradigm, 2012a), 4.

2. William L. O'Neill, *A Better World: The Great Schism: Stalinism and the American Intellectuals* (New York: Simon and Schuster, 1982), 13.

3. Ibid.

4. Wallerstein interview by Rojas 2012a, 4.

5. Ibid., 8.

6. Immanuel Wallerstein, *The Essential Wallerstein* (New York: The New Press, 2000), xv.

7. Immanuel Wallerstein, "Revolution and Order," *Federalist Opinion* 1, no. 7 (1951): 23–26.

8. Ibid., 25–26.

9. Wallerstein interview by Rojas 2012a, 13.

10. Ibid., 6.

11. Wallerstein reflected: "I didn't want to join. In those days, you were drafted. . . . You got exempted through college, and then they drafted you after that. . . . There was no big movement to evade [at the time]." In discussion with the author (May 2010).

12. Wallerstein interview by Williams 2013, 207.

13. Charles Lemert, "Wallerstein and the Uncertain Worlds," in *Uncertain Worlds: World-Systems Analysis in Changing Times* (Boulder: Paradigm, 2012a), 154–156.

14. When asked about this expression (from 2000, xi), Wallerstein added: "I was a product of Columbia sociology, but I was also a heretic. . . . [T]hey tolerated me, because I was a good scholar, and because I was one of the family. But a number of years later, [Paul] Lazarfeld said of me and Terry Hopkins that we were 'His Majesty's loyal opposition'" (interview by Williams 2013, 207).

15. Immanuel Wallerstein, *McCarthyism and the Conservative*, Master of Arts Thesis, 1954. Columbia University, Rare Book and Manuscript Archive.

16. For other works that consider Wallerstein as a New York Intellectual, see: Albert J. Bergesen, "The Columbia Social Essayists," *Journal of World-System Research* 6, no. 2 (2000): 198–213; Harvey J. Kaye, "Totality: Its Application to Historical and Social Analysis by Wallerstein and Genovese," *Historical Reflections* 6, no. 2 (1979): 405–20; Christopher Chase-Dunn and Hiroko Inoue, "Immanuel Wallerstein," *The Wiley-Blackwell Companion to Major Social Theorists, Volume 2, Contemporary Social Theorists, ed.* George Ritzer and Jeffrey Stepinsky (Chichester: John Wiley, 2011).

17. Wallerstein interview by Williams 2013, 207.

18. Wallerstein 1954, 4.

19. Ibid., 5.

20. Wallerstein's practical conservative was similar to Richard Hofstadter's notion of a pseudo-conservative. Wallerstein's thesis cited Hofstadter's then unpublished essay "Dissent and Nonconformity in the Twentieth Century," originally given as a lecture at Barnard College, March 1954 (1954, 5, 13n7). Hofstadter's work appeared in print later that year under the title, "The Pseudo-Conservative Revolt." Hofstadter also cited the younger scholar's thesis in his essay, "Pseudo-Conservatism Revisited" (1965, 84fn5). This supports Wallerstein's modest claim that his own thesis was "well-received" (2000, xvi). Richard Hofstadter, "The Pseudo-Conservative Revolt," in *The Paranoid Style in American Politics* (Cambridge: Harvard University Press, [1954] 1965), 41–65; and, from the same book, "Pseudo-Conservatism Revisited" (1965), 66–91.

21. Wallerstein 1954, 8.

22. Immanuel Wallerstein, letter to Senator Joseph McCarthy, November 14, 1953. Wallerstein Papers, Box 35, Folder: "Thesis MA."

23. Wallerstein 1954, vi.

24. Ibid., 21, 25.

25. Ibid., 50.

26. Ibid., 18, 55–56.

27. Ibid., 97–98.

28. Ibid., v. Consistent with the style at the time, Wallerstein's earliest writings use gendered language. His later writings use gender-neutral language. See,

for example, the 1988 piece "The Ideological Tensions of Capitalism: Universalism Versus Racism and Sexism" (reprinted in Wallerstein 2000). Nonetheless, I have chosen not to sanitize his writing, allowing readers to draw their own conclusions.

29. Wallerstein said that his thesis "was important in understanding what was going on politically in the United States, but then, by extension, actually in many parts of the world, which is still going on" (interview by Williams 2013, 207).

30. Wallerstein 2000, xvii.

31. Wallerstein's dissertation was later published as *The Road to Independence: Ghana and the Ivory Coast* (Paris: Mouton, 1964).

32. Immanuel Wallerstein, *The Emergence of Two West African Nations: Ghana and the Ivory Coast* (PhD Dissertation, Columbia University, 1959), ix.

33. Wallerstein 1959, xii–xiii, 7.

34. Ibid., 279.

35. Ibid., xv.

36. Ibid., 276–77.

37. Wallerstein interview by Rojas 2012a, 4.

38. Perry Anderson interview by Harry Kreisler, "Reflections on the Left from the Left: Conversation with Perry Anderson," *Conversations with History* (2001): https://conversations.berkeley.edu/anderson_2001.

39. Office for National Statistics. "Births Registered in July, August and September, 1938," General Register Office, England and Wales Civil Registration (Vol. 1a, p. 482).

40. B. Anderson 2016, 119.

41. *Burke's Irish Family Records*, ed. Hugh Montgomery-Massingberd (London: Burke's Peerage, 2007).

42. Benedict Anderson, *Language and Power: Exploring Political Cultures in Indonesia* (Ithaca: Cornell University Press, 1990), 2.

43. B. Anderson 2016, 5–6.

44. Ibid., 1.

45. A great deal of Perry Anderson's knowledge about his father came as an adult, reading through the elder Anderson's papers housed at China's Second National Archive. The product of years of research, an essay on Shaemas Anderson appeared in *Spectrum: From Right to Left in the World of Ideas* (London: Verso, 2005).

46. B. Anderson 2016, 12–13.

47. D. Thompson 2007, 9; Elliott 1998, 1.

48. B. Anderson 2016, 14–16.

49. Anderson interview by Kreisler 2001.

50. Anderson interview by Kreisler 2001. Benedict recalled a similar story (B. Anderson 2016, 25).

51. "If I had been born later, I could have become addicted to the television set, and too lazy to go the local theatre" (B. Anderson 2016, 2).

52. Stuart Hall, "The Life and Times of the First New Left," *New Left Review* II/61 (2010): 177.
53. Anderson interview by Kreisler, 2001.
54. Hall 2010, 177.
55. ULR Editors, "Editorial and Contents," *Universities and Left Review* 1 (1957).
56. The piece with Blackburn was "Cuba, Free Territory of America," in *New University* 4, 1960 (cited in Blackledge 2004, 5, and Elliott 1998, 2). The translation was titled, "A Tour with Fidel Castro."
57. Dennis Dworkin, *Cultural Marxism in Postwar Britain: History, the New Left, and the Origins of Cultural Studies* (Durham: Duke University Press, 1997).
58. Harvey J. Kaye, *The British Marxist Historians*, 2nd ed. (New York: St. Martin's, 1995).
59. Dworkin 1997, 16.
60. D. Thompson 2007, 1.
61. Dworkin 1997, 16.
62. Hall 2010, 184.
63. D. Thompson 2007, 5.
64. In order, these were: "Sweden: Mr. Crosland's Dreamland, Part 1," *New Left Review* I/7 (1961a): 4–12; "Sweden: Mr. Crosland's Dreamland, Part 2," *New Left Review* I/9 (1961b): 34–45; and, with Stuart Hall, "Politics of the Common Market," *New Left Review* I/10 (1961): 1–14.
65. NLR Editors, "Notes to Readers," *New Left Review* I/12 (Nov.–Dec. 1961).
66. Robin Blackburn mentioned that there were three individuals who righted the ship. A separate source, however, identified them by name. Robin Blackburn, Letter to Contributors, March 19, 1993; and Christopher Bertram et al., "Resignations from the Editorial Board of *New Left Review*," Feb. 24, 1993. Wallerstein Papers, Box 58, Folder: "New Left Review."
67. The change was announced to readers later on, in two statements in the March–April issue: "To Our Readers" (1964a): 3–4; and "Statement (On Editorial Team)" (1964b): 112.
68. This would be a rarity, since Anderson has at other points allowed several years to pass by without publishing an article of his own. The first article analyzed the Italian Communist Party's reaction to Khrushchev's famous 1956 speech, while the other three focused on Portugal. Perry Anderson, "The Debate of the Central Committee of the Italian Communist Party on the 22nd Congress of the CPSU," *New Left Review* I/13–14 (Jan.–April 1962a): 152–60; Perry Anderson, "Portugal and the End of Ultra Colonialism," *New Left Review* I/15 (May–June 1962b): 83–102; Perry Anderson, "Portugal and the End of Ultra Colonialism 2," *New Left Review* I/16 (July–Aug. 1962c): 88–122; Perry Anderson, "Portugal and the End of Ultra Colonialism 3," *New Left Review* I/17 (Winter 1962d): 85–114; Italian Communist Party, "Text of the Debate of the Central Committee of the

Italian Communist Party on the 22nd Congress of the CPSU," *New Left Review* I/13–14 (Jan.–April 1962): 161–91.

69. The debts that Anderson and the rest of the editorial committee inherited were slowly paid off until 1967, when the NLR produced a surplus. "A Decennial Report" (Unpublished NLR document, 1975), 23.

70. Hall 2010, 189–90.

71. Ibid., 190.

72. Anderson interview by Kreisler, 2001.

73. Perry Anderson, "Conspectus," unpublished manuscript (1964a), 1.

74. Perry Anderson, "The Left in the Fifties," *New Left Review* I/29 (1965a): 11.

75. Ibid., 12.

76. Ibid.

77. NLR Editors, "On Internationalism," *New Left Review* I/18 (1963): 3–4.

78. "A Decennial Report" 1975, 73.

79. Elliott 1998, 13.

80. There is slight disagreement on which articles are part of the Nairn-Anderson theses. The most inclusive listing is as follows, in chronological order: Nairn, "The British Political Elite," no. 23 January–February (1964a); Anderson, "Origins of the Present Crisis," no. 23 January–February (from 1964), referenced here in its reprinted and revised form in *English Questions* (London: Verso, 1992a); Nairn, "The English Working Class," no. 24 March–April (1964b); Nairn, "Hugh Gaitskell," no. 25 May–June (1964c); Nairn, "The Nature of the Labour Party—I," no. 27 September–October (1964d): 38–65; Nairn, "The Nature of the Labour Party—II," no. 28 November–December (1964e); Anderson, "The Left in the Fifties," no. 29 January–February (1965a); and, Nairn, "Labour Imperialism," no. 32 July–August (1965).

81. The editorial team remarked that writings on Britain were a new direction for the journal, away, momentarily, from its global orientation. Readers, however, may see it as a logical extension of NLR's internationalization from the year before, since Anderson and the editors conceived of British socialism as caught up in shifting international structures (NLR Editors 1963, 3).

82. Perry Anderson, "Components of the National Culture," *New Left Review* I/50 (1968): 11fn9.

83. Anderson 1992a, 55fn8.

84. Ibid., 4.

85. Paul Blackledge saw connections between Nairn-Anderson and specific ideas from three works: Gramsci's *Prison Notebooks* and the fight against the state and bourgeois values in Italy, as well as the idea of hegemony; Sartre's *The Communists and Peace*, and what it means to identify as bourgeois or proletarian in France; and, Lukács's *The Destruction of Reason*, and the teleological interpretation of the rise of Nazism in Germany (2004, 14–17). Each of these

works was only later made available to an English-speaking audience. Gramsci's *Prison Notebooks*, written between 1929 and 1935, were only later organized and translated. Lukács's manuscript was composed in the early 1950s. And Sartre's book was originally a series of articles in *Les Tempes Modernes* between 1952 and 1954. Antonio Gramsci, *Selections from the Prison Notebooks*, trans. and ed. Quinton Hoare and Geoffrey Nowell Smith (New York: International Publishers, 1971); Jean-Paul Sartre, *The Communists and Peace* (London: Hamilton, 1968); Georg Lukács, *The Destruction of Reason* (London: Merlin, 1980).

86. "A Decennial Report" 1975, 13–15; Blackledge 2004, 20; Elliott 1998, 13; D. Thompson 2007, 12.

87. Anderson 1992a, 3–4.

88. "The Antinomies of Antonio Gramsci," *New Left Review* I/100 (Nov.–Dec. 1976a): 5–78. See also, *A Zone of Engagement* (London: Verso, 1992b). For comments, see Anderson 1992b, x–xi.

89. In the 2010s, Anderson produced three books dealing with hegemony and other concepts of which Gramsci was an innovator. These were: an intellectual history of hegemony, *The H-Word: The Peripeteia of Hegemony* (London: Verso, 2017a); an updated appraisal, *The Antinomies of Antonio Gramsci* (London: Verso, 2017b); and, to a lesser extent, Anderson's criticism of American hegemony, *American Foreign Policy and Its Thinkers* (London: Verso, 2015).

90. Anderson 1992a, 43.
91. Ibid., 46.
92. Ibid., 30.
93. Ibid., 17.
94. Ibid., 19.
95. Ibid., 30.
96. Ibid., 30–31.
97. Ibid., 23.
98. Ibid., 37.
99. Ibid., 23–27.
100. Anderson 1965a, 4.
101. Anderson 1992a, 47.
102. Anderson 1965a, 4.
103. Anderson 1962b, 1962c, 1962d.
104. Anderson 1962d, 86.

Chapter 2

1. Wallerstein has also mentioned intellectuals such as Schumpeter and Freud, along with the Frankfurt School, as influential for his thinking. Still, his most frequent references, from which one can draw the clearest connections to

his work, are to those listed above. For comparison, see: Wallerstein 2000, xi, xxii; interview by Rojas 2012a, 5; interview by Charles Lemert, "A Discussion of the Itinerary of World-Systems Analysis and Its Uncertainties," in *Uncertain Worlds: World-Systems Analysis in Changing Times* (Boulder: Paradigm, 2012b), 107; and, interview by P. Schouten, "Theory Talk #13: Immanuel Wallerstein on World-Systems, the Imminent End of Capitalism and Unifying Social Science," *Theory Talks* (2008): http://www.theory-talks.org/2008/08/theory-talk-13.html.

2. Some readers, for example, might think to add Terence K. Hopkins or Andre Gunder Frank to the list of intellectual mentors. Hopkins, who was year ahead of Wallerstein in graduate school, served as a kind of instructor for Wallerstein. It was Hopkins, after all, who graded the papers Wallerstein submitted in "Sociological Analysis," a first-year course for Columbia graduate students (Wallerstein 1998a). Frank, too, had been working on relations of dependency for a few years by the time Wallerstein published the *Modern World-System I*. In fact, he wrote an advertising blurb for its dust jacket. Yet neither Hopkins nor Frank revolutionized Wallerstein's thought in the way that others did. This is not to say that Wallerstein did not learn from them, but that they were as much friendships as anything else. Frank has expressed this sentiment too: he, Wallerstein, Samir Amin, and Giovanni Arrighi were "likened" by Frank's wife "to the 'Canasta Club' of the same old ladies in tennis shoes, going around to each other's homes to play" (2000, 218–19 fn1). Immanuel Wallerstein, "Pedagogy and Scholarship," in *Mentoring Methods and Movements: Colloquium in Honor of Terence K. Hopkins by his Former Students*, ed. Immanuel Wallerstein (Binghamton, NY: Fernand Braudel Center, 1998a), 47–52; Andre Gunder Frank, "Immanuel and Me Without Hyphen." *Journal of World Systems Research* 6, no. 2 (2000): 216–31.

3. Three essays are particularly useful for learning Wallerstein's thoughts about Marx: "Marx and History: Fruitful and Unfruitful Emphases," *Thesis Eleven* 8 (1984a): 92–101; and, "Marx and Underdevelopment" and "Marxism as Utopias: Evolving Ideologies," originally published in 1985 and 1986, respectively, and reprinted in *Unthinking Social Science: The Limits of Nineteenth-Century Paradigms*, 2nd ed (Philadelphia: Temple University Press, 2001), 151–84.

4. See Wallerstein: 2001, 152 and 182; and 1984a, 92.

5. Wallerstein interview by Williams 2013, 204.

6. See, for example, Wallerstein's interview with *RT* (October 2011): http://youtu.be/eDgya5clTCY.

7. Wallerstein interview by Rojas 2012a, 19. Elsewhere, he wondered: Who has not been influenced by the likes of Marx and Freud? It was hardly a unique quality. "Most of us have been, at least somewhat, marked by these men." Immanuel Wallerstein, "Frantz Fanon: Reason and Violence," *Berkeley Journal of Sociology* 15 (1970): 223.

8. "Fanon and the Revolutionary Class," originally published in 1979, reprinted in *The Essential Wallerstein* (2000), 14.

9. "Reading Fanon in the 21st Century," *New Left Review* II/57 (May–June 2009a): 124.
10. Ibid.
11. Wallerstein 2000, 22.
12. Ibid., 31.
13. "The Bourgeois(ie) as Concept and Reality," which originally appeared in a 1988 issue of the *New Left Review*, reprinted in Wallerstein 2000, 324–43.
14. Ibid., 317.
15. "Upper," "middle," and "lower" appear throughout Wallerstein's writings. For representative (but not exhaustive) examples of other terms in major works, see: "working" (1989, 63); "capitalist" (1989, 86); "educated" (2011a, 148); "dominant" (1980, 19); and, "privileged" (2011a, 156). *The Modern World-System II: Mercantilism and the Consolidation of the European World-Economy, 1600–1750* (New York: Academic Press, 1980); *The Modern World-System III: The Second Era of Great Expansion of the Capitalist World-Economy, 1730–1840s* (New York: Academic Press, 1989); and, *The Modern World-System IV: Centrist Liberalism Triumphant* (Berkeley: University of California Press, 2011a).
16. Wallerstein 1989, 103.
17. Wallerstein 2000, 316.
18. Ibid., 14.
19. Wallerstein has recalled this statement in slightly different forms (2000, 14; 2009a, 118).
20. Wallerstein 2000, 14.
21. Wallerstein 1970, 225; original underlining.
22. Ibid., 227.
23. Immanuel Wallerstein, *The Uncertainties of Knowledge* (Philadelphia: Temple University Press, 2004a), 87–88.
24. Ibid., 87.
25. See Carlos Antonio Aguirre Rojas, "Immanuel Wallerstein and the Critical 'World-Systems Analysis' Perspective," in *Uncertain Worlds: World-Systems Analysis in Changing Times* (Boulder: Paradigm, 2012b), vii–xl.
26. Braudel was unafraid of quantification and tabulations of agricultural production, characteristics that Wallerstein attributed to two conditions: being born into peasant life, and a genetic affinity for calculation (Braudel's father, after all, worked as a mathematics professor) (Wallerstein 2001, 188). Wallerstein, whose urban upbringing could not have been more different, also displayed a comfort with mathematical and scientific concepts.
27. The original title was *Annales d'histoire économique et sociale*. In 1946, it changed to *Annales: economies, societies, civilizations* (or *Annales: ESC*).
28. Fortune permitted Braudel and Febvre to meet on a ship bound for Europe from Brazil. Their friendship affected Braudel's intellectual trajectory as well as his institutional affiliation. One of the many French citizens captured in

1940, Braudel spent most of World War II in a German military prison. Books and correspondence from Febvre gave Braudel direction. Despite his confinement, Braudel was able to finish his thesis. Like Antonio Gramsci or Marc Bloc, Braudel wrote without notes, and thus forged a contemplative style (Wallerstein 2001, 189). In Wallerstein's opinion, Febvre and Braudel gave new life to the VIe Section of the École Pratique des Hautes Études after the war. In 1963, he created a sister organization, the Maison des Sciences de l'Homme (Wallerstein 2001, 189). The institution, literally, was "the house of the sciences of man," which, despite the name, was not intended to be gender exclusionary. See Immanuel Wallerstein, "Braudel on the *Longue Durée*: Problems of Conceptual Translation" *Review* 32, no. 2 (2009b): 158. For more on the historical context of *Annales*, see the essay "Beyond *Annales?*" reprinted in Wallerstein (2001).

29. Peter Burke, "Introduction," in *Economy & Society in Early Modern Europe: Essays from* Annales (New York: Harper Torchbooks, 1972, 1.

30. Ibid.

31. Ibid., 8.

32. For the former, see Eric R. Dursteler, "Fernand Braudel (1902–1985)," in *French Historians, 1900–2000*, ed. Philip Daileader and Philip Whalen (New York: Wiley-Blackwell, 2010), 62–76; for the latter, see Richard E. Lee, "Fernand Braudel, the *Longue Durée*, and World-Systems Analysis," in *The* Longue Durée *and World-Systems Analysis*, ed. Richard E. Lee (Albany: State University of New York Press, 2012), 1–7.

33. This work consulted two of the four available translations into English of Braudel's "History and the Social Sciences: The *Longue Durée*." For decades, Peter Burke's version was commonly referenced by scholars. Then, to celebrate the fiftieth anniversary of Braudel's article, Wallerstein created his own translation, reading the original article carefully, "paragraph by paragraph" (2009b, 156). See trans. Peter Burke in *Economy & Society in Early Modern Europe: Essays from* Annales (New York: Harper Torchbooks, [1958] 1972), 11–42; and trans. Immanuel Wallerstein, *Review* 32, no. 2 ([1958] 2009): 171–203.

34. Braudel [1958] 2009, 182.

35. Wallerstein 2009b, 161.

36. Braudel [1958] 2009, 187.

37. See, for example Burke's translation (Braudel [1958] 1972, 16).

38. Wallerstein 2009b, 162.

39. Braudel [1958] 2009, 202.

40. Braudel [1958] 1972, 19–20.

41. See Lee's outline of various historical times (2012, 3).

42. Wallerstein 2009b, 163.

43. See, for example: Dale Tomich, "The Order of Historical Time: The *Longue Durée* and Micro-History"; and, Peter J. Taylor, "History and Geography: Braudel's 'Extreme *Longue Durée*' as Generics?" Both works appeared in *The*

Longue Durée, ed. Richard E. Lee (Albany: State University of New York Press, 2012), 9–33 and 35–64, respectively.

44. Wallerstein would later attempt to pair a "space" for each of the "times" Braudel discussed, with the following Time-Space associations: Event—Geopolitical, Cyclical—Ideological, *Longue Durée*—Structural, Very Long-Term—Eternal. See, "The Inventions of TimeSpace Realities: Towards and Understanding of our Historical Systems," a 1988 article reprinted in Wallerstein (2001).

45. Braudel wrote about a "world-economy" as early as 1949 (Vol. I, 387). His works encouraged Wallerstein to think about a system as its own world, not as a system that necessarily covered the planet (which will be discussed in chapter 4). Then, in the late seventies, Braudel provided further details on the meaning of a world-economy. Fernand Braudel, *The Mediterranean and the Mediterranean World in the Age of Philip II*, 2 vols., trans. Sián Reynolds (Berkeley: University of California Press, [1949] 1996); and, Fernand Braudel, *Civilization and Capitalism III: The Perspective of the World*, trans. Sián Reynolds (New York: Harper and Row, [1979a] 1984).

46. Wallerstein 2004a, 89.

47. Karl Polanyi, *The Great Transformation: The Political and Economic Origins of our Time* (Boston: Beacon Press, [1944] 2001), 45.

48. See Fred Block and Margaret R. Somers, "Beyond the Economistic Fallacy: The Holistic Social Science of Karl Polanyi," in *Vision and Method in Historical Sociology*, ed. Theda Skocpol (Cambridge: Cambridge University Press, 1984), esp. 63–64.

49. Polanyi [1944] 2001, 45.

50. Ibid., 50–55.

51. In fact, Wallerstein would equate Polanyi's categories of reciprocity, redistribution, and markets with his own typology of world-systems, what he labeled, in order, as mini-systems, world-empires, and world-economies (Wallerstein 2004a, 89) (to be discussed in chapter 4).

52. In taking up this question, Polanyi presaged the transition debate among Marxists in the 1970s (Block and Somers 1984, 80en12).

53. See Polanyi's example of England's Speenhamland Act and its repeal ([1944] 2001, 81–107), as well as Block and Somers's discussion of its importance for understanding Polanyi (1984, 54–57).

54. Immanuel Wallerstein, *Historical Capitalism with Capitalist Civilization* (London: Verso, 1995a).

55. Polanyi [1944] 2001, 49–50.

56. Block and Somers 1984, 62–79.

57. Polanyi, qtd. in Block and Somers 1984, 62.

58. For a comparison, see Bergesen (2000).

59. As with the discussion on Wallerstein, this section avoids describing the influence of Anderson's peers, such as Tom Nairn or Robin Blackburn. With more difficultly, and perhaps more controversy, the influence of Raymond Wil-

liams and Isaac Deutscher is also left out, having already been well documented by Elliott (1998, 3–5) and Blackledge (2004, 2–9).

60. Frank E. Manuel, "Edward Gibbon: Historien-Philosophe," *Daedalus* 105, no. 3 (1976): 231.

61. Anderson 1974b, 163–68.

62. Manuel 1976, 232.

63. Arnaldo Momigliano, "Gibbon's Contribution to Historical Method," *Historia: Zeitschrift für Alte Geschichte* 2, no. 4 (1954): 450–63.

64. David P. Jordan, "Edward Gibbon: The Historian of the Roman Empire." *Daedalus* 105, no. 3 (1976): 1–12.

65. In one chapter of *The New Old World* ("Theories"), for example, Anderson at one point dismissed most scholarship on a particular subject, and then referred readers to a separate work, described as "the best antidote for such dehydration." Perry Anderson, *The New Old World* (London: Verso, 2009), 89. This style has become more common in recent works.

66. Early in *Passages from Antiquity to Feudalism* and *Lineages of the Absolutist State* (or, *Passages-Lineages*), Anderson outlined the historical story he would pursue over roughly the next eight hundred pages: an exposition of the full effects of the fall of Rome (1974a, 18). London: Verso, 1974a and 1974b, respectively.

67. Anderson 1974a, in the order listed: 76; 132 and 135; and 275.

68. See, for example, Anderson 1974a, 275 fn19.

69. Ibid., 9.

70. Perry Anderson, *Considerations on Western Marxism*, 4th ed. (London: Verso, [1976b] 1984), 1–5.

71. Anderson [1976a] 1984, 8–10 and 11–13, respectively.

72. *Passages-Lineages* often contradicted Marx. For example: he was incorrect on the reproduction of modes of production structures (Anderson 1974b, 479); he "oversimplified" the societies in Eastern Europe (Anderson 1974a, 229); and, while he correctly classified the productive character of pastoral social groups as a separate mode of production, he had mistakenly labeled the Mongols as cattle breeders (Anderson 1974a, 219–20 fn3).

73. Anderson 1974b, 23 fn12.

74. Anderson 1992a, 3.

75. Georg Lukács, *History and Class Consciousness*, trans. Rodney Livingstone (Cambridge: The MIT Press, [1923] 1968), 10.

76. Ibid., 28, 11–14.

77. Ibid., 27.

78. Lukács thought it was "perfectly possible for someone to describe the essentials of an historical event and yet be in the dark about the real nature of that event and of its function in the historical totality, i.e. without understanding it as part of a unified historical process" ([1923] 1968, 12).

79. Lukács [1923] 1968, 28.

80. "But class struggle itself is not a causal prius in the sustentation of order, for *classes are constituted by modes of production, and not vice versa.* The one mode of production of which this will not be true is communism—which, precisely, will abolish classes" (Anderson 1980, 55; original emphasis).

81. Lucio Colletti, "A Political and Philosophical Interview," *New Left Review* I/86 (1974): 3–28.

82. Ibid., 7.

83. Quoted in Dworkin 1997, 51.

84. See, for example, Josef Stalin, "Dialectical and Historical Materialism" (1938): https://www.marxists.org/reference/archive/stalin/works/1938/09.htm.

85. Kaye 1995, 59.

86. Stuart Hall, *Cultural Studies 1983: A Theoretical History*, ed. Jennifer Daryl Slack and Lawrence Grossberg (Durham: Duke University Press, 2016), 46.

87. Ibid., 42–43.

88. Ibid., 39.

89. Ibid., 35.

90. Ibid., 118.

91. For Anderson, Thompson's argument possessed a "circular simultaneity between 'values' and 'interests,' 'want' and 'ought,' 'class struggle' and 'moral conflict,' rooted in the expressive totality of experience" (Anderson 1980, 83).

92. Juliet Mitchell, "Women, The Longest Revolution," *New Left Review* I/40 (1966): 16 fn13.

93. Anderson 1980, 125.

94. Anderson lists nine works inspired by Althusser's methods published in the 1970s alone (1980, 126).

95. See, for example, Anderson's comments on France in *The New Old World* (2009, chapter 4).

96. In practice this meant priority was given to ideas, not to the organization of a movement ("A Decennial Report," 1976, 6; Dworkin 1997, 76).

97. A selection of interviews, reprinted in *Conversations with Jean-Paul Sartre* (London: Seagull, 2006), reveal areas of overlap and disagreement between Anderson and Sartre. The interviews, which originally appeared in the *New Left Review* and *L'Arc* between 1967 and 1975, were conducted by Anderson, Ronald Fraser, Quintin Hoare, and Simone de Beauvoir.

98. Sartre interview by Anderson et al. 2006, 7.

99. Ibid., 48.

100. Ibid., 50.

101. Such contradictions created, for Sartre, a "paradoxical object which is an institutional ensemble that is perpetually detotalized" (interview by Anderson et al. 2006, 51).

102. Anderson 1980, 53, 55.

103. According to Anderson, totalization "is not to reduce everything to the economic, but to analyse the present situation *as a totality*, in which the determination of the crisis in each sector is to be located within that sector (and not in the 'base'), while all the sectors together are structurally integrated in a significant whole—founded by their complex social past." "Socialism and Pseudo-Empiricism." *New Left Review* I/35 (1966): 33; original italics.

104. Blackledge 2004, 57.

105. Stutje 2009.

106. In a letter to Anderson, Mandel wrote: Althusser took "everything which is historical, i.e. dialectical in Marxism, and transformed it into a kind of metaphysical neo-positivism . . . without built-in contradictions, without motion" (quoted in Stutje 2009, 129).

107. Mandel wrote that Anderson was "among the handful of Marxists in the world who have made and are making constructive contributions to the development of theory" (quoted in Stutje 2009, 182).

108. Ernest Mandel, "Trotsky's Marxism: an Anti-Critique," *New Left Review* I/47 (1968): 32–51.

109. Anderson [1976b] 1984, 96.

110. Anderson's comments about the Western Marxists might also have been the product of personal reflection, a belief that he had not sufficiently opposed one-party communism. In a memoir, Tariq Ali described his comrade as being quick to defend the actions of communist parties that took guidance from the Soviet Union (2018, 223). Two of Anderson's traits may have caused others to bristle. One, if confronted over the death toll in the name of socialism, Anderson would note the superior scale of destruction in the name of liberalism (a point summed up well by the title of Mike Davis's book, *Late Victorian Holocausts*). And, two, Anderson regarded the Soviet Union as socialist due to the fact that production was controlled by society, not the private sector (Anderson 1965b, 226–27). To some, his minimalist definition was "obscene," for it ignored the role of proletarian class struggle in the creation of a socialist society (Davidson 2012, 445). For Ali, such an argument had an "icy logic": by grouping the Stalinist form with others, one commits an offense against humane socialists (2018, 224). Paradoxically, the minimalist approach led to strong denunciations of Stalin and a warning to socialists. Stalin's actions, Anderson wrote, "remain, irremediably, part of man's attempt to reach socialism in the twentieth century. For they were socialist, not liberal crimes—a violence consciously decided and willed, a deliberate reproduction and magnification of the violence inherent in an environment of scarcity" (1965b, 227). Mike Davis, *Late Victorian Holocausts*, 2nd ed. (London: Verso, 2017); Neil Davidson, *How Revolutionary Were the Bourgeois Revolutions?* (Chicago: Haymarket, 2012); Tariq Ali, *Street Fighting Years*, 2nd ed. (London: Verso, 2018); Perry Anderson, "Problems of Socialist Strategy,"

in *Towards Socialism, ed.* Perry Anderson and Robin Blackburn (London: The Fontana Library, 1965b), 221-90.

111. Anderson [1976b] 1984, 98-99.
112. Ibid., 100.
113. Blackledge 2004, 57.
114. Blackledge (2004, 59) considers Colletti and Althusser to be similar in terms of how they conceived of totalities. For Colletti's description of totalities, see: *From Rousseau to Lenin: Studies in Ideology and Society*, trans. John Merrington and Judith White (New York: Monthly Review Press, 1972), 14.
115. According to Blackledge, "While Althusser's systems could be condemned for its lack of a purchase on the concrete, Colletti's was marred by the opposite weakness, it tended to collapse analysis into description" (2004, 57).
116. In the course of Anderson's interview, for example, Colletti referenced both Dobb and Hobsbawm (1974, 21, and 16 and 25, respectively).
117. For a comparison of the occasionally overlapping interests and methods of Anderson and the British Marxist Historians, see Kaye (1995, 58-62).
118. Wallerstein interview by Williams 2013, 208.

Chapter 3

1. Carol Fink, Philip Gassert, and Detlef Junker, eds., *1968: The World Transformed* (Cambridge: Cambridge University Press, 1998).
2. Wallerstein, *The Politics of Independence* (Lincoln: University of Nebraska Press, [1961] 2005a).
3. Ibid., 153-63.
4. Wallerstein, *The Politics of Unity* (Lincoln: University of Nebraska Press, [1967] 2005b).
5. Ibid., 223.
6. Robert Friedman, "Introduction," in *Up Against the Ivy Wall: A History of the Columbia Crisis*, ed. Jerry Avorn et al. (New York: Atheneum 1968), 3.
7. Quoted in Jerry Avorn et al., eds., *Up Against the Ivy Wall: A History of the Columbia Crisis* (New York: Atheneum 1968), 25-27.
8. Ibid., 74.
9. Ibid., 75.
10. According to one report: "The paradox of negotiations was . . . clear: the students had been listening to offers they would never consider; the faculty had been promising them things the administration would refuse to accept; and the administration had been making concessions which the Trustees . . . rejected out of hand" (Avorn et al. 1968, 145).
11. Ibid., 155.

12. Quoted in Michael Stern, "Teachers at Columbia Risk Violence as Mediators," *The New York Times*, April 30, 1968.

13. Avorn et al 1968, 175–76.

14. Radical Faculty Group, A Public Affirmation, September 12, 1968, original capitalization. Wallerstein Papers, Box 8, Folder: "Ad Hoc Faculty."

15. Radical Faculty Group, September 12, 1968.

16. Wallerstein was uncomfortable not because of his political views, but because of the campus crisis itself. The unease arose, he said, "not because of what I was writing" (interview by Williams 2013, 207).

17. Reprinted in Wallerstein 2000.

18. And, he added, the radical intellectual "must do this without fatalistic optimism. The revolution is only inevitable because people make it so" (Wallerstein 2000, 38).

19. Wallerstein, *University in Turmoil* (New York: Atheneum, 1969).

20. Ibid., 11.

21. Wallerstein, "Academic Freedom and Collective Expressions of Opinion," *Journal of Higher Education* 42, no. 9 (1971a): 720.

22. Wallerstein 1969, 32–33.

23. This belief in the inseparability between social science and activism became the unifying theme for Wallerstein's first collection of essays, *The Capitalist World-Economy* (Cambridge: Cambridge University Press, 1979a).

24. Wallerstein 1979a, vii; original italics.

25. He concluded: "All good scholarship is polemic (but not all polemic is good scholarship)." Therefore, polemical writing was "the *only possible* road to objectivity" (Wallerstein 1979a, x, xi; original italics).

26. Perry Anderson, "Critique of Wilsonism," *New Left Review* I/27 (Sept.–Oct. 1964b): 3–27.

27. Ibid., 10–11.

28. Ibid., 11.

29. Ibid., 27.

30. Nairn 1965, 3.

31. Ibid., 9.

32. Several writings from the late 1960s show Anderson's reaction to events as they were happening, covering a range of sources. Two publications are especially revealing: the famous "Components of a National Culture" and the NLR editorial "Introduction to the Special Issue on France May 1968." Conclusions are also supported by unpublished documents, including Anderson's manuscript "The Founding Moment," and three NLR internal reports: "A Decennial Report"; "Document A—Theory and Practice: The Coupure of May"; and "Document B—Ten Theses." (Reportedly, Anderson penned another manuscript in 1970, titled, "State and Revolution in the West," which was referenced in Elliott's biography

[1998, 71–86]. It is unclear how well Elliott knew the document; in one passage, he seemed to indicate that he had not seen it [1998, 77]. And other writers who apparently accessed internal NLR documents also could not obtain "State and Revolution," including Blackledge [2004] and D. Thompson [2007], whose 1997 dissertation was supervised by Elliott.) Citations for previously uncited material, in the order listed, are as follows: NLR Editors, "Introduction to the Special Issue on France, May 1968," *New Left Review* I/52 (Nov.–Dec.1968): 1–8; Perry Anderson, "The Founding Moment," unpublished manuscript (1969): 1–137; "Document A—Theory and Practice: The Coupure of May," unpublished NLR document (1968/9a): 1–17; "Document B—Ten Theses," unpublished NLR document (1968/9b): 1–18.

33. NLR Editors 1968, 1.
34. Ibid., 1.
35. On the development of cognitive liberation and its sequel, framing, see Doug McAdam, *Political Process and the Development of Black Insurgency*, 2nd ed. (Chicago: University of Chicago Press, [1982] 1999). On the context of culture and framing, see Mayer N. Zald, "Culture, Ideology, and Strategic Framing," in *Comparative Perspectives on Social Movements, ed.* Doug McAdam, John D. McCarthy, and Mayer N. Zald (Cambridge: Cambridge University Press, 1996), 261–74.
36. NLR Editors 1968, 7.
37. Anderson, 2009, 142, 178, 191, 234, 307, 345, and 510.
38. Ibid., 178.
39. Ibid., 510; original ellipses.
40. Originally published in the July–August issues of the *New Left Review* (I/50, 1968, 3–57), citations refer to its reprint in *English Questions* (1992a).
41. "Document A—Theory and Practice," 1968/9a, 7.
42. Anderson 1992a, 103, or 96–103 for an extended discussion.
43. "Document B—Ten Theses" 1968/9b, 12–14.
44. Ibid., 13–16.
45. Ibid., 16–17.
46. Ibid., 18.
47. "A Decennial Report" 1975, 39, 83–84.
48. Named for soot-covered and stunted miners, *Black Dwarf* engaged in contemporary politics and culture, and took a strong stance against the American war of "imperial narcissism" in Vietnam (Ali, 21 May 2018). Its editor, Tariq Ali (a member of NLR's editorial board), regarded the Vietnam Solidarity Campaign (VSC) as the defining political fight of his generation of leftists (the *new* New Left). Ali also came up with *Black Dwarf*'s most famous headline, spread in large print across its June 1, 1968, issue: "We Shall Fight/ We Will Win/ Paris/ London/ Rome/ Berlin." See: David Edgar's interview with Ali, "That Was the Year That Was," *London Review of Books* 40, no. 10 (2018): 3–10; Tariq Ali's blogpost, "We Shall Fight, We Shall Win" (21 May 2018): http://tariqali.org/archives/3269; and, Ali's reflections in *Street Fighting Years* (2018).
49. "A Decennial Report" 1975, 100.

Chapter 4

1. Lukács [1923] 1968, 198.

2. This work owes a debt to the categories Martin Jay developed in *Marxism and Totality* (Berkeley: University of California Press, 1984).

3. Anderson 1992a, 58fn12.

4. For Roberto Mangabeira Unger: "There is no single tendency in the history of modern social thought more remarkable in its persistence or more far-reaching in its influence than the struggle to formulate a plausible version of the idea of totality." *Knowledge and Politics* (New York: The Free Press, 1975), 125.

5. Hall 2016, 39.

6. Polanyi [1944] 2001.

7. Lukács [1923] 1968, 28.

8. Fredric Jameson, *Valences of the Dialectic* (London: Verso, 2009), 201–22.

9. Unger credited Gottfried Wilhelm Leibniz with this insight (Unger 1975, 127 and 311 en17).

10. Jameson 2009, 211.

11. Jay 1984, 1–80.

12. As Jay notes, the totality for Plato and Aristotle was primarily the governmental institution, both in practicality and potentiality. Yet Plato's and Aristotle's ideas about government were closely connected to society, and Jay also acknowledges an aesthetic dimension to their totalities (1984, 25–26, 300).

13. Joseph Canning, *A History of Medieval Political Thought, 300–1450* (London: Routledge, 1996), 39–42.

14. Allen M. Bass, "The Metaphor of the Human Body in the Political Theory of John of Salisbury: Context and Innovation," in *Metaphor and Rational Discourse*, ed. Bernhard Debatin, Timothy R. Jackson, and Daniel Steurer (Tübingen: Max Niemeyer Verlag, 1997), 201–13.

15. Canning 1996, 110–12.

16. John wrote: "Take away the assistance of the feet from the most robust body, and it cannot proceed on its own power, but must crawl on its hands shamefully, inefficiently, and with great difficulty, or else be moved with the help of brute animals" (qtd. in Bass 1997, 209).

17. According to Jay, in rejecting the hierarchical structure of the medieval world, Enlightenment thinkers also became mechanistic and antimetaphysical. They saw great importance in individual reason, the ego, downplaying the world beyond the rational self: "[T]he psychology of the Enlightenment has been identified with egoism and intellectualism, and not with that affective attachment to entities beyond the self which is the source of much holistic thinking" (1984, 30).

18. Lukács [1923] 1971, 27.

19. Jay's (1984) intellectual history also makes this point.

20. Scott Malcomson, quoted in Gregory Elliott, "Olympus Mislaid? A Profile of Perry Anderson," *Radical Philosophy* no. 71 (1995): 5.

21. "Document B—Ten Theses" 1968/9b, 1.
22. Readers may be surprised to hear that Wallerstein used Marxist terminology for totalities. See, therefore, "Civilizations and Modes of Production: Conflicts and Convergences," reprinted in *The Politics of the World-Economy: The States, the Movements, and the Civilizations* (Cambridge: Cambridge University Press, 1984b), 163.
23. Wallerstein interview by Rojas 2012a, 26.
24. For more on Wallerstein's transition away from states to the world-system, see the "intermission" that follows this chapter.
25. Immanuel Wallerstein, "The Rise and Future Demise of the World Capitalist System: Concepts for Comparative Analysis," *Comparative Studies in Society and History* 16, no. 4 (1974a): 390.
26. See Wallerstein's book, *The Uncertainties of Knowledge* (2004a), especially the essay, "The Itinerary of World-Systems Analysis, or How to Resist Becoming a Theory."
27. Wallerstein 1974a, 390.
28. Wallerstein kept his definition simple: "it is a 'world-*economy*' because the basic linkage between the parts of the system is economic, although this was reinforced to some extent by cultural links and eventually . . . by political arrangements." *The Modern World-System I: Capitalist Agriculture and the Origins of the European World-Economy in the Sixteenth Century* (New York: Academic Press, 1974b), 15.
29. Wallerstein 1974a, 390.
30. Wallerstein had a much earlier date for the arrival of capitalism than many other scholars, including Anderson. For his justification, see *The Modern World-System III* (1989). For his dating in the inaugural volume, see Wallerstein 1974b, 63 and 270.
31. Wallerstein seemed to realize as much in later years, when he described world-systems as an attempt to *unthink* basic assumptions about studying the social world. *Unthinking Social Science*, 2nd ed. Philadelphia: Temple University Press, 2001.
32. Charles E. Bidwell, letter to Immanuel Wallerstein, June 19, 1973. Wallerstein Papers, Box 98, Folder: "The Rise and Future Demise of the World Capitalist System: Concepts for Comparative Analysis."
33. The other reviewer, however, was favorable, but thought that the journal was not the appropriate place for publication (Bidwell letter, June 19, 1973).
34. Wallerstein 1974a.
35. "Prologue to the 2011 Edition," in *The Modern World-System I: Capitalist Agriculture and the Origins of the European World-Economy in the Sixteenth Century*, 2nd ed. (Berkeley: University of California Press, 2011b), xvii.
36. Wallerstein 1974b.
37. Wallerstein 2011b, xvii.

38. Immanuel Wallerstein, letter to David Solomon, March 10, 1975. Wallerstein Papers, Box 37, Folder: "McGill—Department of Sociology, David Solomon."
39. Goldfrank 2000, 158.
40. "Report on an Intellectual Project: The Fernand Braudel Center, 1976–1991," available online at: binghamton.edu/fbc/about-fbc/intellectual-report.html.
41. Charles Tilly, "Anthropology, History, and the *Annales*," *Review* 1, no. 3/4 (1978): 207–13; Charles Tilly, "The Old New Social History and the New Old Social History," *Review* 7, no. 3 (1984): 363–406; Eric Hobsbawm, "Comments," *Review* 1, no. 3/4 (1978); Rodney Hilton, "Towns in English Feudal Society," *Review* 3, no. 1 (1979): 3–20; Fernand Braudel, "A Model for the Analysis of the Decline of Italy," trans. Immanuel Wallerstein, *Review* 2, no. 4 (1979b): 647–62; Karl Polanyi, "The Economistic Fallacy," trans. Harry W. Pearson, *Review* 1, no. 1 (1977): 9–18; N. D. Kondratieff, "The Long Waves in Economic Life," trans. W. F. Stolper, *Review* 2, no. 4 ([1926] 1979): 519–62.
42. Immanuel Wallerstein, "The Tasks of Historical Social Science: An Editorial," *Review* 1, no. 1 (1977): 4.
43. See: "From Feudalism to Capitalism: Transition or Transitions?" (reprinted in Wallerstein 1979a). See also: "Kondratieff Up or Kondratieff Down?" *Review* 2, no. 4 (1979b): 663–73.
44. See Wallerstein's introduction to the first issue of *Review* (1977), as well as his article with Michael Hechter, "Social Rank and Nationalism: Some African Data," *The Public Opinion Quarterly* 34, no. 3: 360–70. In addition, Part II of *The Capitalist World-Economy* (1979a) is devoted to race and class.
45. "There Is No Such Thing as Sociology," *The American Sociologist* 6, no. 4 (1971b): 328; "A World-System Perspective on the Social Sciences," reprinted in Wallerstein 1979a; Research Working Group on Cyclical Rhythms and Secular Trends, "Cyclical Rhythms and Secular Trends of the Capitalist World-Economy: Some Premises, Hypotheses, and Questions," *Review* 2, no. 4 (1979): 483–500.
46. Wallerstein 1980.
47. See, for example: Walter Rodney, *How Europe Underdeveloped Africa* (Baltimore: Black Classic Press, [1972] 2011); Andre Gunder Frank, *Latin America: Underdevelopment or Revolution* (New York: Monthly Review, 1969).
48. Immanuel Wallerstein, "World System Versus World-Systems: A Critique," in *The Modern World System: Five Hundred Years or Five Thousand?*, ed. Andre Gunder Frank and Barry K. Gills (London: Routledge, 1993), 295.
49. Dissatisfied with his 1974 account of the transition from feudalism to capitalism, Wallerstein later published an expanded and revised history. Still, he claimed that he had not fundamentally changed his views. For the article, see: "The West, Capitalism, and the Modern World-System," *Review* 15, no. 4 (1992): 561-619.
50. Wallerstein 1974b, 18–20.
51. "Civilization" is mentioned in two places, Wallerstein 1974b, 18 and 36.

52. "Prologue to the 2011 Edition," in *The Modern World-System II: Mercantilism and the Consolidation of the European World-Economy 1600–1750* (Berkeley: University of California Press, 2011c): xiii–xxvii.

53. Wallerstein 1984b, 169.

54. Ibid., 159.

55. Wallerstein 1974b, 36–37.

56. Ibid., 33–34.

57. After striking in the mid-fourteenth century, the plague did not end for about 350 years (Wallerstein 1974b, 34fn64, 35fn77).

58. Ibid., 35, 37.

59. Ibid., 37–38.

60. For *ceaseless*, see "World System Versus World-Systems: A Critique," in *The Modern World System: Five Hundred Years or Five Thousand?*, ed. Andre Gunder Frank and Barry K. Gills (London: Routledge, 1993), 293. For *endless*, see *World-Systems Analysis: An Introduction* (Durham: Duke University Press, 2004b), 24.

61. For the system to function, it did not matter how the value was stored or accumulated. At one conference, Wallerstein said: "I think of capital as stored value. You can store value in money, in the multiple forms of money, you can store value in capital stock. There is nothing magical about capital stock. And if it is better to store it in money, people will keep the capital stock and store it in money. And therefore the problem of capital is indeed not merely to accumulate, but to prevent its de-valorization." Immanuel Wallerstein, as transcribed in *The World We Are Entering, 2000–2050*, ed. Wallerstein and Arman Clesse (The Netherlands: Dutch University Press, 2002), 84.

62. Wallerstein 1974b, 46.

63. "Semiperipheral Countries and the Contemporary World Crisis," reprinted in Wallerstein 1979a.

64. See the issues of conceptualization and measurement outlined by Nicole Bousquet, "Core, Semiperiphery, Periphery: A Variable Geometry Presiding over Conceptualization," in *Routledge Handbook of World-Systems Analysis*, ed. Salvatore J. Babones and Christopher Chase-Dunn (London: Routledge, 2012), 123–24.

65. See the striking similarities between two such semiperipheral areas, Scotland and the Basque region, that also experienced surges in support for micro-nationalist parties, in Cyrus Ernesto Zirakzadeh, "Economic Changes and Surges in Micro-Nationalist Voting in Scotland and the Basque Region of Spain," *Comparative Studies in Society and History* 31, no. 2 (1989): 318–39.

66. He wrote: "It is . . . not meaningful to speak of semiperipheral production processes" (Wallerstein 2004b, 29).

67. See Christopher Chase-Dunn, *Global Formation: Structures of the World-Economy*, 2nd ed. (Lanham, MD: Rowman and Littlefield, 1998), esp. ch. 2.

68. For an overview, see Wallerstein's essay, "An Historical Perspective on the Emergence of the New International Order: Economic, Political, Cultural Aspects," reprinted in *The Capitalist World Economy* (1979a, 269–82).

69. Wallerstein 2001, 260–61.

70. Wallerstein 1974b, 63.

71. The moment, for Wallerstein, was a dramatic one: "What tumbled was not merely a particular state structure. It was more than the tragic abdication of Charles V amid the tears of his knights. What tumbled was the world-system. For a hundred years, Europe was enjoying a new prosperity. Men had tried to profit from it in the ways of old. But technological advance and the upsurge of capitalist elements had already progressed too far to make it possible to recreate political empires that would match the economic arenas. The year 1557 marked, if you will, the defeat of that attempt, and the establishment of a balance of power in Europe which would permit states which aimed at being nations (let us call them nation-states) to come into their own and to batten on the still flourishing world-economy" (1974b, 184).

72. Wallerstein 1974b, 99.

73. Ibid., 99; original italics.

74. Immanuel Wallerstein, "Testimony given at hearings on 'Underdevelopment in Africa' of House of Representatives, Committee on International Relations, Subcommittee on Africa," September 7, 1977. Wallerstein Papers, Box 52, Folder: "House of Representatives' Subcommittee on Africa."

75. Wallerstein reiterated his academic position: "The only development we ought to be discussing is that of the system as a whole" (Wallerstein testimony, September 7, 1977, 5).

76. Wallerstein testimony, September 7, 1977, 5; original underlining.

77. Ibid., 5–6; original underlining.

78. The objective was to "attain what Hegel called a *concrete universality*," which was a goal shared by Sartre (Anderson 1965a, 12; original italics).

79. Ibid.

80. "Document B—Ten Theses" 1968/9b, 4, 11.

81. Ibid., 1–2.

82. Ibid., 2, 5.

83. Anderson 1974a and 1974b.

84. Anderson published two cultural pieces under the pen name of Richard Merton. One compared the Rolling Stones and the Beatles (in 1968), and the other compared the Beach Boys and Bob Dylan (in 1970). See: Elliott (1998, 60) and Ali (May 21, 2018).

85. Anderson 1974a, 97.

86. Other factors included the overall weight of the urban economy as well as the structural limits of technological innovation (Ibid., 76–82).

87. Ibid., 99.
88. Ibid., 102–103, 107, 127.
89. Ibid., 117.
90. Ibid., 131.
91. Ibid., 122.
92. Ibid., 132.
93. Ibid., 152.
94. Ibid., 227.
95. Ibid., 201.
96. Anderson 1974b, 428–29.
97. Over centuries, the Russian economy transformed into a capitalist mode of production, but the Russian state remained feudal (Anderson 1974b, 359).
98. Anderson 1974b, 420.
99. Ibid., 458–61.
100. Ibid., 422.
101. Wallerstein 1992.
102. Andre Gunder Frank, "The World Economic System in Asia before European Hegemony," *The Historian* 56, no. 4 (1994): 259–76.
103. See, for example: Andre Gunder Frank, "A Theoretical Introduction to 5,000 Years of World System History," *Review* 13, no. 2 (1990): 155–248; Janet Abu-Lughod, *Before European Hegemony: The World System A.D. 1250–1350* (Oxford: Oxford University Press, 1989); Robert A. Denemark, "World System History: From Traditional Politics to the Study of Global Relations," *International Studies Review* 1, no. 2 (1999): 45–73.
104. Barry K. Gills and Andre Gunder Frank, "The Cumulation of Accumulation," as contributors to their edited volume, *The Modern World System: Five Hundred Years or Five Thousand* (London: Routledge, 1993), 81–114.
105. Their view was summarized rather well by K. Ekholm and J. Friedman, whose essay, "'Capital' Imperialism and Exploitation in Ancient World Systems," was reprinted in *The Modern World System: Five Hundred Years or Five Thousand* (London: Routledge, 1993), 59–80.
106. Wallerstein 1993, 293.
107. Immanuel Wallerstein, letter to Andre Gunder Frank, August 23, 1989, original underlining. Wallerstein Papers, Box 50, Folder: "Andre Gunder Frank."
108. Theda Skocpol and Margaret Somers, "The Uses of Comparative History in Macrosocial Inquiry," *Comparative Studies in Society and History* 22, no. 2 (1980): 190.
109. Ira Katznelson, "Periodization and Preferences: Reflections on Purposive Action in Comparative Historical Social Science," in *Comparative Historical Analysis in the Social Sciences*, ed. James Mahoney and Dietrich Rueschemeyer (Cambridge: Cambridge University Press 2003), 270–301, esp. 274–276.
110. Ibid., 276.

111. Katznelson believed institutions, at critical junctions, could serve as a bond (ibid., 278).

Intermission I:
Immanuel Wallerstein's New Pair of Glasses

1. Wallerstein 1974a and 1974b.
2. Wallerstein interview by Williams 2013, 207.
3. This is the heading of the first section of *The Essential Wallerstein* (2000).
4. In order: Terence K. Hopkins and Immanuel Wallerstein, "The Comparative Study of National Societies," *Social Science Information* 6, no. 5 (1967): 25–58; Immanuel Wallerstein, "Three Paths of National Development in Sixteenth-Century Europe," *Studies in Comparative International Development* 7, no. 2 (1972): 95–101; and Immanuel Wallerstein, "Africa in a Capitalist World," originally published in 1973, but cited as *The Essential Wallerstein* (New York: The New Press, 2000), 39–68.
5. In the original article, Hopkins and Wallerstein actually wrote: "[I]t is a *contect* for its constituent members." I substituted *context*, assuming that this was their intention all along. But they could have also meant *contection*, or "covering up," implying that each type of analysis possessed constituent units. Regardless, *contect* or *context*, their overall meaning may have been the same. Hopkins and Wallerstein 1967, 27; my emphasis.
6. Ibid., 30.
7. Ibid., 34.
8. Ibid.
9. Arend Lijphart, "Comparative Politics and the Comparative Method," *American Political Science Review* 65, no. 3 (1971): 686.
10. Wallerstein [1967] 2005b, 225.
11. In the 1960s, the Left was popular among some in the professional classes and among many in what Wallerstein called the "pariah classes"; but it was less popular for the middle classes and skilled workers, who, he thought, could be pulled to the right in times of crisis (1969, 115).
12. Ibid., 144–45.
13. Wallerstein 1972.
14. Ibid., 96.
15. Wallerstein interview by Williams 2013.
16. Wallerstein 2000, 39–68.
17. Ibid., 39.
18. Ibid., 45.
19. Wallerstein summarized: "How can a movement be simultaneously one of 'national liberation' and one of 'class struggle,' if the unit of analysis is

not larger than the colonial territory—at the very minimum that of the imperial political framework?" (2000, 46).

20. The idea, he reflected, was to turn an adjective into an adjectival noun. It was to make "world" more than a mere description of the system. Despite the limitations of English, Wallerstein may have considered himself fortunate. In German, differentiation could only be made contextually; such was the case with Fritz Rörig, whose writings in the 1920s influenced Braudel, but whose audience remained limited (Wallerstein 2004a, 88–89).

21. Wallerstein 1993, 294–95.
22. Wallerstein 2000, 56.
23. Wallerstein 2004a, 89.
24. Wallerstein 2000, 63–64.
25. Ibid., 52.

Chapter 5

1. See, for example, Robert Brenner's account, emphasizing a Long Downturn, in *The Economics of Global Turbulence* (London: Verso, 2006).

2. For a critique of neoliberalism, see: David Harvey, *A Brief History of Neoliberalism* (Oxford: Oxford University Press, 2005).

3. See Vijay Prashad, *The Poorer Nations* (London: Verso, 2012).

4. In 1978, Wallerstein was expectant of a socialist future: "I believe . . . we are living in the early moments of a long systemic change—the transformation of the capitalist world-economy to a socialist world-government" (reprinted in 1984b, 167). This prediction appeared in several articles, such as Wallerstein's piece, "Crisis as Transition," in *Dynamics of Global Crisis*, ed. Samir Amin et al. (New York: Monthly Review, 1982), 11–54. See also several articles reprinted in *The Politics of the World-Economy* (Wallerstein 1984b): "The Dialectics of Civilizations in the Modern World-System" (from 1978); "World Networks and the Politics of the World-Economy," (from 1979); and, "The Future of the World-Economy" (from 1980).

5. He pondered, in a 1984 article: "We are living in the . . . sea-change . . . from capitalism to something else (most probably socialism)" (184). "The Development of the Concept of Development," reprinted later that year in *The Politics of the World-Economy*.

6. In 1988, Wallerstein wrote: "While [capitalist] demise is certain . . . what comes after the transition is historically open" (reprinted in 1991, 106). See *Geopolitics and Geoculture* (Cambridge: Cambridge University Press, 1991).

7. Christopher Chase-Dunn stands out as one who sees world-systems as historically linked, like water in small ponds flowing into streams, lakes, rivers, and oceans. For this image, see: Christopher Chase-Dunn and Bruce Lerro, *Social*

Change: Globalization From the Stone Age to the Present (Boulder: Paradigm, 2014), 78.

8. Ilya Prigogine, "Time, Structure and Fluctuations," Nobel Lecture (1977): http://www.nobelprize.org/nobel_prizes/chemistry/laureates/1977/prigogine-lecture.html.

9. Wallerstein interview by Rojas 2012a, 31.

10. Ilya Prigogine interview by Hans Ulrich Obrist, "Science and Art," trans. Gregory Ball, *Review* 28, no. 2 (2005): 117.

11. Ilya Prigogine, *The End of Certainty: Time, Chaos, and the New Laws of Nature* (New York: The Free Press, 1997), 19. See also Ilya Prigogine and Isabelle Stengers, *Order out of Chaos: Man's New Dialogue with Nature* (London: Verso, 2017).

12. Ilya Prigogine, "The Laws of Chaos," trans. Richard Lee, *Review* 19, no. 1 (1996): 1–9.

13. Ibid., 6.

14. Prigogine 1997, viii.

15. Wallerstein interview by Williams 2013.

16. Wallerstein interview by Rojas 2012a, 30.

17. Prigogine approved of applying his terminology to social systems: "I always found remarkable that the neolithic bifurcation emerged everywhere about the same period about ten thousand years ago, but that it emerged in different forms in the Middle East, in China or in Precolumbian America. This is similar to the branches of bifurcations which appear in chemical or physical systems." "The Networked Society," *Journal of World-Systems Research* 6, no. 1 (2000): 896.

18. Immanuel Wallerstein, "End of the Road for Runaway Factories?" *Commentary* no. 351 (April 15, 2013): http://www.iwallerstein.com/road-runaway-factories/.

19. The first English translation of Kondratieff's article, "The Long Waves in Economic Life," by W. F. Stolper, was the lead article in the November 1935 issue of *The Review of Economic Statistics* (17, no. 6: 105–15).

20. See George Garvy, "Kondratieff's Theory of Long Cycles," *The Review of Economics and Statistics* 25, no. 4 (1943): 203–20.

21. "Long Waves as Capitalist Process," *Review* 7, no. 4 (1984c): 559.

22. The title of the unpublished essay also captured his view: "Why Is the Study of Long Waves Controversial?" Wallerstein Papers, Box 94, Folder: "Why Is the Study of Long Waves Controversial?"

23. Wallerstein 1984c, 562.

24. Waves, Wallerstein acknowledged, were quite difficult to measure. In place of profit-rates, others used price fluctuations (which Kondratieff preferred), the rate of technological innovation, patterns of industrial production, or shifts in gold reserves. For Wallerstein, these other factors were too approximate, that is, too far removed from the real fluctuations of the world-economy. "All of these,

I have little doubt myself, go up and down in complex interlinkage with the Kondratieffs, but they are Plato's shadow in the cave." (1984c, 564).

25. For a summary and explanation of logistical cycles, see Wallerstein 2011c, xiii–xv.

26. Wallerstein (2011c, xiii–xv) identified the following logistical cycles spanning the transition between the middle ages and modern world:

A-phase: 1000 (or 1100)–1250
B-phase: 1250 (or 1300)–1450
A-phase: 1450–1600 (or 1650)
B-phase: 1600 (or 1650)–1700 (or 1750)

Then, following the seventeenth-century downturn was another upswing in the eighteenth century. Other waves, such as the Kondratieff, were unique to the modern world-system.

27. Wallerstein 1980, 2–34.
28. Ibid., 221–22.
29. Ibid., 125.
30. Ibid., 233 fn346.
31. Sweden developed a strong, effective, mercantilist state. It built an impressive army, increased wealth through iron and shipbuilding, and constrained the lower nobility by bring them into government service. War with Russia in 1700, however, revealed Sweden's weaknesses, and it lost its eastern Baltic possessions to Russia, part of its German possessions to Prussia, and of course, the profits that came from those lands (Wallerstein 1980, 217–24). Thus, it is noteworthy that Sweden's rise was limited by a force external to the world-economy. Russia had not yet been incorporated into the modern world-system. For Wallerstein, world-systems were not totally self-contained entities. Contact between world-systems can occur by trading luxury goods or even going to war.
32. Wallerstein 1980, 233.
33. Ibid., 158.
34. Ibid., 185.
35. Ibid., 187.
36. Ibid., 142, 144 fn79, 145 fn81.
37. Wallerstein 1974b, 400; 1980, 134–42.
38. Cost-shifting happened throughout the periphery. Wallerstein disliked the label "refeudalization." He thought it was better to think of this process as the "inflation of the nobility" or "the commercialization of the fief." These expressions were coined by László Makki and Emilio Sereni, respectively (quoted in Wallerstein 1980, 142 and 147). Whatever the term, the process was more about the upper strata's economic and political authority than a transition in the mode of production. In other words, the return to serfdom was a capitalist process, not a rejection of it.
39. Wallerstein 1980, 137, 289.
40. Ibid., 167.

41. American Indians, more susceptible to disease, could not be pressed in large numbers into slave captivity. Thus, it is well known, European producers enslaved African peoples instead (Wallerstein 1980, 173).

42. Ibid., 139.

43. For my take on the structure of the Soviet Union, and the timing of its demise, see: Gregory P. Williams, "When Opportunity Structure Knocks: Social Movements in the Soviet Union and Russian Federation," *Social Movement Studies* 9, no. 4 (2010): 443–60.

44. Wallerstein 2011c, xiv.

45. For my extended remarks on marking the boundaries of world-systems, see: Gregory P. Williams, "Will We Know It When We See It? Contemplating Emergent World-Systems," *Journal of Globalization Studies* 9, no. 1 (2018a): 129–49.

46. Wallerstein 1989, 129.

47. Wallerstein 1974b, 315.

48. Wallerstein 1989, 151–52.

49. Ibid., 137.

50. Ibid., 157.

51. Wallerstein, in a work with Terence K. Hopkins, claimed that "no external zone was a state prior to incorporation, but all developed state structures as part of the integration process." Some areas, such as Russia or Japan, arguably possessed state institutions prior to incorporation. But states were nonetheless rare in external areas prior to incorporation. "Capitalism and the Incorporation of New Zones into the World-Economy," *Review* 10, no. 5/6 (1987): 778.

52. Wallerstein 1989, 171.

53. Ibid., 188.

54. Ibid., 178.

55. Wallerstein 2011a, xvi.

56. Hopkins and Wallerstein 1987, 771–73; Wallerstein 1984b, 102–103.

57. Thomas Piketty also regarded the postwar years as an exception, though without the language of Kondratieff waves. See: *Capital in the Twenty-First Century*, trans. Arthur Goldhammer (Cambridge: The Belknap Press of Harvard University Press, 2014).

58. From "The Future of the World-Economy" (reprinted in Wallerstein 1984b).

59. Wallerstein interview by *RT* (2011).

60. Wallerstein believed systems had unique rules and did not join Christopher Chase-Dunn and others in their efforts to compare world-systems over time. However, Wallerstein did think such comparisons were fruitful when limited to the births and deaths of systems. See his 1994 essay, "Hold the Tiller Firm: On Method and Unit of Analysis" (reprinted in Wallerstein 2000).

61. From Polanyi (and as mentioned in chapter 2), Wallerstein would occasionally describe capitalism as involving the commodification of everything. See, for example, *Historical Capitalism with Capitalist Civilization* (1995a).

62. This is the example Wallerstein gave in a talk at Swarthmore College, "Crisis and Upsurge in Movements" (April 8, 2012): http://theprogressparadox.wordpress.com/.

63. "I will not say that eliminating the priority given to the endless accumulation of capital will automatically ensure equality of race, gender, and nation. What I will say is that it would eliminate one the most potent reasons for the inequalities. . . . Perhaps with the elimination—or at least reduction—of economic fears, at the very least the murderous element may disappear." Immanuel Wallerstein, *Utopistics: Or, Historical Choices of the 21st Century* (New York: The New Press, 1998b), 76.

64. Wallerstein 1998b, 74–75.

65. Ibid., 75–76.

66. Ibid., 75.

67. "Antisystemic Movements, Yesterday and Today," *Journal of World-Systems Research* 20, no. 2 (2014): 172.

68. Wallerstein believed that "the last thirty or forty years has borne out my views. Not everyone would agree with that, but more people agree with that today than they would have thirty or forty years ago" (interview by Williams 2013, 206).

69. Wallerstein 1980; 1989.

70. Wallerstein 1998b; 2014.

71. See, for example, Wallerstein's remarks at one conference: "If you ask me the question, which I get asked regularly . . . are you optimistic or pessimistic? I now have a very standard answer, it is fifty-fifty. That is my answer, that is where I am, fifty-fifty, and it depends on us" (Wallerstein and Clesse 2002, 150).

72. "NLR 1975–1980" (Unpublished NLR document, 1980, 1–92), 4.

73. *Considerations on Western Marxism*, 4th ed. (London: Verso, [1976b] 1984); *Arguments within English Marxism* (London: Verso, 1980); *In the Tracks of Historical Materialism* (London: Verso, 1983).

74. Wallerstein interview by Williams 2013, 205.

75. Originally published in *Past and Present*, Brenner's article, "Agrarian Class Structure and Economic Development in Pre-Industrial Europe," became the subject of debate in articles in that journal as well as the *New Left Review*. A collection later appeared in book form as *The Brenner Debate*. Robert Brenner, "Agrarian Class Structure and Economic Development in Pre-Industrial Europe," in *The Brenner Debate*, ed. T. H. Aston and C. H. E. Philpin (Cambridge: Cambridge University Press, [1976] 1985), 10–63.

76. Among the several sources Elliott (1998, 79) provides as evidence is Brenner's kind thanks to Anderson for comments on a rebuttal to critics. Robert Brenner, "The Agrarian Roots of European Capitalism," in *The Brenner Debate*, ed. T. H. Aston and C. H. E. Philpin (Cambridge: Cambridge University Press, 1985), 213–327. Another is Anderson's praised-filled review of Brenner's research in the *London Review of Books*: "Maurice Thomson's War" (1993) 15, no. 1: 13–17.

77. Perry Anderson, letter to Immanuel Wallerstein, January 17, 1976. Wallerstein Papers, Box 67, Folder: "P. Anderson."

78. The general direction of Anderson's view on the bourgeois revolutions can be found in two sources: his essay, "The Notion of Bourgeois Revolution," (given as a lecture in 1976 and published in Anderson 1992a); and, his article, "The Antinomies of Antonio Gramsci" (1976a), that described apparent contradictions within the *Prison Notebooks*. For Wallerstein's critique of Anderson's position, see his interview with Williams 2013.

79. Anderson 1992a, 113.

80. Ibid., 110–13.

81. Anderson 1983, 27.

82. Anderson 2000, 17.

83. E. P. Thompson, *The Making of the English Working Class* (New York: Vintage, [1963] 1966).

84. Anderson 1980.

85. Ibid., 56.

86. Ibid., 31–32.

87. Ibid., 56.

88. In his opinion, intellectuals must consider the "actualization of a tangible socialist future" (Anderson 1983, 99). For too long, advocates of historical materialism had ignored questions about socialist democracy's political structure, economy, and culture (including its educational system). It also seemed wise to think about what the conduct of international relations among socialist democracies might look like. This would necessarily be a speculative enterprise.

89. Anderson 1980, 22; original italics.

90. Anderson 1983, 103.

91. Anderson [1976b] 1984, 20.

92. Anderson 1983, 97; original italics.

93. Anderson was concerned about the status of women. Gender inequality, he thought, might persist even after the implementation of socialism. He noted that the women's struggle predated the labor movement, even class relations (Anderson 1992b, 357).

94. See Anderson 1983, 84–96.

95. Anderson 2005, 300.

96. See, for example, Robert Brenner and Mark Glick, "The Regulation Approach: Theory and History," *New Left Review* I/188 (1991): 45–117.

97. Anderson 1992b, 353.

98. Perry Anderson, *The Origins of Postmodernity* (London: Verso, 1998), 77.

99. Over his career, Anderson developed a fondness for obscure words. Some of the more interesting ones include: "hebetude" (1974a, 26); "filial," "catenary," "dethesaurized" (1974b, 440, 502, 525); "morphological," "miasma" (1992a, 26, 31); "speleological" (1992b, 252); and, "tyros" (2009, 164).

100. "NLR 1975–1980," 90.
101. Ibid., 91–92.
102. Ibid., 56.
103. Ibid., 91.
104. One report described Anderson in opposition to most of the collective, especially Ronald Fraser, with behavior that was at times intolerable ("A Decennial Report," 42, 55). Anderson wrote that he would have resigned earlier if he did not think it would further destabilize the journal ("NLR 1975–1980," 87). Yet his self-doubt and blame in these internal documents were not new.
105. Anderson routinely clashed with his managing editor, Quintin Hoare who, in turn, fought with Robin Blackburn when the latter filled in for Anderson to produce issue 103 (May–June 1977). Once, Anderson blocked Hoare from replying to Nairn's "The Modern Janus." On another occasion, he pushed for the rapid acceptance of an essay by Terry Eagleton (on the writings of Raymond Williams). He then delayed publication of a response by Anthony Barnett, an editorial committee member who thought that the NLR had too hastily accepted Eagleton's piece. Anderson only later admitted that Barnett had been right all along, and that NLR would have benefited from his public critique ("NLR 1975–1980," 86). On another occasion, he wavered on a piece submitted by Geras, first pressing for acceptance, then, to Geras's surprise, reversing course after talking with other editors. See: Tom Nairn, "The Modern Janus," *New Left Review* I/94 (Nov.–Dec. 1975): 3–29; Terry Eagleton, "Criticism and Politics: The Work of Raymond Williams," *New Left Review* I/95 (Jan.–Feb. 1976): 3–23; Anthony Barnett, "Raymond Williams and Marxism: A Rejoinder to Terry Eagleton," *New Left Review* I/99 (Sept.–Oct. 1976): 47–64; Norman Geras, "Literature of Revolution," *New Left Review* I/113–114 (Jan.–April 1979): 3–41.
106. According to Anderson, problems within the committee were a product of the journal's success. This was the thesis of his internal report, "NLR 1975–1980," an unpublished document (1980): 1–92.
107. "NLR 1975–1980," 4.
108. "A Decennial Report," after all, had encouraged fruitful intellectual liberty and candor in the writings of editorial committee members, which perhaps primed the *Review* for infighting ("NLR 1975–1980," 8).
109. Letters from Immanuel Wallerstein (January 22, 1977) and Sheldon W. Grebstein (Dean of Arts and Sciences, March 10, 1977, and June 15, 1977) gave Anderson a wide range of options. Wallerstein Papers, Box 67, Folder: "P. Anderson."
110. Anderson committed in a letter to Wallerstein, March 28, 1977. This was confirmed in a letter to Anderson from Dean Grebstein, June 15, 1977. Wallerstein Papers, Box 67, Folder: "P. Anderson."

111. Immanuel Wallerstein, letters to Anderson, April 24, 1978, and May 16, 1979.

112. Perry Anderson, "Book-Lists," undated. Wallerstein Papers, Box 67, Folder: "P. Anderson."

113. Perry Anderson, letter to Immanuel Wallerstein, August 8, 1980. Wallerstein Papers, Box 67, Folder: "P. Anderson."

114. "NLR 1980–1983," 24.

115. Anthony Barnett, "Iron Britannia," *New Left Review* I/134 (1982): 5–96.

116. Anderson saw the Falklands piece to be rather different than work by Thompson, who, in the former's opinion, tried to be universally appealing but tended to exaggerate and write with outdated colloquialisms ("NLR 1980–1983," 20). According to Anderson, Barnett's style conveyed an intelligence and ease for a wider audience. In addition, Anderson remarked, the introductory "Themes" section was the first time the *New Left Review* had produced an authentic editorial. "NLR 1980–1983" (unpublished NLR document, 1983, 1–72).

117. D. Thompson 2007, 117.

118. According to Duncan Thompson (2007, 117 and 211 en90), Blackburn even expressed skepticism in an unpublished paper.

119. On the eve of his departure as lead editor, Anderson prepared a report, "NLR 1980–1983," on what he called Phase VII in the history of the *New Left Review*. As in other documents, he noted internal divisions, and, once again, Anderson wrote that his second-guessing had exacerbated internal tensions ("NLR 1980–1983," 2). The editors prepared a draft for a new constitution, but it would not be finalized for another year, after Robin Blackburn had taken the helm. (See "Charter," unpublished NLR document, 1983/4, 1–11). Meanwhile, the financial well-being of the journal had slid a bit due to wastefulness and inattention ("NLR 1980–1983," 6–10).

120. Elliott 1998, 170.

Chapter 6

1. This was Georgi M. Derluguian's assessment in *Bourdieu's Secret Admirer in the Caucasus: A World-System Biography* (Chicago: The University of Chicago Press, 2005), 6.

2. Twice in the decade, the Russian economy expanded: in 1997, when it grew by 1.4%; and, in 1998, the year of Russia's turnaround, when the economy grew by 6.4%. See the World Bank's comparison at data.worldbank.org.

3. According to Derluguian, Wallerstein in fact predicted the end of the Soviet Union, at one point indicating as much in conversation. There is some evidence for this, such as a 1976 article in which Wallerstein pointed to a "new

inter*state* political alignment of forces at the world level" that "may not come until 1990" (reprinted in 1979a, 138). Georgi Derluguian, "What Communism Was," in *Does Capitalism Have a Future?*,ed. Wallerstein et al. (Oxford: Oxford University Press, 2013), 99–129.

4. Wallerstein 1989, 184.

5. Immanuel Wallerstein, "What Cold War in Asia? An Interpretive Essay," in *The Cold War in Asia: The Battle for Hearts and Minds*, ed. Zheng Yangwen, Hong Liu, and Michael Szonyi (Leiden: Brill, 2010), 15–24.

6. Ibid., 20.

7. Wallerstein 2014, 164.

8. Soviet intervention in Afghanistan, Wallerstein admitted, may be the exception to this rule. Yet behavior and outcomes still fit the model: the Americans did not intervene directly, and the Soviet Union left without making any gains. And like Washington's war in Vietnam, Moscow eventually withdrew from Afghanistan (2010, 23).

9. Giovanni Arrighi, Terence K. Hopkins, and Immanuel Wallerstein, *Antisystemic Movements* (London: Verso, 1989), 104.

10. Wallerstein's writings on social protest reveal a Weberian element to his thought. For Weber, classes were economic divisions within society and status groups were honorific positions. Classes were created by property in the premodern world and wealth in the modern world. Status groups, he thought, could be the product of class, of race, or by achievements (such as knighthood). See Max Weber, "Class, Status, Party," in *Essays in Sociology*, trans. and ed. H. H. Gerth and C. Wright Mills (Oxford: Oxford University Press, 1946), 180–95.

11. Arrighi, Hopkins, and Wallerstein 1989, 104.

12. Ibid., 104–105.

13. Ibid., 106.

14. Giovanni Arrighi, Terence K. Hopkins, and Immanuel Wallerstein, "1989, The Continuation of 1968," *Review* 15, no. 2 (1992): 221–42.

15. This typology was described in several writings. The three clearest descriptions can be found in Wallerstein (1984b, 104; 1995a, 67–69) and Arrighi, Hopkins, and Wallerstein (1989).

16. Wallerstein 1989, 121.

17. Wallerstein 1984b, 127.

18. Wallerstein 2011a, 143.

19. Ibid., 1.

20. Ibid., 23.

21. "The powerful and the privileged lost nothing that was of fundamental importance to them, and they slept more peacefully at night." Immanuel Wallerstein, *After Liberalism* (New York: The New Press, 1995b), 256.

22. Wallerstein 2011a, 92.

23. Wallerstein 1995b, 256.

24. Wallerstein characterized the liberal-imperial state as follows: "What distinguished the liberal-imperial state was its commitment to intelligent reform by the state that would simultaneously advance economic growth (or rather the accumulation of capital) and tame the dangerous classes (by incorporating them into the citizenry and offering them a part, albeit a small part, of the imperial economic pie)" (2011a, 137).

25. Wallerstein 1995b, 240.

26. Ibid., 239.

27. Ibid., 240.

28. Ibid., 223.

29. Immanuel Wallerstein, *The Decline of American Power* (New York: The New Press, 2003), 19.

30. Immanuel Wallerstein, "Global Left vs. Global Right: 1945 to Today," Commentary No. 449 (15 May 2017): http://iwallerstein.com/global-left-vs-global-right-from-1945-to-today/.

31. Wallerstein interview by Williams 2013, 206.

32. Wallerstein 1995b, 7.

33. Anderson 2017a, 18–23.

34. Anderson (2017a, 108) figured that out of the world-systems project at SUNY Binghamton, Arrighi had imbued a Gramscian element into Wallerstein's writings, and, in the other direction, a Braudelian element had gone into Arrighi's writings. Wallerstein did not list Gramsci as a major influence, but Anderson's assessment was logical. His conclusion may have been controversial, however, since many neo-Gramscians in international relations (IR) consider Wallerstein's writings too determinist and too economistic. For various perspectives, see Stephen Gill, ed. *Gramsci, Historical Materialism and International Relations* (Cambridge: Cambridge University Press, 1993). For Anderson's impression of neo-Gramscian IR, see *The H-Word* (2017a, ch. 10).

35. See: "The Three Instances of Hegemony in the History of the Capitalist World-Economy," originally published in 1983, reprinted in Wallerstein 2000, 255.

36. Wallerstein 1980, 39–45, 53–57.

37. Ibid., 46.

38. Ibid., ch. 3.

39. Wallerstein 2000, 256.

40. Wallerstein 2000, 257.

41. Anderson 2005; 2015.

42. Anderson noted that Oakeshott, Strauss, and Hayek, who were all born around 1900, believed inequality was important and shared suspicions about popular sovereignty: "What they all in the end sought to restrain was democracy—seen and feared through the prisms of their theories of law, as the abyss of its absence . . . the mystery of lawlessness" (2005, 26).

43. Anderson 1992b.

44. Anderson 2005, 28.
45. Anderson 1998, 100.
46. Perry Anderson, "The River of Time," *New Left Review* II/26 (2004a): 72.
47. Fredric Jameson, "Future City," *New Left Review* II/21 (2003): 76.
48. Anderson 2004a, 74.
49. Anderson 1998, 88, 100.
50. Anderson [1976b] 1984, 52–54.
51. Anderson 2000, 18.
52. Ibid., 19.
53. Intellectuals may not like to admit resignation, but, Anderson reminded, it was possible ("as a matter of logic") that some leftists will succumb to the political situation, "without any belief in the chance of an alternative" to capitalism (Anderson 2000, 13fn5).
54. "The underlying attitude is: capitalism has come to stay, we must make our peace with it" (Anderson 2000, 13).
55. Ibid.
56. "Arms and Rights: The Adjustable Centre" (2005) originally appeared in *New Left Review* and was reprinted later that year in *Spectrum*. Citations refer to the book.
57. Anderson 2005, 165.
58. Ibid., 174.
59. Anderson considered Hobsbawm's writings to be a kind of autobiography of the twentieth century (Anderson 2005, 278).
60. Ibid., 317.
61. In Anderson's opinion, Hobsbawm's prose, at times, was "reduced to clutching at straws of Stiglitz and Sen, as if Nobel Prizes were tokens of intellectual hope" (ibid., 318). Anderson was referring, of course, to Hobsbawm's *The Age of Extremes* (1994) and *Interesting Times: A Twentieth-century Life* (New York: The New Press, 2002).
62. *The Age of Revolution: 1789–1848* (London: Weidenfeld & Nicolson, 1962); *The Age of Capital: 1848–1875* (London: Weidenfeld & Nicolson, 1975); *The Age of Empire:1875–1914* (London: Weidenfeld & Nicolson, 1987).
63. Anderson 2005, 299–310.
64. Ibid., 312, 315.
65. Anderson 2000, 31.
66. Ibid., 16.
67. Ibid., 15.
68. Ibid.
69. Mark Garnett, "New Left Review," *Times Literary Supplement*, March 23, 2001: 25.
70. Boris Kagarlitsky, "The Suicide of *New Left Review*," *International Socialism* 88 (2000): 127–33.

71. Ibid., 132–33.
72. Ibid., 129.
73. MR Editors, "Socialism: A Time to Retreat?" *Monthly Review* (September 2000): 4, 5.
74. Gilbert Achcar, "The 'Historical Pessimism' of Perry Anderson," in *International Socialism* 88 (2000): 137.
75. Gregory Elliott, *Ends in Sight: Marx/Fukuyama/Hobsbawm/Anderson* (London: Pluto, 2008), 111.
76. Ibid., 128.
77. See Fukuyama's essay (1989), and expanded book, *The End of History and the Last Man* (New York: The Free Press, 1992).
78. Anderson 1992b, 332–36.
79. Ibid., 336.
80. Ibid., 358.
81. To the contrary, the end of history was more of a "structure of feeling, the precipitate of a certain common historical experience" (Anderson 1992b, 279). This was Lutz Niethammer's conclusion, whose book was finished simultaneously to Fukuyama's article in *The National Interest* (1989). Lutz Niethammer, *Posthistoire: Has History Come to an End?*, trans. Patrick Camiller (London: Verso, [1989] 1993).
82. Anderson 1992b, 293.
83. Ibid., 301.
84. Ibid., 304.
85. Ibid., 318.
86. Ibid., 319; emphasis added.
87. Ibid., 316.
88. Ibid., 324.
89. Ibid., 351–52.
90. Ibid., 355.
91. Ibid., 356.
92. Francis Fukuyama, "The Neoconservative Moment," *The National Interest*, Summer (2004): 57–68. This piece was later revised and expanded into *America at the Crossroads* (New Haven: Yale University Press, 2006).
93. Anderson 2015, 248–49.
94. Ibid., 252.
95. Ibid.
96. Anderson 1992b, 367–68.
97. Ibid., 368–69.
98. Ibid., 370.
99. Ibid., 371.
100. Ibid., 372.
101. Ibid., 372–75.

Intermission II:
Perry Anderson's Clear-Headed Radicalism

1. Anderson 2000.
2. For more on Anderson's view of the advance of capitalist culture, see *The Origins of Postmodernity* (1998).
3. Anderson 2017a.
4. Anderson 1974a; 1974b.
5. Anderson 2017a, 180.
6. Ibid., 1–2.
7. Anderson (2017a, 119), referencing Xunzi.
8. Ibid., 122, 125–26.
9. As shown in this work, Anderson addressed Gramsci in the 1960s (with the Nairn-Anderson theses), in the 1970s (Anderson 1976a; "A Decennial Report" 1975), and in a companion book released alongside *The H-Word*, an edited reprint of his article of the same name from forty-one years prior, titled *The Antinomies of Antonio Gramsci* (2017b). Even as he downplayed Gramsci's significance for his intellectual development, Anderson never really let go. For more on Anderson's interpretation of the Italian thinker, see Blackledge (2004, 80–85).
10. Anderson 2017a, 16, 19.
11. Anderson 1976a, 20.
12. Anderson 2017a, 80–81.
13. Ibid., ch. 8.
14. Ibid., 107–16.
15. See, Giovanni Arrighi, *The Long Twentieth Century* (London: Verso [1994] 2010).
16. Anderson 2017a, 73.
17. Ibid., 74.
18. Qtd. in Anderson 2017a, 140.
19. Anderson 2017a, ch. 10.
20. Ibid., 152.
21. Ibid., 115–16.
22. Bruce Robbins, "The Long Goodbye: Perry Anderson's realism," in *The Nation* (May 3, 2018): https://www.thenation.com/article/perry-anderson-the-long-goodbye/.
23. For my comparison of thinkers based on conceptions of the past and the future, see: Gregory P. Williams, "Old Ideas for New Times: Radical History in International Political Economy," *Perspectives on Global Development and Technology* 17, no. 4 (2018b): 429–50.
24. Robbins 2018, ¶15.
25. These were discussed in chapters 6 and 2.
26. See, for example Anderson 2015, 197–217, 253.

27. According to Anderson, Guha only erred by making the same judgment after independence, which relied on more democratic mechanisms (2017a, 99–107).
28. *Arguments within English Marxism* (Anderson 1980).
29. Anderson 2017a, 182.

Chapter 7

1. See, for example, Tariq Ali, *The Clash of Fundamentalisms* (London: Verso, 2002); Susan Buck-Morss, *Thinking Past Terror* (London: Verso, 2006); and Solomon Hughes, *War on Terror, Inc.* (London: Verso, 2008).
2. See: Philip Mirowski, *Never Let a Serious Crisis Go to Waste: How Neoliberalism Survived the Financial Meltdown* (London: Verso, 2013); Antony Lowenstein, *Disaster Capitalism* (London: Verso, 2015).
3. Anderson 2017b, 27.
4. Wallerstein's writings on knowledge accumulation appeared in four books: *Unthinking Social Science* (1991), *The End of the World As We Know It* (Minneapolis: University of Minnesota Press, 1999), *The Uncertainties of Knowledge* (2004a), and, with several coauthors, *Open the Social Sciences* (Stanford: Stanford University Press, 1996). He also edited a book on disciplinary divisions with Richard E. Lee, *Overcoming the Two Cultures* (Boulder: Paradigm, 2004).
5. When asked about his numerous essays, Wallerstein responded: "In my other writings I have dealt with the material that will be in volume five [of *The Modern World-System*] and maybe six, and so forth. And maybe I don't need to write it, but it isn't done as systematically, and I think as persuasively as it should be done. So, if I were to die tomorrow, my views on the twentieth century, and even on the twenty-first, exist in all kinds of articles. But the volume doesn't exist. So I will try" (interview with Williams 2013, 205).
6. Anderson [1976b] 1984, 1980, 1983, 1992a, 1992b, 2005.
7. On Europe: Perry Anderson and Patrick Camiller, eds. *Mapping the West European Left* (London: Verso, 1994); Peter Gowan and Perry Anderson, eds. *The Question of Europe* (London: Verso, 1997). On Russia: "Perry Anderson reflects on his experience of the Moscow coup, and of its failure, and considers Gorbachev's failure and success," *London Review of Books* 13, no. 18 (1991): 5–8; and, "Russia's Managed Democracy," *London Review of Books* 29, no. 2 (2007): 3–12. On Brazil: "The Dark Side of Brazilian Conviviality," *London Review of Books* 16, no. 22 (1994): 3–8; "The Cardoso Legacy: Lula's Inheritance," *London Review of Books* 24, no. 24 (2002): 18–22; "Crisis in Brazil," *London Review of Books* 38, no. 8 (2016): 15–22. On China: "Stand-Off in Taiwan," *London Review of Books* 26, no. 11 (2004b): 12–17; "Two Revolutions," *New Left Review* II/ 61 (2010a): 59–96; "Sinomania," *London Review of Books* 32, no. 2 (2010b): 3–6; and, "Sino-Americana," *London Review of Books* 34, no. 3 (2012b): 20–22. On India:

The Indian Ideology (New Delhi: Three Essays Collective, 2012c). And, on the Arab world: "On the Concatenation in the Arab World," *New Left Review* II/68 (2011): 5–15; and, Anderson's interview with Suleiman Mourad, *The Mosiac of Islam* (London: Verso, 2016b).

    8. Immanuel Wallerstein *European Universalism: The Rhetoric of Power* (New York: The New Press, 2006).

    9. These lectures later appeared as Wallerstein 2006.

    10. Bonar Ludwig Hernandez, "The Las Casas-Sepúlveda Controversy: 1550–1551" (undated), archived at https://web.archive.org/web/20150421063702/http://userwww.sfsu.edu/epf/journal_archive/volume_X%2C_2001/hernandez_b.pdf.

    11. Wallerstein 2006, 11.
    12. Ibid., 5.
    13. Ibid., 7.
    14. Ibid., 8.
    15. Ibid., 24–25.
    16. Ibid., 8.
    17. Ibid., 6.
    18. Ibid., 20.

    19. "The Great Libyan Distraction," Commentary No. 302 (April 1, 2011): http://www.iwallerstein.com/great-libyan-distraction/; and "The Very Risky Bet of Hollande in Mali: The Probably Long-Term Disaster," Commentary No. 346 (February 1, 2013): http://www.iwallerstein.com/risky-bet-hollande-mali-probable-longterm-disaster/.

    20. Wallerstein, April 1, 2011.
    21. Ibid.
    22. Wallerstein 2006, 29.
    23. Wallerstein 2006, 47.

    24. Wallerstein wrote: "We may start with the paradoxical argument that there is nothing so ethnocentric, so particularist, as the claim of universalism" (2006, 40).

    25. Ibid., 45–46.
    26. Ibid., 49.
    27. Ibid., 80.

    28. Immanuel Wallerstein, letter to the News Editor, January 17, 1972. Wallerstein Papers, Box 58, Folder: "The New York Times." The article in question was a brief piece, "Facts on Republic of Ghana," from three days prior (available at https://nyti.ms/2MDLFe5).

    29. Ibid.

    30. E. Debrah, Ghana's ambassador to the United States, who also received a copy of Wallerstein's letter to the *Times*, praised Wallerstein for "coming to the defence at least as a scholar of Ghanaians at this time." E. Debrah, letter to

Immanuel Wallerstein, January 24, 1972. Wallerstein Papers, Box 58, Folder: "The New York Times."

31. James L. Greenfield, letter to Immanuel Wallerstein, 25 January 25, 1972. Wallerstein Papers, Box 58, Folder: "The New York Times."

32. Immanuel Wallerstein, letter to the James L. Greenfield, February 8, 1972. Wallerstein Papers, Box 58, Folder: "The New York Times."

33. Grace Lichtenstein, "'Transitional' Crown Heights Now in Midst of Comeback," *The New York Times* (August 1, 1974): https://nyti.ms/2MHiCX5.

34. Immanuel Wallerstein, letter to the editor, August 1, 1974. Wallerstein Papers, Box 58, Folder: "The New York Times."

35. George Palmer, letter to Immanuel Wallerstein, August 23, 1974. Wallerstein Papers, Box 58, Folder: "The New York Times."

36. Immanuel Wallerstein, letter to George Palmer, August 29, 1974. Wallerstein Papers, Box 58, Folder: "The New York Times."

37. See Lori L. Tharps's op-ed, "The Case for Black With a Capital B," *The New York Times* (November 18, 2014): http://nyti.ms/11hYFJC.

38. Comprised of twelve previously published essays in the *London Review of Books*, one from the *New Left Review*, and new introductory and concluding material, the result was a single argument greater than its individual contributions. I make this point in my review of Anderson's book. See Gregory P. Williams, "Review of P. Anderson, *The New Old World*," *Socialist History* 39 (2011): 100–103.

39. Anderson 2009, xiv.

40. Perry Anderson, "After the Event," *New Left Review* II/73 (2012a): 52.

41. NLR Editors, "Turmoil in Europe," *New Left Review* II/73 (2012): 18.

42. Anderson 2009, 20.

43. Moreover, larger lessons were always background, never foreground. Two edited volumes helped Anderson to place his vision of European history alongside that of other scholars (Anderson and Camiller 1994; Gowan and Anderson 1997).

44. Anderson 2009, 98.

45. Ibid., 12–17, 540.

46. Elsewhere, Anderson noted that Hayek would not completely approve, even though it formed largely in line with his views (2009, 540–41).

47. Anderson 2009, 66.

48. Ibid., 67.

49. Ibid., 547.

50. Ibid., 67.

51. Ibid., 133.

52. Ibid., 518.

53. Ibid., 475–76.

54. Ibid., 518.

55. In the twentieth century, "totalitarian creeds—exacerbated nationalism, fascism, bolshevism—shattered Europe in successive catastrophic conflicts" (Anderson 2009, 519).
56. Ibid.
57. Ibid.
58. Ibid.
59. Williams 2011, 102.
60. Habermas received harsh treatment throughout *The New Old World*. Anderson portrayed him as out of touch, sliding from Hegelian Marxism to a kind of Kantian pragmatism, unaware of lower-class interests or needs (2009, 513).
61. Ibid., 49.
62. Ibid., 56.
63. Ibid., 57.
64. Ibid., 58.
65. Ibid., 60.
66. Ibid., 539.
67. Ibid., 536–37.
68. Ibid., 538.
69. Ibid., 538–39.
70. "Once the space of political choice is narrowed so drastically, a certain decathexis of the public sphere"—a withdrawal of the public sphere's mental energy—"is bound to ensue" (Ibid., 542).
71. "Why the system will still win," *Le Monde Diplomatique*, March (2017c), ¶8.
72. Anderson nonetheless sympathized with the dilemmas of the Left: their concerns of a non-xenophobic, "humane internationalism," combined with their worries of regression to pre–World War nationalism (2017c).
73. Anderson 2009, 355, 393, 545.
74. Ibid., 355.
75. Ibid., 373.
76. Ibid., 403.
77. Ibid., 405–406.
78. Ibid., 407.
79. Ibid., 408.
80. Ibid., 417.
81. Ibid., 418–19.
82. Ibid., 393–94.
83. Ibid., 464.
84. Ibid., 391.
85. Ibid., 472.
86. Anderson 2017c.
87. Anderson 2009, 543–47.

88. See Anderson 2017c, and "Passing the Baton," *New Left Review* II/103 (2017d): 41–64.

Conclusion

1. Anderson 2005, 278.
2. Anderson 2017b, 13.
3. Georgi Derluguian, "Spaces, Trajectories, Maps: Towards a World-Systems Biography of Immanuel Wallerstein," *Journal of World-Systems Research* 21, no. 2 (2015): 449.
4. Shenhav 2015, 57.
5. Theodore A. Wilson, "Individuals, Narratives, and Diplomatic History," in *Presidents, Diplomats, and Other Mortals*, ed. Garry Clifford and Theodore A. Wilson (Columbia: University of Missouri Press, 2007), 1–11.
6. In the fall of 1973, Wallerstein sent (at Brenner's request) a copy of his "slightly messy" book manuscript along with an outline of the project and "a paper which will explain further the theoretical assumptions" (a reference, presumably, to "Rise and Future Demise"). The exchange lasted about four months: Brenner's letters are dated September 27, 1973, October 9, 1973, and January 28, 1974; Wallerstein's letters in return are dated October 3, 1973, October 24, 1973 (delayed due to a strike at McGill), and February 1, 1974. Wallerstein Papers, Box 44, Folder: "Robert Brenner."
7. Rodney Hilton et al., *The Transition from Feudalism to Capitalism* (London: Verso, 1976).
8. Brenner [1976] 1985 and 1977.
9. See: Robert Brenner, "The Origins of Capitalist Development: a Critique of Neo-Smithian Marxism." *New Left Review* I/104 (1977): 25–92.
10. Wallerstein 2011b, xx.
11. Brenner's quotations from Wallerstein's text even omitted the hyphen from *world-system* and *world-economy*, which, for Wallerstein, were important indicators of his use of totalities instead of an examination of a smaller scale (the nation-state) or a larger scale (the whole planet). See Brenner 1977, 30, 53, 54.
12. T. Aston and C. E. Philpin, eds., *The Brenner Debate* (Cambridge: Cambridge University Press, 1985); Robert A. Denemark and Kenneth P. Thomas, "The Brenner-Wallerstein Debate," *International Studies Quarterly* 32, no. 1 (1988): 47–65; Robert A. Denemark, "Core-Periphery Trade: The Debate with Brenner over the Nature of the Link and its Lessons," *Humboldt Journal of Social Relations* 18, no. 1 (1992): 119–45.
13. Alexander Anievas and Kerem Nişancioğlu, *How the West Came to Rule* (London: Pluto Press, 2015).
14. Anderson 1980, 137.

15. Calling the term *coup* overblown, Anderson responded with his own characterization: *abdication* (1980, 137).

16. In response to the Tom Nairn and Perry Anderson theses, Thompson wrote: "Our authors bring to this analysis the zest of explorers. They set out on their circumnavigation by discarding, with derision, the old speculative charts. . . . [O]ur explorers are heroic and missionary. We hold our breath in suspense as the first Marxist landfall is made upon this uncharted Northland. . . . There is a sense of rising suspense as they—the First White Marxists—approach the astonished aborigines." E. Thompson, "The Peculiarities of the English," in *The Poverty of Theory and Other Essays* (New York: Monthly Review [1965] 1978), 248.

17. Anderson opened his essay with lines to match Thompson: "In a voice choking with anger, Edward Thompson has denounced the historical and theoretical work on British society developed in this review. In twenty years of public life, no other group or individual has earned the kind of unprovoked attack he has launched over some fifty pages. . . . Certainly, no opponent on the Right has ever aroused this fixity of passion and rancor. It has been reserved, apparently, for fellow-socialists" (1966, 2).

18. Thompson [1963] 1966, 9.

19. Anderson's rebuttal came years after Thompson's book, in a work titled *Arguments Within English Marxism* (1980).

20. Anderson 2005, 180.

21. Harvey 2005, 19–20.

22. Monbiot 2016, 4.

23. Razmig Keucheyan, *The Left Hemisphere*, trans. Gregory Elliott (London: Verso, 2013), 59.

24. Molly Andrews, *Shaping History: Narratives of Political Change* (Cambridge: Cambridge University Press, 2007), 66.

25. Alain Badiou, *The Communist Hypothesis* (London: Verso, 2015), 29.

26. For those familiar with Keucheyan's typology of critical theorists, rather broadly conceived, Wallerstein and Anderson would also be labeled "innovators" or "expects"—that is, resisters who continued to innovate theoretically or mounted criticism against dominant explanations of economics and society (2013, 59–69).

27. "The Falsity of False Consciousness," Commentary No. 445 (March 15, 2017): http://iwallerstein.com/the-falsity-of-false-consciousness/.

28. Anderson 2017c.

29. Christopher Chase-Dunn explained this point in his article, "Interstate System and Capitalist World-Economy: One Logic or Two?" *International Studies Quarterly* 25, no. 1 (1981): 19–42.

30. Two classic works in this genre, with opposing conclusions, are Susan Strange's *The Retreat of the State: The Diffusion of Power in the World Economy* (Cambridge: Cambridge University Press, 1996), and Robert Gilpin's *War and Change in World Politics* (Cambridge: Cambridge University Press, 1981).

31. Sarah Bakewell, *At the Existentialist Café* (New York: Other Press, 2016), 217.
32. Ibid.

Bibliography

"A Decennial Report." 1975. Unpublished *New Left Review* document: 1–131.

Abu-Lughod, Janet. 1989. *Before European Hegemony: The World System A.D. 1250–1350*. Oxford: Oxford University Press.

Achcar, Gilbert. 2000. "The 'Historical Pessimism' of Perry Anderson." *International Socialism* 88: 135–41.

Ali, Tariq. 2002. *The Clash of Fundamentalisms*. London: Verso.

———. 2018, May 21. "We Shall Fight, We Shall Win": http://tariqali.org/archives/3269.

———. 2018a. Interview by David Edgar. "That Was the Year That Was." *London Review of Books* 40 (10): 3–10.

———. 2018b. *Street Fighting Years*, 2nd ed. London: Verso.

Amin, Samir. 2013. *The Implosion of Contemporary Capitalism*. New York: Monthly Review.

Anderson, Benedict. 1990. *Language and Power: Exploring Political Cultures in Indonesia*. Ithaca: Cornell University Press.

———. 2016. *A Life beyond Boundaries*. London: Verso.

Anderson, Perry. [Undated]. "Book-Lists." Binghamton University, Wallerstein Papers, Box 67, Folder: "P. Anderson."

———. 1961a. "Sweden: Mr. Crosland's Dreamland, Part 1." *New Left Review* I/7 (January–February): 4–12.

———. 1961b. "Sweden: Mr. Crosland's Dreamland, Part 2." *New Left Review* I/9 (May–June): 34–45.

———. 1962a. "The Debate of the Central Committee of the Italian Communist Party on the 22nd Congress of the CPSU." *New Left Review* I/13–14 (January–April): 152–60.

———. 1962b. "Portugal and the End of Ultra-Colonialism." *New Left Review* I/15 (May–June): 83–102.

———. 1962c. "Portugal and the End of Ultra-Colonialism 2." *New Left Review* I/16 (July–August): 88–122.

———. 1962d. "Portugal and the End of Ultra-Colonialism 3." *New Left Review* I/17 (Winter): 85–114.
———. 1964a. "Conspectus." Unpublished manuscript: 1–7.
———. 1964b. "Critique of Wilsonism." *New Left Review* I/27 (September–October): 3–27.
———. 1965a. "The Left in the Fifties." *New Left Review* I/29 (January–February): 3–18.
———. 1965b. "Problems of Socialist Strategy." In *Towards Socialism*, edited by Perry Anderson and Robin Blackburn, 221–90. London: The Fontana Library.
———. 1966. "Socialism and Pseudo-Empiricism." *New Left Review* I/35 (January–February): 2–42.
———. 1968. "Components of the National Culture." *New Left Review* I/50 (July–August): 3–57.
———. 1969. "The Founding Moment." Unpublished manuscript: 1–137.
———. 1974a. *Passages from Antiquity to Feudalism*. London: Verso.
———. 1974b. *Lineages of the Absolutist State*. London: Verso.
———. 1976, January 17. Letter to Immanuel Wallerstein. Binghamton University, Wallerstein Papers, Box 67, Folder: "P. Anderson."
———. 1976, December 9. Letter to Immanuel Wallerstein. Binghamton University, Wallerstein Papers, Box 67, Folder: "P. Anderson."
———. 1976a. "The Antinomies of Antonio Gramsci." *New Left Review* I/100 (November–December): 5–78.
———. [1976b] 1984. *Considerations on Western Marxism*, 4th ed. London: Verso.
———. 1977, March 28. Letter to Immanuel Wallerstein. Binghamton University, Wallerstein Papers, Box 67, Folder: "P Anderson."
———. 1980, August 8. Letter to Immanuel Wallerstein. Binghamton University, Wallerstein Papers, Box 67, Folder: "P Anderson."
———. 1980. *Arguments within English Marxism*. London: Verso.
———. 1983. *In the Tracks of Historical Materialism*. London: Verso.
———. 1991. "Perry Anderson reflects on his experience of the Moscow coup, and of its failure, and considers Gorbachev's failure and success." *London Review of Books* 13, no. 18: 5–8.
———. 1992a. *English Questions*. London: Verso.
———. 1992b. *A Zone of Engagement*. London: Verso.
———. 1993. "Maurice Thomson's War." *London Review of Books* 15, no. 21: 13–17.
———. 1994. "The Dark Side of Brazilian Conviviality." *London Review of Books* 16, no. 22: 3–8.
———. 1998. *The Origins of Postmodernity*. London: Verso.
———. 2000. "Renewals." *New Left Review* II/1 (January–February): 5–24.
———. 2002. "The Cardoso Legacy: Lula's Inheritance." *London Review of Books* 24, no. 24: 18–22.
———. 2004a. "The River of Time," *New Left Review* II/26 (March–April): 67–77.

———. 2004b. "Stand-Off in Taiwan," *London Review of Books* 26, no. 11: 12–17.
———. 2005. *Spectrum: From Right to Left in the World of Ideas*. London: Verso.
———. 2007. "Russia's Managed Democracy." *London Review of Books* 29, no. 2: 3–12.
———. 2009. *The New Old World*. London: Verso.
———. 2010a. "Two Revolutions." *New Left Review* II/61 (January–February): 59–96.
———. 2010b. "Sinomania." *London Review of Books* 32, no. 2: 3–6.
———. 2011. "On the Concatenation in the Arab World." *New Left Review* II/68 (March–April): 5–15.
———. 2012a. "After the Event." *New Left Review* II/73 (January–February): 49–61.
———. 2012b. "Sino-Americana." *London Review of Books* 34, no. 3: 20–22.
———. 2012c. *The Indian Ideology*. New Delhi: Three Essays Collective.
———. 2015. *American Foreign Policy and Its Thinkers*. London: Verso.
———. 2016a. "Crisis in Brazil," *London Review of Books* 38, no. 8: 15–22.
———. 2016b. Interview with Suleiman Mourad. *The Mosaic of Islam*. London: Verso.
———. 2017a. *The H-Word: The Peripeteia of Hegemony*. London: Verso.
———. 2017b. *The Antinomies of Antonio Gramsci*. London: Verso.
———. 2017c. "Why the System Will Still Win," *Le Monde Diplomatique* (March).
———. 2017d. "Passing the Baton," *New Left Review* II/103 (January–February): 41–64.
Anderson, Perry, and Patrick Camiller, eds. 1994. *Mapping the West European Left*. London: Verso.
Anderson, Perry, and Robin Blackburn. 1960. "Cuba, Free Territory of America." *New University* 4.
Anderson, Perry, Ronald Fraser, Quintin Hoare, and Simone de Beauvoir. 2006. *Conversations with Jean-Paul Sartre*. London: Seagull.
Anderson, Perry, and Stuart Hall. 1961. "Politics of the Common Market." *New Left Review* I/10 (July–August): 1–14.
Andrews, Molly. 2007. *Shaping History: Narratives of Political Change*. Cambridge: Cambridge University Press.
Anievas, Alexander, and Kerem Nişancioğlu. 2015. *How the West Came to Rule*. London: Pluto Press.
Arrighi, Giovanni. [1994] 2010. *The Long Twentieth Century*. London: Verso.
Arrighi, Giovanni, Terence K. Hopkins, and Immanuel Wallerstein. 1989. *Antisystemic Movements*. London: Verso.
———. 1992. "1989, The Continuation of 1968." *Review* 15, no. 2: 221–42.
Aronowitz, Stanley. 2006. *Left Turn*. Boulder: Paradigm.
———. 2012. *Taking It Big: C. Wright Mills and the Making of Political Intellectuals*. New York: Columbia University Press.

Aston, T., and C. E. Philpin, eds. 1985. *The Brenner Debate*. Cambridge: Cambridge University Press.
Avorn, Jerry L., et al. 1968. *Up Against the Ivy Wall*. New York: Atheneum.
Badiou, Alain. 2015. *The Communist Hypothesis*. London: Verso.
Bakewell, Sarah. 2016. *At the Existentialist Café*. New York: Other Press.
Barfield, Thomas. 2010. *Afghanistan: A Cultural and Political History*. Princeton: Princeton University Press.
Barnett, Anthony. 1976. "Raymond Williams and Marxism: A Rejoinder to Terry Eagleton." *New Left Review* I/99 (September–October): 47–64.
———. "Iron Britannia." 1982. *New Left Review* I/134 (July–August): 5–96.
Bartlett, Robert. 1994. *The Making of Europe*. Princeton: Princeton University Press.
Bass, Allen M. 1997. "The Metaphor of the Human Body in the Political Theory of John of Salisbury: Context and Innovation." In *Metaphor and Rational Discourse*, edited by Bernhard Debatin, Timothy R. Jackson, and Daniel Steurer, 201–13. Tübingen: Max Niemeyer Verlag.
Bergesen, Albert J. 2000. "The Columbia Social Essayists." *Journal of World-Systems Research* 6, no. 2: 198–213.
Bertram, Christopher, et al. 1993, February 24. "Resignations from the Editorial Board of *New Left Review*." Binghamton University, Wallerstein Papers, Box 58, Folder: "New Left Review."
Best, Jacqueline, and Matthew Paterson. 2010. *Cultural Political Economy*. London: Routledge.
Bidwell, Charles E. 1973, June 19. Letter to Immanuel Wallerstein. Binghamton University, Wallerstein Papers, Box 98, Folder: "The Rise and Future Demise of the World Capitalist System: Concepts for Comparative Analysis."
Blackburn, Robin. 1993, March 19. Letter to Contributors. Binghamton University, Wallerstein Papers, Box 35, Folder: "New Left Review."
Blackledge, Paul. 2004. *Perry Anderson, Marxism and the New Left*. London: Merlin.
Block, Fred, and Margaret R. Somers. 1984. "Beyond the Economistic Fallacy: The Holistic Social Science of Karl Polanyi." In *Vision and Method in Historical Sociology*, edited by Theda Skocpol, 47–84. Cambridge: Cambridge University Press.
Bousquet, Nicole. 2012. "Core, Semiperiphery, Periphery: A Variable Geometry Presiding over Conceptualization." In *Routledge Handbook of World-Systems Analysis*, edited by Salvatore J. Babones and Christopher Chase-Dunn, 123–24. London: Routledge, 2012.
Braudel, Fernand. [1949] 1996. *The Mediterranean and the Mediterranean World in the Age of Philip II*, 2 vols. Translated by Sián Reynolds. Berkeley: University of California Press.
———. [1958] 1972. "History and the Social Sciences: The *Longue Durée*." Translated by Peter Burke. In *Economy & Society in Early Modern Europe: Essays from* Annales, 11–42. New York: Harper Torchbooks.

———. [1958] 2009. "History and the Social Sciences: The *Longue Durée*." Translated by Immanuel Wallerstein. *Review* 32, no. 2: 171–203.
———. [1979a] 1984. *Civilization and Capitalism III: The Perspective of the World*. Translated by Siàn Reynolds. New York: Harper and Row.
———. 1979b. "A Model for the Analysis of the Decline of Italy." Translated by Immanuel Wallerstein. *Review* 2, no. 4: 647–62.
Brenner, Robert. 1973, September 27. Letter to Immanuel Wallerstein. Binghamton University, Wallerstein Papers, Box 44: Folder: "Robert Brenner."
———. 1973, October 9. Letter to Immanuel Wallerstein. Binghamton University, Wallerstein Papers, Box 44: Folder: "Robert Brenner."
———. 1974, January 28. Letter to Immanuel Wallerstein. Binghamton University, Wallerstein Papers, Box 44: Folder: "Robert Brenner."
———. [1976] 1985. "Agrarian Class Structure and Economic Development in Pre-Industrial Europe." In *The Brenner Debate*, edited by T. Aston and C. E. Philpin, 10–63. Cambridge: Cambridge University Press.
———. 1977. "The Origins of Capitalist Development: a Critique of Neo-Smithian Marxism." *New Left Review* I/104: 25–92.
———. 1985. "The Agrarian Roots of European Capitalism." In *The Brenner Debate: Agrarian Class Structure and Economic Development in Pre-Industrial Europe*, edited by T. Aston and C. E. Philpin, 213–327. Cambridge: Cambridge University Press.
———. 2006. *The Economics of Global Turbulence*. London: Verso.
Brenner, Robert, and Mark Glick. 1991. "The Regulation Approach: Theory and History." *New Left Review* I/188 (July–August): 45–117.
Buck-Morss, Susan. 2006. *Thinking Past Terror*. London: Verso.
Bush, George W. 2008, September 24. "President Bush's Speech to the Nation on the Economic Crisis." *The New York Times*: https://nyti.ms/2ow5DdD.
Burke's Irish Family Records. 2004. Edited by Hugh Montgomery-Massingberd. London: Burke's Peerage.
Cafruny, Alan, Leila Simona Talani, and Gonzalo Pozo Martin, eds. 2016. *The Palgrave Handbook of Critical International Political Economy*. London: Palgrave.
Canning, Joseph. 1996. *A History of Medieval Political Thought, 300–1450*. London: Routledge.
Carr, Edward Hallett. 1961. *What Is History?* New York: Random House.
"Charter." 1983/4. Unpublished *New Left Review* document: 1–11.
Chase-Dunn, Christopher. "Interstate System and Capitalist World-Economy: One Logic or Two?" *International Studies Quarterly* 25, no. 1 (1981): 19–42.
———. 1998. *Global Formation: Structures of the World-Economy*, 2nd ed. Lanham, MD: Rowman and Littlefield.
Chase-Dunn, Christopher, and Hiroko Inoue. 2011. "Immanuel Wallerstein." In *The Wiley-Blackwell Companion to Major Social Theorists, Volume 2, Contemporary Social Theorists*, edited by George Ritzer and Jeffrey Stepinksy, 395–411. Chichester: John Wiley.

Chase-Dunn, Christopher, and Bruce Lerro. 2014. *Social Change: Globalization from the Stone Age to the Present.* Boulder: Paradigm.

Cohen, Benjamin J. 2008. *International Political Economy: An Intellectual History.* Princeton: Princeton University Press.

Colletti, Lucio. 1972. *From Rousseau to Lenin: Studies in Ideology and Society.* Trans. John Merrington and Judith White. New York: Monthly Review.

———. 1974. "A Political and Philosophical Interview." *New Left Review* I/86: 3–28.

Davidson, Neil. 2012. *How Revolutionary Were the Bourgeois Revolutions?* Chicago: Haymarket.

Davis, Mike. 2017. *Late Victorian Holocausts: El Niño Famines and the Making of the Third World,* 2nd ed. London: Verso.

Debrah, E. 1972, January 24. Letter to Immanuel Wallerstein. Binghamton University, Wallerstein Papers, Box 58, Folder: "The New York Times."

Denemark, Robert A. 1992. "Core-Periphery Trade: The Debate with Brenner over the Nature of the Link and its Lessons." *Humboldt Journal of Social Relations* 18, no. 1: 119–45.

———. 1999. "World System History: From Traditional Politics to the Study of Global Relations." *International Studies Review* 1, no. 2: 43–75.

Denemark, Robert A., and Kenneth P. Thomas. 1988. "The Brenner-Wallerstein Debate." *International Studies Quarterly* 32, no. 1: 47–65.

Derluguian, Georgi M. 2005. *Bourdieu's Secret Admirer in the Caucasus: A World-System Biography.* Chicago: The University of Chicago Press.

———. 2013. "What Communism Was." In *Does Capitalism Have a Future?* by Immanuel Wallerstein et al., 99–129. Oxford: Oxford University Press.

———. 2015. "Spaces, Trajectories, Maps: Towards a World-Systems Biography of Immanuel Wallerstein." *Journal of World-Systems Research* 21, no. 2: 448–59.

Drezner, Daniel. 2014. *The System Worked.* Oxford: Oxford University Press.

"Document A—Theory and Practice: The Coupure of May." 1968/9a. Unpublished *New Left Review* document: 1–17.

"Document B—Ten Theses." 1968/9b. Unpublished NLR document: 1–18.

Dursteler, Eric R. 2010. "Fernand Braudel (1902–1985)." In *French Historians, 1900–2000,* edited by Philip Daileader and Philip Whalen, 62–76. New York: Wiley-Blackwell.

Dworkin, Dennis. 1997. *Cultural Marxism in Postwar Britain.* Durham: Duke University Press.

Eagleton, Terry. 1976. "Criticism and Politics: The Work of Raymond Williams." *New Left Review* I/95 (January–February): 3–23.

Ekholm, K., and J. Friedman. 1993. "'Capital' Imperialism and Exploitation in Ancient World Systems." In *The Modern World System: Five Hundred Years or Five Thousand,* 59–80. London: Routledge.

Elliott, Gregory. 1995. "Olympus Mislaid? A Profile of Perry Anderson." *Radical Philosophy* 71 (May/June): 5–19.

---. 1998. *Perry Anderson: The Merciless Laboratory of History*. Minneapolis: University of Minnesota Press.

---. 2008. *Ends in Sight: Marx/Fukuyama/Hobsbawm/Anderson*. London: Pluto.

"Facts on Republic of Ghana." 1972, January 14. *The New York Times:* https://nyti.ms/2MDLFe5.

Fink, Carole, Philipp Gassert, and Detlef Junker, eds. 1998. *1968: The World Transformed*. Cambridge: Cambridge University Press.

Frank, Andre Gunder. 1969. *Latin America: Underdevelopment or Revolution*. New York: Monthly Review.

---. 1990. "A Theoretical Introduction to 5,000 Years of World System History." *Review* 13, no. 2: 155–248.

---. 1994. "The World Economic System in Asia before European Hegemony." *The Historian* 56, no. 4: 259–76.

---. 2000. "Immanuel and Me With-Out Hyphen." *Journal of World-Systems Research* 6, no. 2: 216–31.

Friedman, Robert. 1968. "Introduction." In *Up Against the Ivy Wall*, edited by Jerry L. Avorn et al., 3–22. New York: Atheneum.

Fukuyama, Francis. 1989. "The End of History?" *The National Interest* (Summer): 3–18.

---. 1992. *The End of History and the Last Man*. New York: The Free Press.

---. 2004. "The Neoconservative Moment." *The National Interest* (Summer): 57–68.

---. 2006. *America at the Crossroads: Democracy, Power, and the Neoconservative Legacy*. New Haven: Yale University Press.

Geras, Norman. 1979. "Literature of Revolution." *New Left Review* I/113–114 (January–April): 3–41.

Garnett, Mark. 2001, March 23. "New Left Review." *Times Literary Supplement*: 25.

Garraty, John A. 1957. *The Nature of Biography*. New York: Alfred A. Knopf.

Garvy, George. 1943. "Kondratieff's Theory of Long Cycles." *The Review of Economics and Statistics* 25, no. 4: 203–20.

Geithner, Timothy F. 2014. *Stress Test*. New York: Crown.

Gill, Stephen, ed. 1993. *Gramsci, Historical Materialism, and International Relations*. Cambridge: Cambridge University Press.

Gills, Barry K., and Andre Gunder Frank. 1993. "The Cumulation of Accumulation." In *The Modern World System: Five Hundred Years or Five Thousand*, edited by Andre Gunder Frank and Barry K. Gills, 81–114. London: Routledge.

Gilpin, Robert. 1981. *War and Change in World Politics*. Cambridge: Cambridge University Press.

Goldfrank, Walter L. 2000. "Paradigm Regained? The Rules of Wallerstein's World-System Method." *Journal of World-Systems Research* 6, no. 2: 150–95.

———. 2012. "Wallerstein's World-System: Roots and Contributions." In *Routledge Handbook of World-Systems Analysis*, edited by Salvatore J. Babones and Christopher Chase-Dunn, 97–103. London: Routledge.

Goodin, Robert E., and Charles Tilly, eds. 2006. *The Oxford Handbook of Contextual Political Analysis*. Oxford: Oxford University Press.

Gowan, Peter, and Perry Anderson, eds. 1997. *The Question of Europe*. London: Verso.

Gramsci, Antonio. 1971. *Selections from the Prison Notebooks*. Translated and edited by Quinton Hoare and Geoffrey Nowell Smith. New York: International Publishers.

Grebstein, Sheldon W. 1977, March 10. Letter to Perry Anderson. Binghamton University, Wallerstein Papers, Box 67, Folder: "P. Anderson."

———. 1977, June 15. Letter to Perry Anderson. Binghamton University, Wallerstein Papers, Box 67, Folder: "P. Anderson."

Greenfield, James L. 1972, January 25. Letter to Immanuel Wallerstein. Binghamton University, Wallerstein Papers, Box 58, Folder: "The New York Times."

Hall, Stuart. 2010. "The Life and Times of the First New Left." *New Left Review* II/61 (January–February): 177–96.

———. 2016. *Cultural Studies 1983: A Theoretical History*. Edited by Jennifer Daryl Slack and Lawrence Grossberg. Durham: Duke University Press.

———. 2017. *Familiar Stranger: A Life between Two Islands*, with Bill Schwarz. Durham: Duke University Press.

Harvey, David. 2005. *A Brief History of Neoliberalism*. Oxford: Oxford University Press.

Hernandez, Bonar Ludwig. [Undated]. "The Las Casas-Sepúlveda Controversy: 1550–1551": https://history.sfsu.edu/sites/default/files/images/2001_Bonar%20Ludwig%20Hernandez.pdf.

Hilton, Rodney. 1979. "Towns in English Feudal Society." *Review* 3, no. 1: 3–20.

———, et al. 1976. *The Transition from Feudalism to Capitalism*. London: Verso.

Hobsbawm, Eric. 1962. *The Age of Revolution: 1789–1848*. London: Weidenfeld & Nicolson.

———. 1975. *The Age of Capital: 1848–1875*. London: Weidenfeld & Nicolson.

———. 1987. *The Age of Empire: 1875–1914*. London: Weidenfeld & Nicolson.

———. 1978. "Comments." *Review* 1, no. 3/4.

———. 1994. *The Age of Extremes*. New York: Vintage.

———. 2002. *Interesting Times: A Twentieth-century Life*. New York: The New Press.

———. 2012, January 19. Interview by Jeremy Paxman. "Newsnight." *BBC News*: http://news.bbc.co.uk/2/hi/programmes/newsnight/9682626.

Hofstadter, Richard. [1954] 1965. "The Pseudo-Conservative Revolt." In *The Paranoid Style in American Politics*, 41–65. Cambridge: Harvard University Press.

———. 1965. "Pseudo-Conservatism Revisited." In *The Paranoid Style in American Politics*, 66–91. Cambridge: Harvard University Press.

Hopkins, Terence K., and Immanuel Wallerstein. 1967. "The Comparative Study of National Societies," *Social Science Information* 6, no. 5: 25–58.

———. 1987. "Capitalism and the Incorporation of New Zones into the World-Economy." *Review* 10, no. 5/6: 763–79.

Hughes, Solomon. 2008. *War on Terror, Inc*. London: Verso.

Italian Communist Party. 1962. "Text of the Debate of the Central Committee of the Italian Communist Party on the 22nd Congress of the CPSU." *New Left Review* I/13–14 (January–April): 161–91.

Jacoby, Russell. [1987] 2000. *The Last Intellectuals*. New York: Basic Books.

Jameson, Fredric. 2003. "Future City." *New Left Review* II/21 (May–June): 65–79.

———. 2009. *Valences of the Dialectic*. London: Verso.

Jay, Martin. 1984. *Marxism and Totality*. Berkeley: University of California Press.

Jervis, Robert. 2008. "Bridges, Barriers, and Gaps: Research and Policy." *Political Psychology* 29, no. 4: 571–92.

Jordan, David P. 1976. "Edward Gibbon: The Historian of the Roman Empire." *Daedalus* 105, no. 3: 1–12.

Kagarlitsky, Boris. 2000. "The Suicide of *New Left Review*." *International Socialism* 88: 127–33.

Katznelson, Ira. 2003. "Periodization and Preferences: Reflections on Purposive Action in Comparative Historical Social Science." In *Comparative Historical Analysis in the Social Sciences*, edited by James Mahoney and Dietrich Rueschemeyer, 270–301. Cambridge: Cambridge University Press.

Kaye, Harvey J. 1979. "Totality: Its Application to Historical and Social Analysis by Wallerstein and Genovese." *Historical Reflections* 6, no. 2: 405–20.

———. 1995. *The British Marxist Historians*, 2nd ed. New York: St. Martin's.

Keucheyan, Razmig. 2013. *The Left Hemisphere*. Translated by Gregory Elliott. London: Verso.

Kondratieff, Nikolai. [1926] 1935/1979. "The Long Waves in Economic Life." Translated by W. Stolper. *The Review of Economics and Statistics* 17, no. 6: 5–15; *Review* 2, no. 4: 519–62.

Kreisler, Harry. 2001. Interview with Perry Anderson. "Reflections on the Left from the Left." *Conversations with History* (April 27): https://conversations.berkeley.edu/anderson_2001.

Kunkel, Benjamin. 2014. *Utopia or Bust*. London: Verso.

Lee, Richard E. 2012. "Fernand Braudel, the *Longue Durée*, and World-Systems Analysis." In *The Longue Durée and World-Systems Analysis*, edited by Richard E. Lee, 1–7. Albany: State University of New York Press.

———, and Immanuel Wallerstein, eds. 2004. *Overcoming the Two Cultures: Science versus the Humanities in the Modern World-System*. Boulder: Paradigm.

Lemert, Charles. 2012a. "Wallerstein and the Uncertain Worlds." In *Uncertain Worlds: World-Systems Analysis in Changing Times*, 151–93. Boulder: Paradigm.

———. 2012b. Interview with Immanuel Wallerstein. "A Discussion of the Itinerary of World-Systems Analysis and Its Uncertainties." In *Uncertain Worlds: World-Systems Analysis in Changing Times*, 101–49. Boulder: Paradigm.

Lichtenstein, Grace. 1974, August 1. "'Transitional' Crown Heights Now in Midst of Comeback." *The New York Times*: https://nyti.ms/2MHiCX5.

Lijphart, Arend. 1971. "Comparative Politics and the Comparative Method." *American Political Science Review* 65, no. 3: 682–93.

Lukács, Georg. [1923] 1968. *History and Class Consciousness*. Cambridge: The MIT Press.

———. 1980. *The Destruction of Reason*. London: Merlin.

Mandel, Ernest. 1968. "Trotsky's Marxism: an Anti-Critique." *New Left Review* I/47: 32–51.

Manuel, Frank E. 1976. "Edward Gibbon: Historien-Philosophe." *Daedalus* 105, no. 3: 231–45.

Marshall, Stephen H. 2011. *The City on the Hill from Below: The Crisis of Prophetic Black Politics*. Philadelphia: Temple University Press.

McAdam, Doug. [1982] 1999. *Political Process and the Development of Black Insurgency*, 2nd ed. Chicago: University of Chicago Press.

Merton, Richard. 1968. "Comment [on Alan Beckett's 'Stones']." *New Left Review* I/47: 29–31.

———. 1970. "Comment [on Andrew Chester's 'For a Rock Aesthetic']." *New Left Review* I/59 (January–February): 88–96.

Mitchell, Juliet. 1966. "Women, the Longest Revolution." *New Left Review* I/40: 11–37.

Momigliano, Arnaldo. 1954. "Gibbon's Contribution to Historical Method." *Historia: Zeitschrift für Alte Geschichte* 2, no. 4: 450–63.

Monbiot, George. 2016. *How Did We Get into This Mess? Politics, Equality, Nature*. London: Verso.

MR Editors. 2000. "Socialism: A Time to Retreat?" *Monthly Review* (September): 1–7.

Murphy, Craig N. 2009. "Do the Left-Out Matter?" *New Political Economy* 14, no. 3: 357–65.

Murphy, Craig N., and Douglas R. Nelson. 2001. "International Political Economy: A Tale of Two Heterodoxies." *British Journal of Politics and International Relations* 3, no. 3: 393–412.

Nairn, Tom. 1964a. "The British Political Elite." *New Left Review* I/23 (January–February): 19–25.

———. 1964b. "The English Working Class." *New Left Review* I/24 (March–April): 43–57.

———. 1964c. "Hugh Gaitskell." *New Left Review* I/25 (May–June): 63–68.

———. 1964d. "The nature of the Labour Party—I." *New Left Review* I/27 (September–October): 38–65.

―――. 1964e. "The nature of the Labour Party—II." *New Left Review* I/28 (November–December): 33–62.

―――. 1965. "Labour Imperialism." *New Left Review* I/32 (July–August): 3–15.

―――. 1975. "The Modern Janus." *New Left Review* I/94 (November–December): 3–29.

Nelson, Stephen C., and Peter J. Katzenstein. 2014. "Uncertainty, Risk, and the Financial Crisis of 2008." *International Organization* 68, no. 2: 361–92.

Niethammer, Lutz. [1989] 1993. *Posthistoire: Has History Come to an End?* Translated by Patrick Camiller. London: Verso.

Nietzsche, Friedrich. [1874] 1980. *On the Advantage and Disadvantage of History for Life*. Translated by Peter Preuss. Indianapolis: Hackett.

"NLR 1975–1980." 1980. Unpublished *New Left Review* document: 1–92.

"NLR 1980–1983." 1983. Unpublished *New Left Review* document: 1–72.

NLR Editors. 1961. "Notes to Readers." *New Left Review* I/12 (November–December).

―――. 1963. "On Internationalism." *New Left Review* I/18 (January–February): 3–4.

―――. 1964a. "To Our Readers." *New Left Review* I/24 (March–April): 3–4.

―――. 1964b. "Statement (On Editorial Team)." *New Left Review* I/24 (March–April): 112.

―――. 1968. "Introduction to the Special Issue on France, May 1968" *New Left Review* I/52 (November–December): 1–8.

―――. 2012. "Turmoil in Europe." *New Left Review* II/73 (January–February): 18.

Nye, Joseph S. 2008. "Bridging the Gap between Theory and Policy." *Political Psychology* 29, no. 4: 593–603.

―――. 2009, April 13. "Scholars on the Sidelines." *The Washington Post*: http://www.washingtonpost.com/wp-dyn/content/article/2009/04/12/AR2009041202260.html.

Office for National Statistics. "Births Registered in July, August and September, 1938." General Register Office. England and Wales Civil Registration 1a: 482.

O'Neill, William L. 1982. *A Better World—The Great Schism: Stalinism and the American Intellectuals*. New York: Simon and Schuster.

Palmer, George. 1974, August 23. Letter to Immanuel Wallerstein. Binghamton University, Wallerstein Papers, Box 58, Folder: "The New York Times."

Piketty, Thomas. 2014. *Capital in the Twenty-First Century*. Translated by Arthur Goldhammer. Cambridge: The Belknap Press of Harvard University Press.

Polanyi, Karl. [1944] 2001. *The Great Transformation: The Political and Economic Origins of our Time*. Boston: Beacon Press.

―――. 1977. "The Economistic Fallacy." Translated by Harry W. Pearson. *Review* 1, no. 1: 9–18.

Prashad, Vijay. 2012. *The Poorer Nations*. London: Verso.

Prigogine, Ilya. 1977. "Time, Structure and Fluctuations," Nobel Lecture (1977): http://www.nobelprize.org/nobel_prizes/chemistry/laureates/1977/prigogine-lecture.html.

———. 1996. "The Laws of Chaos." Translated by Richard Lee. *Review* 19, no. 1: 1–9.

———. 1997. *The End of Certainty: Time, Chaos, and the New Laws of Nature*. New York: The Free Press.

———. 2000. "The Networked Society." *Journal of World-Systems Research* 6, no. 1: 892–98.

———. 2005. Interview by Hans Ulrich Obrist. "Science and Art." Translated by Gregory Ball. *Review* 28, no. 2: 115–28.

———, and Isabelle Stengers. 2017. *Order Out of Chaos: Man's New Dialogue with Nature*. London: Verso.

Radical Faculty Group. 1968, September 12. A Public Affirmation. Binghamton University, Wallerstein Papers, Box 8, Folder: "Ad Hoc Faculty."

Ragin, Charles and Daniel Chirot. 1984. "The World System of Immanuel Wallerstein: Sociology and Politics as History." In *Vision and Method in Historical Sociology*, edited by Theda Skocpol, 276–312. Cambridge: Cambridge University Press.

"Report on an Intellectual Project: The Fernand Braudel Center, 1976–1991." 1991. http://binghamton.edu/fbc/about-fbc/intellectual-report.html.

Research Working Group on Cyclical Rhythms and Secular Trends. 1979. "Cyclical Rhythms and Secular Trends of the Capitalist World-Economy: Some Premises, Hypotheses, and Questions." *Review* 2, no. 4: 483–500.

Robbins, Bruce. 2018. "The Long Goodbye: Perry Anderson's realism." *The Nation* (May): https://www.thenation.com/article/perry-anderson-the-long-goodbye/.

Rodney, Walter. [1972] 2011. *How Europe Underdeveloped Africa*. Baltimore: Black Classic Press.

Rojas, Carlos Antonio Aguirre. 2012a. Interview with Immanuel Wallerstein. "The World-Systems Analysis Perspective." In *Uncertain Worlds: World-Systems Analysis in Changing Times*, 1–100. Boulder: Paradigm.

———. 2012b. "Immanuel Wallerstein and the Critical 'World-Systems Analysis' Perspective." In *Uncertain Worlds: World-Systems Analysis in Changing Times*, vii–xl. Boulder: Paradigm.

Rosenau, James N. 1989. "Mapping and Organizing the Journeys." In *Journeys through World Politics: Autobiographical Reflections of Thirty-Four Academic Travelers*, edited by Joseph Kruzel and James N. Rosenau, 1–12. Lexington, MA: Lexington Books.

RT. 2011. Interview with Immanuel Wallerstein (October 9): http://youtu.be/eDgya5clTCY.

Sartre, Jean-Paul. 1960. "A Tour with Fidel Castro." Translated by Perry Anderson. *New University* 4.

———. 1968. *The Communists and Peace*. London: Hamilton.

Shenhav, Shaul R. 2015. *Analyzing Social Narratives*. London: Routledge.

Schouten, P. 2008. Interview with Immanuel Wallerstein. "Theory Talk #13: Immanuel Wallerstein on World-Systems, the Imminent End of Capitalism and Unifying Social Science." *Theory Talks*: http://www.theory-talks.org/2008/08/theory-talk-13.html.

Schwartz-Shea, Peregrine, and Dvora Yanow. 2012. *Interpretive Research Design*. New York: Routledge.

Skocpol, Theda, and Margaret Somers. 1980. "The Uses of Comparative History in Macrosocial Inquiry." *Comparative Studies in Society and History* 22, no. 2: 174–97.

Srnicek, Nick, and Alex Williams. 2015. *Inventing the Future*. London: Verso.

Stalin, Josef. 1938. "Dialectical and Historical Materialism": https://www.marxists.org/reference/archive/stalin/works/1938/09.htm.

Stern, Michael. 1968, April 30. "Teachers at Columbia Risk Violence as Mediators." *The New York Times*: 37.

Strange, Susan. 1996. *The Retreat of the State: The Diffusion of Power in the World Economy*. Cambridge: Cambridge University Press.

Streeck, Wolfgang. 2014. "How Will Capitalism End?" *New Left Review* II/87 (May–June): 35–64.

Stutje, Jan Willem. *Ernest Mandel: A Rebel's Dream Deferred*. Translated by Christopher Beck and Peter Drucker. London: Verso.

Taylor, Peter J. 2012. "History and Geography: Braudel's 'Extreme *Longue Durée*' as Generics?" In *The Longue Durée*, edited by Richard E. Lee, 33–64. Albany: State University of New York Press.

Tharps, Lori L. 2014, November 18. "The Case for Black with a Capital B," *The New York Times*: http://nyti.ms/11hYFJC.

Thompson, Duncan. 2007. *Pessimism of the Intellect? A History of* New Left Review. London: Merlin.

Thompson, E. P. [1963] 1966. *The Making of the English Working Class*. New York: Vintage.

———. [1965] 1978. "The Peculiarities of the English." In *The Poverty of Theory and Other Essays*, 245–301. New York: Monthly Review.

Tilly, Charles. 1978. "Anthropology, History, and the *Annales*." *Review* 1 (3/4): 207–13.

———. 1984. "The Old New Social History and the New Old Social History." *Review* 7, no. 3: 363–406.

Tomich, Dale. 2012. "The Order of Historical Time: The *Longue Durée* and Micro-History." In *The Longue Durée*, edited by Richard E. Lee, 9–33. Albany: State University of New York Press.

ULR Editors. 1957. "Editorial and Contents." *Universities and Left Review* 1 (Spring).

Unger, Roberto Mangabeira. 1975. *Knowledge and Politics*. New York: The Free Press.

———. 2009. *The Left Alternative*. London: Verso.

Wallerstein, Immanuel. [Undated]. "Why is the Study of Long Waves Controversial?" Binghamton University, Wallerstein Papers, Box 94, Folder: "Why is the Study of Long Waves Controversial?"

———. 1951. "Revolution and Order." *Federalist Opinion* 1, no. 7: 23–26.

———. 1953, November 14. Letter to Senator Joseph McCarthy. Binghamton University, Wallerstein Papers, Box 35, Folder: "Thesis MA."

———. 1954. "McCarthyism and the Conservative." Master of Arts Thesis. Columbia University, Rare Book and Manuscript Archive.

———. 1959. *The Emergence of Two West African Nations: Ghana and the Ivory Coast.* PhD Dissertation, Columbia University.

———. [1961] 2005a. *Africa: The Politics of Independence.* Lincoln: University of Nebraska Press.

———. 1964. *The Road to Independence: Ghana and the Ivory Coast.* Paris: Mouton.

———. [1967] 2005b. *Africa: The Politics of Unity.* Lincoln: University of Nebraska Press.

———. 1969. *University in Turmoil: The Politics of Change.* New York: Atheneum.

———. 1970. "Frantz Fanon: Reason and Violence." *Berkeley Journal of Sociology* 15: 222–31.

———. 1971a. "Academic Freedom and Collective Expressions of Opinion," *Journal of Higher Education* 42, no. 9: 713–20.

———. 1971b. "There Is No Such Thing as Sociology." *The American Sociologist* 6, no. 4: 328.

———. 1972, January 17. Letter to the News Editor. Binghamton University, Wallerstein Papers, Box 58, Folder: "The New York Times."

———. 1972, February 8. Letter to the James L. Greenfield. Binghamton University, Wallerstein Papers, Box 58, Folder: "The New York Times."

———. 1972. "Three Paths of National Development in Sixteenth-Century Europe." *Studies in Comparative International Development* 7, no. 2: 95–101.

———. 1973, October 3. Letter to Robert Brenner. Binghamton University, Wallerstein Papers, Box 44: Folder: "Robert Brenner."

———. 1973, October 24. Letter to Robert Brenner. Binghamton University, Wallerstein Papers, Box 44: Folder: "Robert Brenner."

———. 1974, February 1. Letter to Robert Brenner. Binghamton University, Wallerstein Papers, Box 44: Folder: "Robert Brenner."

———. 1974, August 1. Letter to the Editor. Binghamton University, Wallerstein Papers, Box 58, Folder: "The New York Times."

———. 1974, August 29. Letter to George Palmer. Binghamton University, Wallerstein Papers, Box 58, Folder: "The New York Times."

———. 1974a. "The Rise and Future Demise of the World Capitalist System: Concepts for Comparative Analysis." *Comparative Studies in Society and History* 16, no. 4: 387–415.

———. 1974b. *The Modern World-System I: Capitalist Agriculture and the Origins of the European World-Economy in the Sixteenth Century.* New York: Academic Press.

———. 1975, March 10. Letter to David Solomon. Binghamton University, Wallerstein Papers, Box 37, Folder: "McGill—Department of Sociology, David Solomon."

———. 1977, January 22. Letter to Perry Anderson. Binghamton University, Wallerstein Papers, Box 67, Folder: "P. Anderson."

———. 1977, September 7. "Testimony given at hearings on 'Underdevelopment in Africa' of House of Representatives, Committee on International Relations, Subcommittee on Africa." Binghamton University, Wallerstein Papers, Box 52, Folder: "House of Representatives' Subcommittee on Africa."

———. 1977. "The Tasks of Historical Social Science: An Editorial." *Review* 1, no. 1: 3–7.

———. 1978, April 24. Letter to Perry Anderson. Binghamton University, Wallerstein Papers, Box 67, Folder: "P. Anderson."

———. 1979, May 16. Letter to Perry Anderson. Binghamton University, Wallerstein Papers, Box 67, Folder: "P. Anderson."

———. 1979a. *The Capitalist World-Economy.* Cambridge: Cambridge University Press.

———. 1979b. "Kondratieff Up or Kondratieff Down?" *Review* 2, no. 4: 663–73.

———. 1980. *The Modern World-System II: Mercantilism and the Consolidation of the European World-Economy, 1600–1750.* New York: Academic Press.

———. 1982. "Crisis as Transition." In *Dynamics of Global Crisis*, by Samir Amin, et al., 11–54. New York: Monthly Review.

———. 1984a. "Marx and History: Fruitful and Unfruitful Emphases." *Thesis Eleven* 8: 92–101.

———. 1984b. *The Politics of the World-Economy: The States, the Movements, and the Civilizations.* Cambridge: Cambridge University Press.

———. 1984c. "Long Waves as Capitalist Process." *Review* 7, no. 4: 559–75.

———. 1989, August 23. Letter to Andre Gunder Frank. Binghamton University, Wallerstein Papers, Box 50, Folder: "Andre Gunder Frank."

———. 1989. *The Modern World-System III: The Second Era of Great Expansion of the Capitalist World-Economy, 1730–1840s.* New York: Academic Press.

———. 1991. *Geopolitics and Geoculture: Essays on the Changing World-system.* Cambridge: Cambridge University Press.

———. 1992. "The West, Capitalism, and the Modern World-System." *Review* 15, no. 4: 561–619.

———. 1993. "World System Versus World-Systems: A Critique." In *The Modern World System: Five Hundred Years or Five Thousand?* edited by Andre Gunder Frank and Barry K. Gills, 292–96. London: Routledge.

———. 1995a. *Historical Capitalism with Capitalist Civilization*, 2nd ed. London: Verso.

———. 1995b. *After Liberalism*. New York: The New Press.

———. 1998a. "Pedagogy and Scholarship." In *Mentoring Methods and Movements: Colloquium in Honor of Terence K. Hopkins by his Former Students*, edited by Immanuel Wallerstein, 47–52. Binghamton, NY: Fernand Braudel Center.

———. 1998b. *Utopistics: Or, Historical Choices of the 21st Century*. New York: The New Press.

———. 1999. *The End of the World as We Know It: Social Science for the 21st Century*. Minneapolis: University of Minnesota Press.

———. 2000. *The Essential Wallerstein*. New York: The New Press.

———. 2001. *Unthinking Social Science*, 2nd ed. Philadelphia: Temple University Press.

———. 2003. *The Decline of American Power*. New York: The New Press.

———. 2004a. *The Uncertainties of Knowledge*. Philadelphia: Temple University Press.

———. 2004b. *World-Systems Analysis: An Introduction*. Durham: Duke University Press.

———. 2006. *European Universalism: The Rhetoric of Power*. New York: The New Press.

———. 2009a. "Reading Fanon in the 21st Century." *New Left Review* II/57 (May–June): 117–25.

———. 2009b. "Braudel on the *Longue Durée*: Problems of Conceptual Translation." *Review* 32, no. 2: 155–70.

———. 2010. "What Cold War in Asia? An Interpretive Essay." In *The Cold War in Asia: The Battle for Hearts and Minds*, edited by Zheng Yangwen, Hong Liu, and Michael Szonyi, 15–24. Boston: Brill.

———. 2011, April 1. "The Great Libyan Distraction." Commentary No. 302: http://www.iwallerstein.com/great-libyan-distraction/.

———. 2011a. *The Modern World-System IV: Centrist Liberalism Triumphant, 1789–1914*. Berkeley: University of California Press.

———. 2011b. "Prologue to the 2011 Edition." In *The Modern World-System I: Capitalist Agriculture and the Origins of the European World-Economy in the Sixteenth Century*, 2nd ed., xvii–xxx. Berkeley: University of California Press.

———. 2011c. "Prologue to the 2011 Edition." In *The Modern World-System II: Mercantilism and the Consolidation of the European World-Economy 1600–1750*, xiii–xxvii. Berkeley: University of California Press.

———. 2012, April 8. "Crisis and Upsurge in Movements." Keynote address for The Progress Paradox: Critical Perspectives on Development at Swarthmore College. Swarthmore, PA: http://theprogressparadox.wordpress.com/.

———. 2013, February 1. "The Very Risky Bet of Hollande in Mali: The Probably Long-Term Disaster." Commentary No. 346: http://www.iwallerstein.com/risky-bet-hollande-mali-probable-longterm-disaster/.

———. 2013, April 15. "End of the Road for Runaway Factories?" Commentary no. 351: http://www.iwallerstein.com/road-runaway-factories/.

———. 2014. "Antisystemic Movements, Yesterday and Today," *Journal of World-Systems Research* 20, no. 2: 158–72.

———. 2017, March 15. "The Falsity of False Consciousness." Commentary No. 445: http://iwallerstein.com/the-falsity-of-false-consciousness/.

———. 2017, May 15. "Global Left vs. Global Right: 1945 to Today." Commentary No. 449: http://iwallerstein.com/global-left-vs-global-right-from-1945-to-today/.

———, and Armand Clesse, eds. 2002. *The World We Are Entering, 2002–2050*. The Netherlands: Dutch University Press.

Wallerstein, Immanuel, et al. 1996. *Open the Social Sciences: Report of the Gulbenkian Commission on the Restructuring of the Social Sciences*. Stanford: Stanford University Press.

Wallerstein, Immanuel, and Michael Hechter. 1970. "Social Rank and Nationalism: Some African Data." *The Public Opinion Quarterly* 34, no. 3: 360–70.

Walt, Stephen M. 2005. "The Relationship between Theory and Policy in International Relations." *Annual Review of Political Science* 8: 23–48.

———. 2009, April 15. "The Cult of Irrelevance." *Foreign Policy*: http://walt.foreignpolicy.com/posts/2009/04/15/the_cult_of_irrelevance.

Weber, Max. 1946. "Class, Status Party." In *Essays in Sociology*. Translated and edited by H. Gerth and C. Wright Mills, 180–195. Oxford: Oxford University Press.

Weiss, Thomas G., and Elizabeth R. DeSombre. 2010. Call for Papers: "Theory vs. Policy? Connecting Scholars and Practitioners," International Studies Association: www.isanet.org.

Wilson, Theodore A. 2007. "Individuals, Narratives, and Diplomatic History." In *Presidents, Diplomats, and Other Mortals*, edited by J. Garry Clifford and Theodore A. Wilson, 1–11. Columbia: University of Missouri Press.

Williams, Gregory P. 2010. "When Opportunity Structure Knocks: Social Movements in the Soviet Union and Russian Federation." *Social Movement Studies* 9, no. 4: 443–60.

———. 2011. "Review of P. Anderson, *The New Old World*." *Socialist History* 39: 100–103.

———. 2013. Interview with Immanuel Wallerstein. "Retrospective on the Origins of World-Systems Analysis." *Journal of World-Systems Research* 19, no. 2: 202–10.

———. 2018a. "Will We Know It When We See It? Contemplating Emergent World-Systems," *Journal of Globalization Studies* 9, no. 1: 129–49.

———. 2018b. "Old Ideas for New Times: Radical History in International Political Economy." *Perspectives on Global Development and Technology* 17, no. 4: 429–50.

Wolf, Martin. 2014. *The Shifts and the Shocks*. New York: Penguin.

Zald, Mayer N. 1996. "Culture, Ideology, and Strategic Framing." In *Comparative Perspectives on Social Movements*, edited by Doug McAdam, John D.

McCarthy, and Mayer N. Zald, 261–74. Cambridge: Cambridge University Press.

Zirakzadeh, Cyrus Ernesto. 1989. "Economic Changes and Surges in Micro-Nationalist Voting in Scotland and the Basque Region of Spain." *Comparative Studies in Society and History* 31, no. 2: 318–39.

———. 2013. For What Do We Cheer? Nietzsche, Moral Stands, and Social Movement Research." *New Political Science* 35, no. 3: 492–506.

Žižek, Slavoj. 2012. "Don't Act. Just Think." *Big Think* (28 August): http://bigthink.com/videos/dont-act-just-think.

Index

Abu-Lughod, Janet, 87, 204n103
Ad Hoc Faculty Group, 57–59
Africa, 19–20, 34, 45, 57, 59, 108–110
  colonization of, 34, 209n41
  decolonization of, 17, 20–23, 39–41
  and development, 79, 93–96, 153
  and postcolonial states, 55–56, 77
  and Wallerstein's development,
    22–23, 91, 93, 97, 168
Africa Studies Association, 73, 91,
  95–96
agency, 14, 63, 144, 174–175
  increase over time, 100, 115, 119,
    171–172
  limitations of, 50, 88–89
  meaning of, 181n25
  in systemic transformation, 9–11,
    110–112
Albright, Madeleine, 161
al-Mahdi, Sadiq, 30
Almond, Gabriel, 137
Althusser, Louis, 46, 52, 145
  criticism of, 51, 195n106
  and structuralism, 48–51, 194n94
  and totalities, 196n114–115
Amin, Samir, 4, 74, 189n2
Amsterdam, 129
ancient world, 9–10, 46, 69–70, 72,
  82, 169

Anderson, Benedict, 24–25, 28, 131,
  182–183n37, 185n50
Anderson, Perry, *passim but see
  especially,* 8–12, 168–170,
  174–175
  early life, 24–25
  as editor of *New Left Review*,
    28–30, 50, 117–119, 133
  at Oxford, 26
  as professor at UCLA, 119, 174
Andrew, Molly, 173
Angola, 34
anti-Semitism, 22
antisystemic movements, 124, 127
Armenian genocide, 161
Aronowitz, Stanley, 5
Arrighi, Giovanni, 4, 189n2, 215n34
Attlee, Clement, 27

Badiou, Alain, 173
Bakewell, Sarah, 177
Barfield, Thomas, 182n37
Barnett, Anthony, 117, 212n105
base, 51, 71, 113
  and totalities, 195n103
  See also mode of production,
    superstructure
Beauvoir, Simone de, 139
Beck, Ulrich, 158

Bell, Daniel, 20–21
Binghamton University
    Anderson teaching at, 118
    archives at, 2, 182n30
    and Arrighi's Gramscian
        perspective, 215n34
    Fernand Braudel Center at, 2, 14,
        67, 99–100, 119, 124, 169, 173
    Wallerstein joining, 73
    Wallerstein retiring from, 174
BISA (British International Studies
    Association), 3
Blackburn, Robin, 26, 117–119,
    186n66, 192n59, 212n105,
    213n118–119
Black Dwarf, 65, 198n48
Blackledge, Paul
    on Lucio Colletti, 52
    on Nairn-Anderson, 187–188n85,
        218n9
    on *New Left Review*, 197–198n32
    on Raymond Williams and Isaac
        Deutscher, 192–193n59
    on totalities, 196n114–115
Block, Fred, 45
bourgeoisie, 106, 127, 139, 155
    and hegemony, 31
    ideology of, 47, 70, 126, 187n85
    meaning of, 40
    revolution of, 32–33, 85, 100,
        113–114, 118, 171, 211n78
Brandt, Willy, 99
Braudel, Fernand, 37–38, 74
    and holism, 45
    influences on, 191n26, 191–192n28,
        206n20
    set of sets, 92
    and space and time, 43, 41–43, 68,
        92, 96, 192n44–55
    translations of, 191n33
    See also Binghamton University

Brenner, Robert, 4, 116, 131
    and Anderson, 113–114, 210n75,
        210–211n76
    debate with Wallerstein, 170–171,
        223n6, 223n11
Brzezinski, Zbigniew, 130
Bush, George W., 1

Campaign for Nuclear Disarmament, 29
capitalism, *passim but see especially*,
        75, 172
    defined, 75–76, 171, 179n3, 200n30,
        209n61
    end of, 64–66, 81–82, 103, 175
    functions of, 10–11, 40, 44
    history of, 43, 78–80, 84–87, 108,
        114, 170, 201n49
    justifications for, 121–125
    opposition to, 3–4, 14–15, 133–135,
        216n53–54
    and postcolonialism, 94–95
    stability of, 2–5, 103–104, 130–132
    See also postcapitalism, world-
        economy
Caribbean, 107
Carr, E. H., 5, 12 182n33
civilization
    and antiquity, 82
    and European Union, 156–158, 161
    and rhetorical power, 148
    and world-systems, 75, 92, 201n51
Charles V, 78–79, 88, 149, 166
    abdication of, 203n71
Chase-Dunn, Christopher, 206, 224n29
    and comparative world-systems,
        209n60
China
    and Anderson's cosmopolitanism,
        30, 185n45
    Anderson's reflections on, 13, 17,
        24–25, 148

and hegemony, 142–143
and protests, 81
and world-systems, 72, 78, 95, 109t
Chinese Maritime Customs, 24
classes
  conflict between, 32–34
  consciousness of, 172, 175
  corporate, 33
  hegemony of, 31–32
  lower, 125–127, 159–160, 171–172, 215n24
  terminology of, 40, 190n15
  upper, 31–32, 125, 172
  working, 52, 61, 117, 126–127
  See also lower strata, upper strata
Clinton, Bill, 161
cognitive liberation, 62, 198n35
Cohen, Benjamin, 3–4
Cohen, Samuel, 57
Cold War, *passim but see especially*, 8, 11, 157, 169
  meaning of, 122–123, 132–133
  narratives of, 29, 34, 80, 168
  and Vietnam, 55
Colletti, Lucio, 13, 196n115–116
  and Anderson, 52, 196n114
  on communist parties, 48
colonialism, 26, 75, 91
  end of, 33–34
  legacy of, 2, 33, 96, 157
  See also decolonization
Columbia University
  archives, ix, 182n30
  Columbia Essayists, 5, 45, 184n16
  IDA (Institute for Defense Analysis), 57, 59
  protests at, 14, 57–59, 91, 97, 127
  Radical Faculty Group, 59
  and Wallerstein as professor, 28, 55, 71

  and Wallerstein as student, 20–22, 38, 45, 184n14, 189n2
communism
  anticommunism, 20, 22, 34
  and class struggle, 194n80
  East European (one party), 10, 15, 26, 121, 134, 138, 140
  future of, 173
  reputation of, 29
  Soviet, 18, 27, 195n110
  and student Left, 63
  See also Marxism, socialism
Communist Party Historians Group, 26–28
complex totality. See totalities
conjoncture (cyclical phase), 42 177
  See also conjuncture
conjuncture, 63, 79, 114–115, 131
  meaning of, 25, 42
  See also conjoncture
conservatism
  and amateurism, 32
  and ideological battles, 59–60, 65, 137, 148
  and order, 130
  origins of, 125–126
  and policy, 35
  sophisticated versus practical, 20–22, 184n20
  twentieth century, 127–128, 173
  See also neoconservatism
Conservative Party, 31, 34, 61
Cordier, Andrew, 59
core
  defined, 41, 74, 77–78
  in eighteenth century, 108–109t
  emergence, 94
  and liberalism, 126, 128–129, 148–149, 154, 175
  and production, 171
  in seventeenth century, 105–107

core *(continued)*
  unequal exchange, 96
  in Western Europe, 79
  See also periphery, semiperiphery
cosmopolitanism, 17, 24, 35
Cournot, Antoine-Augustin, 135
Cox, Robert, 3, 143, 180n12
CPC (Communist Party of China), 123
CPGB (Communist Party of Great Britain), 26–27, 48, 117
CPSU (Communist Party of Soviet Union), 48, 51
Cuba, 64, 123
CUP (Committee of Union and Progress), 160
Cyprus, 160–162

dangerous classes, 125–126, 215n24
Debrah, E., 220n30
decolonization, 22–23, 30, 34, 41, 53, 55, 61, 167
Denemark, Robert A., 87
Defoe, Daniel, 129
de Gaulle, Charles, 62
Derluguian, Georgi, 166, 213n3
Derrida, Jacques, 131
Deutscher, Isaac, 52, 192–193n59
development
  beliefs about, 11, 42, 126
  economic, 63, 80, 89, 126
  and end of history, 135, 137
  of Europe, 83–85
  international, 4
  as relational process, 23, 44, 99, 167
  and stages, 6, 74, 82
  Wallerstein's critique of, 56, 65, 79, 93–96, 176
  of world-system, 74, 77, 203n75
dialectical materialism. *See* materialism
Dobb, Maurice, 52, 170, 196n116

egalitarian world-system, 111
Egypt, 26
  See also Suez
Elliott, Gregory, 114, 134, 192–193n59, 210n76
  and Anderson's unpublished manuscripts, 197–198n32
end of history, 134–137, 217n81
  See also Fukuyama, Francis
England
  Anderson's childhood in, 17, 25
  class antagonisms within, 106, 124, 171, 192n53
  and communist party, 26, 48
  and English Revolution, 138
  and European Union, 159–160
  hegemony of, 129, 126, 129, 142
  Leveller movement in, 138
  mercantilism of, 105–106, 109t
  New Left Review on, 30, 33
  socialism in, 30
  state development of, 94
entropy, 31, 88, 101, 110
Eton College, 25, 45
EU (European Union), 63, 154–162
  See also Europe
Europe, *passim but see especially*, 14–15
  and capitalism, 75–79, 81–85, 105–109t
  communist parties of, 48–49, 121
  and hegemony, 128–130
  ideas of, in developing world, 39–41
  imperialism of, 23, 56, 72
  integration of (*see* EU)
  universalism, and, 149–152

Fanon, Frantz
  on classes in postcolonial world, 39–40
  and particularism and universalism, 41, 149
  and resisting labels, 39

Far Right, 7, 20, 127, 160, 167, 175
fascism, 27–28, 157, 222n55
  and antifascism, 18
feudalism, 9–10, 44, 156t, 170
  in Asia, 7, 85–86
  as civilization (Wallerstein), 75
  end of, 75–76, 83, 105, 201n49
  as mode of production (Anderson), 83–84
France
  and colonialism, 23
  geopolitics of, 78–79, 109t, 129, 151
  intellectual life of, 31, 45
  and liberalism, 126
  and mercantilism, 105–107
  protests in, 62–63, 197n32
  and socialism, 26, 168
  welfare state of, 156
Frank, Andre Gunder, 4, 74, 189n2
  and world system history, 87
Fraser, Ronald, 28, 50, 194n97, 212n104
Friedman, Thomas, 130
Fukuyama, Francis, 130, 134–138
  See also end of history

Garraty, John, 6
Gauchet, Marcel, 158
George, Alexander, 10
Ghana, 19, 22–23, 39, 56, 153
Gibbon, Edward, 13, 37, 46
Gills, Barry K., 87
Gilpin, Robert, 3
Global South, 123
Gramsci, Antonio, 5, 166
  and Anderson, 218n9
  on hegemony, 32, 128–129, 142–143
  and Nairn-Anderson theses, 31, 188n85
  and Wallerstein, 128, 215n34
  writing style, 190–191n28

Great Britain. See England
Greenfield, James, 221n31
Guha, Ranajit, 142, 145, 219n27

Habermas, Jürgen, 131–132, 158, 222n60
Halliday, Fred, 117
Hall, Stuart
  as editor of New Left Review, 28, 30
  on hegemony, 142
  memoir of, 182n37
  at Oxford, 25–26
  on totalities, 49, 68
Hayek, Friedrich von, 43, 130, 156, 215n42
hegemony, passim but see especially, 4, 15
  American, 20, 41, 80, 132, 167
  Anderson's history of, 141–145
  British, 129
  of a class, 32–34
  cycles of, 77–78, 129
  Dutch, 128–129
  Gramsci on (see Gramsci)
  of a state, 128
Hill, Christopher, 27, 30
Hilton, Rodney, 27
Hispanic America, 79, 107, 109t
historical materialism. See materialism
Hoare, Quintin, 50, 212n105
Hobsbawm, Eric, 4, 196n116
  Anderson's assessment of, 52, 144, 166
  on capitalism, 8, 116, 131–132
  on Marxism, 48
  and Past and Present, 27
  and Review, 74
Hofstadter, Richard, 45, 184n20
Hollande, François, 151
Hopkins, Terence, 166
  at Binghamton, 73
  at Columbia, 184n14, 189n2

Hopkins, Terence *(continued)*
  on incorporation, 209n51
  on pluri-national studies, 92t-93, 205n5
  and *Review*, 74
House of Representatives, 161
human agency. *See* agency
humanism, 13, 49-50
  See also structuralism
Hungary, 25, 38, 45, 109t, 168

imperialism, 23, 47, 65, 72, 81, 86
inequality, 7, 22, 81, 159
  and gender, 211n93
  in a postcapitalist system, 112
  in precapitalist systems, 111, 125
  and race, 154
  support for, 215n42
internationalism, 143, 222n72
International Organization, 3-4
International Socialism, 133
IPE (international political economy), 3-4, 9, 11, 179n6
Ireland, 13, 17, 24-25
ISA (International Studies Association), 3
Ivory Coast, 22-23

Jacoby, Russell, 180n14
Jameson, Fredric, 68, 117-118, 131, 176
Jervis, Robert, 10
John of Salisbury, 69-70, 199n16

Kagarlitsky, Boris, 133-134
Katzenstein, Peter, 3
Katznelson, Ira, 88-89
Kemal Atatürk, 161
Keohane, Robert, 3, 143
Keucheyan, Razmig, 173
Keynes, John Maynard, 33, 131, 172
Khrushchev, Nikita, 48, 186n68

Kindleberger, Charles, 3
Kirk, Grayson, 57-58
Kojève, Alexandre, 135
Kondratieff, Nikolai, 74, 104
  methods of, 207-208n24
  and waves, 104-105, 110, 116, 209n57
  See also long waves
Krasner, Stephen, 3
Krauthammer, Charles, 137

Labour Party
  and Attlee government, 27
  historical weaknesses of, 32-34
  and *New Left Review*, 61, 117
  and Wilson government, 61, 168
Laclau, Ernesto, 142, 170
Las Casas, Bartolomé de, 150-151
Lazarfeld, Paul, 20, 184n14
Left Book Club, 26
Lenin, Vladimir (Leninism), 48, 64, 126, 140
Leonard, Mark, 158
Lerners, Daniel, 137
Levellers, 138-139
liberalism
  crimes of, 195n110
  as defense of capitalism, 122, 125-130
  and English Marxism, 30
  and Enlightenment, 38
  history of, as model for socialism, 139
  of postwar generation, 99
  and Turkey, 161
  See also neoliberalism
Libya, 151
Lipset, Seymour Martin, 20
London, 24, 129
London Review of Books, 117, 221n38
long waves, 77, 104-105
  See also Kondratieff, Nikolai

Louis Napoleon, 126
lower strata, 5, 40, 106, 144
  See also classes, upper strata
Lukács, Georg, 5, 31
  on totalities, 47–48, 67, 71, 193n78
  and Western Marxism, 51

Mandel, Ernest, 51–52, 195n106–107
Mann, Michael, 131
markets
  as economy type, 23, 43–45, 65, 76, 86, 92, 113, 156, 170, 192n51
  in Great Recession, 1–2, 7
  ideology of, 9, 15, 135
  and neoliberalism, 99, 108, 121, 130–131, 140, 143, 147, 172–173
  and postcapitalism, 112
  unpredictability of, 165
Marx, Karl, 4–5, 13, 127, 193n72
  influence on radicals, 37–39, 42, 189n7
  social science of, 42–43, 47
  and totalities, 200n22
  See also Marxism
Marxism
  and Anderson, 24, 46–47, 50–53, 114, 117, 144, 176
  and British historians, 4, 13, 46–48, 50, 52, 166, 171, 196n117, 224n16
  and communist parties, 27, 48, 116
  and radicals, 5
  as social science, 5, 37–38, 43, 51, 70–71, 170, 195n106, 200n22
  and Wallerstein, 38–39, 42, 189n7
  Western, 29–31, 51, 62, 81, 113, 118, 131, 133, 148, 171, 195n110, 222n60
  See also communism, Marx, socialism
Marxism Today, 117
materialism, 46–48, 172, 211n88
  historical or dialectical, 52
  and Soviet Union, 116

McCarthy, Joseph (McCarthyism), 21–23, 167
McGill University, 59, 223n6
McNamara, Robert, 99
mercantilism, 105–106, 129
Merton, Richard, 203n84
Miliband, Ralph, 118
Mills, C. Wright, 5, 20, 45
Milward, Alan, 155
Mitchell, Juliet, 49
MKT (Kuomintang), 123
mode of production
  and capitalism, 208n38
  and classes, 194n80, 115
  importance of, 48, 51
  and Marxism, 144, 193n72
  in Russian absolutism, 204n97
  transformation of, 82–83, 86, 115
  See also base, superstructure
modernity, *passim but see especially*, 9, 14–16
  as accident, 78–79
  as capitalism, 43–44, 72, 95–96, 171, 179n3
  crisis of, 110
  European, 67, 71, 85, 155–156t
  forced labor of, 85, 107
  inequality of, 125
  as macrohistorical outcome, 46, 75, 82, 169–170, 208n26
  science of, 101–102
  society of, 122, 124–125, 131, 138, 159
  states system of, 81–82, 129
  uniqueness of, 86–89, 214n10
  wage labor of, 84–85
modernization theory, 41, 56, 74, 82, 93, 137, 157
Mollet, Guy, 26
Monbiot, George, 12
Monthly Review, 134
Monnet, Jean, 156

Morris, John, 27
Mouffe, Chantel, 142
Mozambique, 34
Myrdal, Gunnar, 6

Nairn, Tom, 4, 131, 193n59, 212n105
 and popular issues, 117
 and theses with Anderson, 30–31,
  187n80, 187n85, 224n16
 on Wilson government, 61
Napoleon Bonaparte, 136
Nationalism, 34, 91, 166
 in Africa, 22–23, 55, 96–97
 and Anderson, 24–25
 Turkish, 160, 162
nation-state. *See* states
neoconservatism, 137
 See also conservatism
neoliberalism, *passim but see
  especially*, 14–15, 99
 Anderson's response to, 113–114
 and freedom, 172–173
 and the Left, 132, 173
 survival of, 147
 types of, 162
 Wallerstein's response to, 103
 See also liberalism
New Deal, 172
New England, 109t
New Left, 5, 26, 28–30, 119, 198n48
New Left Books. *See* Verso Books
New Left Review (NLR), *passim but
  see especially*, 2, 14, 15
 creation of, 28
 financial rescue of, 28–29, 113
 objectives of, 29–30, 117–119,
  133–134
 Sartre's influence on, 50
 as vanguard organization, 64–65
New Reasoner, 27–28
New Statesman, 117
New University, 26

New York (city)
 as center of capitalism, 19–20, 129
 intellectuals of, 45
 and protests, 55, 57–59
 and Wallerstein's childhood, 13,
  18–24
New York Times
 Wallerstein's criticisms of, 74, 153–154
Nietzsche, Friedrich, 5, 163, 180n17,
  180n19
1956
 and conjunctures, 26, 29, 177
 events of, 25–27, 45, 168
 secret speech of, 48
1968, *passim but see especially*, 55–66
nobility, 32, 76, 84–85, 106–107,
  208n31, 208n38
 See also classes
notables, 125–127
 See also classes
Nye, Joseph, 143
Nyerere, Julius, 56

Oakeshott, Michael, 130, 215n42
Obama, Barack, 145, 151
OECD (Organisation for Economic
  Co-operation and Development),
  139
Office of Political Warfare, 25
Ottoman Empire, 108–109t, 160–161
Oxford University, 25–28, 30, 45, 168

Past and Present, 27, 210n75
PCC (Communist Party of Cuba), 64
PCF (French Communist Party), 64
PCI (Italian Communist Party), 48,
  142
Pearson, Gabriel, 26
periphery
 defined, 74, 77
 eighteenth century membership,
  109t

incorporation into, 78
and nineteenth and twentieth
  centuries, 126, 148–149, 175
seventeenth-century burden,
  106–107
sixteenth century membership, 79,
  94
and unequal exchange, 96, 105
Polanyi, Karl, 5, 13, 37–38, 74,
  192n53, 209n61
  on modes of economic behavior,
    43–45, 192n51
  and transition debate, 192n52
  and unequal exchange, 96
Portugal, 34, 77–78, 106–107, 109t,
  186n68
postcapitalism, 7–9, 16
  as egalitarianism, 111, 138–140, 173
  as socialism, 206n5–6
Prigogine, Ilya, 38, 101–103, 119,
  173–174, 207n17
proletariat, 32, 47, 69, 77, 187n85
  and antisystemic movements, 124,
    165
  and class struggle, 195n110
  as defined by Fanon, 39–40
  English, 33, 105–106
  and hegemony, 142
  and liberalism, 125, 127
  in periphery, 107
  rule of, 51

radicalism
  clear-headed, 15, 141, 144–145
  as ideology, 125–127, 133
  as political economy, 4, 147
Reagan, Ronald, 14, 99, 103, 172–
    173
Review, 2, 73–74
Rifkin, Jeremy, 158
Robbins, Bruce, 144
Rosenau, James, 6

Rosdolsky, Roman, 52
RPE (radical political economy), 4–7,
  16, 165, 176
RSSF (Revolutionary Socialist
  Students' Federation), 65
Rudd, Mark, 57
Russia
  as absolutist state, 85, 204n97
  incorporation of, 108–109t
  Marxism in, 116
  post-Soviet, 121
  See also Soviet Union
Rwandan genocide, 152

Samuel, Raphael, 26
Sartre, Jean-Paul
  influence on Anderson, 5, 13, 26,
    52, 118, 194n97
  influence on Nairn-Anderson
    theses, 31, 187–188n85
  on structures, 50–51, 194n101,
    203n78
  and totalization, 37, 45–46, 68
Saville, John, 27
Schmitt, Carl, 130
second scramble, 56
semiperiphery
  antisystemic movements of, 124,
    202n65
  defined, 41, 74, 77, 94
  in eighteenth century, 109t
  European origins, 78
  and mercantilism, 106–107
  and Russia, 108
  and unequal exchange, 96, 105
Sen, Amartya, 131, 216n61
Sepúlveda, Juan Ginés de, 150–151
serfdom
  as coerced cash-crop labor, 107,
    208n38
  as extra-economic coercion, 83–85
Skocpol, Theda, 88

slavery
  and capitalism, 107
  as mode of production, 10, 82–83, 86
Smith, Adam, 43–44, 170
socialism, *passim but see especially*, 7–9
  and antisystemic movements, 57, 59, 62–63, 168
  Cold War rhetoric about, 33–34, 169
  future of, 138–139
  and gender, 211n93
  ideology of, 125–126, 134
  and Left parties, 26, 33, 195n110
  at *New Left Review*, 30, 61–64, 134, 187n81
  as postcapitalist system, 65, 72, 100–101, 119, 171–176, 206n5
  strategy for, 64, 67
  See also communism, Marxism
Socialist Challenge, 117
socialist society
  creation of, 195n110
  organization for, 119
Somers, Margaret, 45, 88
sovereignty, 84, 121, 142, 156
Soviet Union
  in Cold War, 122–123
  and end of history, 136
  intervention in Hungary, 168
  and parade of sovereignties, 108, 121–122, 127
  and self-determination, 126
  socialism in, 116, 195n110
  See also Russia, Stalin
Spain
  and Jesuit Order, 138
  slide to semiperiphery, 106–107, 109t
  universalism of, 149–151
  and world-empire ambitions, 78–79, 88, 167

Stalin, Josef (Stalinism), 5
  and Cold War rhetoric, 27, 29, 34, 139
  crimes of, 5, 18–19
  debates over, 17–20, 48, 50–51
  geopolitics of, 17–18, 123
  and socialism, 116, 195n110
  and Soviet trajectory, 26–27, 48, 50–51
states, *passim but see especially*, 3–4
  absolutist, 85–86
  demise of, 64–65, 81
  Polanyi on, 44
  postcolonial, 22–23, 34, 40, 56
  system of, 9–10
  as unit of analysis, 41, 70–72, 82, 91–97
  welfare, 26, 61
Stiglitz, Joseph, 131, 216n61
Strange, Susan, 3, 143
Strauss, Leo, 130, 137, 215n42
structuralism
  defense and critique of, 48–50, 88–89, 110, 115
  defined, 5, 50–53, 119, 181n25
  and totalities, 68, 73, 195n103
  See also humanism
Students for a Democratic Society, 57
Suez, 25–26, 168
  See also Egypt
superstructure, 48, 51, 71, 113
  See also base, mode of production
Sweezy, Paul, 170

Taylor, Charles, 26
Tet Offensive, 55
  See also Vietnam
Thatcher, Margaret, 14, 99, 103, 172–173
Thatcherism, 132, 173
third world, 74, 79, 116
  and movements, 19, 62, 65–67, 123

and nationalism, 14, 168
as part of complex totality, 29, 81
Thompson, Dorothy, 27
Thompson, E. P.
  and Anderson, 115, 118, 144,
    171–172, 194n91, 224n16–17
  humanism of, 48–52
  Marxism of, 4
  at the *New Reasoner*, 27
  and writing style, 213n116
Tilly, Charles, 73–73, 182
Times Literary Supplement, 133
totalities, *passim but see especially*, 9,
    82–83, 169–170, 194n91
  complex totality, 50, 81, 93, 176
  defined, 6, 68, 70, 195n103
  history of, 68–70, 199n4, 199n12
  in-itself and for-itself, 157, 158t
  as mode of production, 70, 200n22
  open or closed, 9, 72, 86–89,
    100–101
  theorists of, 37–38, 45, 47–53,
    67–70, 196n114
  as unit of analysis, 16, 70–71,
    223n11
  See also totalization, world-systems
totalization, 9, 37, 50–51, 68–69, 70,
    80–82, 144, 195n103
  See also totalities, world-systems
transition debate, 171, 192
  See also Brenner, Robert
Trotsky, Leon, 51–52
Truman, David, 58
Turkey, 160–162

UCLA (University of California at
    Los Angeles), 73, 119, 174
underdevelopment, 75, 167
United Kingdom. *See* England
United States, *passim but see
    especially*, 80
  and Cold War, 122–123, 127

EU as junior partner to, 156
McCarthyism and global power,
    21–22
universalism of, 151
Universities and Left Review, 26, 28
University of British Columbia, 149
upper strata, 107–108, 128, 208n38
  See also classes, lower strata

Verso (New Left Books), 2, 113
Vietnam, 26, 123, 127, 198n48, 214n8
  See also Tet Offensive

Wallerstein, Beatrice, 55
Wallerstein, Immanuel, *passim but
    see especially*, 8–12, 165–169,
    174–176
  as Binghamton professor, 73–74, 174
  as Columbia professor, 55–60
  as Columbia student, 20, 22, 38, 45,
    184n14, 189n2
  death of, 175
  early life of, 18–20
  influences, 38–45
  and Yale, 174
Washington Consensus, 99
Weber, Max, 131, 214n10
Westin, Alan, 58
Wilson, Harold, 61, 168
Wilson, Woodrow (Wilsonism), 126,
    140
World Assembly of Youth, 19
World Bank, 99
world-economy, *passim, but see
    especially*, 72
  Braudel's description of, 43, 192n45
  hegemonic capital of, as center of
    trade, 129
  incorporation into, 103–104,
    108–109t, 171, 209n51
  Wallerstein's definition of, 72, 200n28
  zones of, 77

world-economy *(continued)*
  See also capitalism, world-empire, world-system
world-empire
  and Charles V, 78–79, 106
  as distinct from imperialism, 72
  and Germany, 167
  and late feudalism, 75
  and transformation, 78
  as type of world-system, 72, 96, 192n51
  See also world-economy, world-systems

world-systems, *passim, but see especially*, 70–72
  hyphen debate on, 71, 86–88, 96
  stages of, 74
  as totalities, 71–72
  types, 72, 96, 111
  See also totalities, totalization

Yale University, 174, 182n30
Yalta, 122–123
Young Adult Council, 19
Young Turks, 160

www.ingramcontent.com/pod-product-compliance
Lightning Source LLC
Chambersburg PA
CBHW020644230426
43665CB00008B/315